D1548544

THE AFRICAN AMERICAN CHURCH COMMUNITY IN ROCHESTER, NEW YORK 1900–1940

THE AFRICAN AMERICAN CHURCH COMMUNITY IN ROCHESTER, NEW YORK
∼1900–1940∼

by

Ingrid Overacker

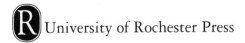
University of Rochester Press

First published 1998

University of Rochester Press
668 Mt. Hope Avenue
Rochester, NY 14620   USA

and at P.O. Box 9
Woodbridge, Suffolk IP12 3DF
United Kingdom

ISBN 1–878822 89–6

Library of Congress Cataloging-in-Publication Data

Overacker, Ingrid, 1953–
    The African American church community in Rochester, New York,
1900–1940 / by Ingrid Overacker.
        p.   cm.
    Includes bibliographical references and index.
    ISBN 1–878822–89–6 (alk. paper)
    1. Afro-American churches—New York (State)—Rochester.   2. Afro-
Americans—New York (State)—Rochester—Religion.   3. Afro-American
women—New York (State)—Rochester—Religion.   I. Title.
BR563.N4094   1998
277.47′890821′08996073—DC21   98–7283
                                                                              CIP

British Library Cataloguing-in-Publication Data
A catalogue record for this book is
available from the British Library

Designed and typeset by Cornerstone Composition Services
Printed in the United States of America
This publication is printed on acid-free paper

To
My Father, John Wendall Overacker

and to

Deborah Mullen
Joseph Crockett
Carol Gomez

~

CONTENTS

~

ACKNOWLEDGMENTS

Many individuals have helped to bring this work to fruition. I am most grateful to Professor Mary Young, who has guided me throughout and who I esteem as teacher, mentor, and friend. Professors Larry Hudson and Brenda Meehan gave painstaking attention to the manuscript. It benefited from their comments and advice. Professor Ayala Gabriel advised me about field work, challenged my thinking on gender issues, and has given me an abundance of collegial and personal support.

I was fortunate to have colleagues and professors in the History Department at the University of Rochester who challenged and supported me along the way. Professor Eugene Genovese first cracked open my mind. Professor Christopher Lasch and Professor Jules Benjamin provoked and nurtured my intellect. Mary Conable and Norm Gayford loaned me a computer and made their home a refuge. Kathy Kelly, Cathy Mason, Cathy Tumber, David Steigerwald, and David Chappell provided the comraderie and collegial support without which no student can survive graduate school.

I have been fortunate also in finding support from friends in other academic fields. Harold Wechsler, my employer, mentor, and friend, has been a constant support. He has encouraged my heart and spirit, given me time off, and insisted I make my own work my priority. He also read every chapter and provided insightful comments. Dale Dannefer invited me to teach a course in the Graduate School of Education and Human Development, and has brought me groceries and loaned me his car. Other members of the faculty in the Graduate School of Education and Human Development have treated me as one of their own. Julia Smith has become a friend. Hank Allen, Warren Crichlow, and Karen Mackie have offered encouragement and friendship as well. The staff at the Ed School, most particularly Dorothea Horton, have also supported me.

My close friends have made it possible for me to work. They have listened to me, sometimes at four in the morning, taken care of me when I was ill, created a study where I could work, and even read the manuscript. Jackie Barnes, Linda Berkes, Kathy Buckwell, Joseph Crockett, Elaine Dannefer, Kathy Fraser, James Frackenpohl, Pam Klainer, Jim Thorne, Phyllis Tolbert, Sharon Turner, and Anne Waasdorp have taught me the meaning of community. Rachel and Michael Dannefer, Jason and Andrew Frackenpohl, and Katie Buckwell have lightened my spirit too many times to count.

Many people helped me during the course of my research. Professors Frederick Jefferson and Jesse Moore helped me contact African Americans in the Rochester community. Alean Rush, Kay Jordan, Eugene DuBois, Mildred Reynolds, and Dr. Juanita Pitz also provided important contacts. Charles Frazier, the historian of Memorial A.M.E. Zion, was invaluable. The staff of the local history department of Rundell Public Library were gracious and help-ful. Reviewers of the manuscript offered important points for revision and further research.

I offer my most sincere thanks to those women and men who gave me their time and told me their stories. Without them, this work would not have been possible.

PART I

Context

~~~

INTRODUCTION

Three interrelated theses guide the analysis of the history of the African American church community[1] in Rochester, New York, from 1900 through 1940. The first thesis asserts that Christian *faith*[2] motivated African American women and men to challenge the oppressive conditions they faced in Rochester. The second maintains that the study of *local* African American church communities is an essential avenue through which to trace the connections between the expression of faith and the resistance to oppression. The voices of lay people provide the evidence for an interpretation of the church, and the issues it addressed, from the standpoint of those who built the church, implemented its programs, and gathered to worship in its sanctuary. The third thesis argues for the essential and primary role of *women* in the development of local African American church communities and the faith that resided within them. While this book is not only, or even primarily, about women, it does maintain the absolutely fundamental role women played within the local community and without which that community could not have endured. African American women worked in partnership with African American men, and according to their understanding of their role as women, to instill and model a faithful response to the extreme challenges facing them in Rochester, New York. Therefore, the chapter on the women in the local church communty in Rochester is the anchoring chapter of this book.

THE AFRICAN AMERICAN CHURCH COMMUNITY IN ROCHESTER—A PEOPLE OF FAITH

Despite its reputation as a seat of abolition and progressive reform movements, Rochester placed social, economic, and political limitations upon the lives of its African American citizens. African American churches devised institutional structures and practices to better material conditions and challenge prevailing racial norms. Personal interviews and church records suggest that in Rochester, the church was the primary site of such efforts not only because it was the most significant social institution[3] in the African American community, but also because its members were people of faith who interpreted Christian mandates so that they could both take care of each other and face environmental challenges. This study employs the evidence of personal interviews from the members of four local congregations—Memorial A.M.E. Zion, Trinity Presbyterian, Mt. Olivet Baptist, and St. Simon's Episcopal churches—to examine the connections among the faith testimonies of church members, the theological framework espoused in the African American churches, internal church organizations and practices, and the examples of individual lives. The results reveal a community of women and men who relied on a God of justice, personally present in their day-to-day lives, who called them to work for racial equality and liberation. Such faith acknowledged the practical realities with which they had to contend, and informed strategies and programs to address both personal development and social engagement. The African American church in Rochester housed that faith and provided the forum for an articulation of its mandates.

The thesis that the laity in a local African American church community relied upon faith to motivate them to continue to challenge racism during the first four decades of the twentieth century departs from traditional historical interpretation. This interpretation, based primarily on the evidence of nationally prominent male clergy, regretfully dismisses or bitterly excoriates the church for failing to address the pressing social and political issues crucial to the lives and futures of African Americans from the turn of the century to the advent of World War II. Scholarly treatment of the African American church community during this time period also does not give adequate attention to the role of faith as a motivating force in the lives of lay people within local communities fraught with racial oppression and discrimination. In their denunciations of the church as accomodationist, other-worldly, and inwardly focused, scholars have not examined what the women and men who occupied the pews within local congregations believed, and how they may have applied those beliefs to their efforts to better their own and each other's conditions.

Scholars in many fields have established the importance of the church as a vehicle for community cohesion within the African American community, while debating the relative merits of its centrality.[4] While most scholars extol African American churches and their leaders as primary forces in African American social and political struggles, some cast a different light on the central role of the churches during the first four decades of the twentieth century. Joseph

Washington, Gayraud Wilmore, and Ernest Morial argue that the early twentieth century African American church, across the board, turned its back on its militant heritage, became accommodationist and otherworldly, and eschewed social and political protest. Washington argues that, "in that era of decline in the quest for freedom, the Negro minister remained the spokesman for the people with this difference—faced by unsurmountable obstacles, he succumbed to the cajolery and bribery of the white power structure and became its foil. Instead of freedom he preached moralities and emphasized rewards in the life beyond."[5] Gayraud Wilmore concurs.

> With a basically rural orientation, most Black churches retreated into enclaves of moralistic, revivalistic Christianity which tried to fend off the encroaching secular gloom and the social pathology of the ghetto. As far as challenging the white society or seeking to mobilize Blacks against poverty and oppression, most Black congregations were too other-worldly, apathetic, or involved in the business of "being church" to deal with such problems.[6]

Ernest Morial echoes these themes when he argues that, "as a result of the loss of civil rights for blacks during the closing decades of the nineteenth century, the black churches in general took on characteristics which differ from former days. The major emphasis now was salvation for the world to come with little or no organized effort to better the present life of black Christians by working to regain lost rights."[7]

This interpretation of the church as retreating, accommodationist, and otherworldly permeates the writings of historians and sociologists such as C. Eric Lincoln, Jacqueline Jones, and John Hope Franklin. Franklin claims that "although church membership was increasing, the organized religious bodies were going through a period that was critical for blacks as for whites. The conservative element, devoting its attention to denouncing the sins of the young people and concerned largely with otherworldliness, was in control."[8] He tempers his remarks with the example of institutional churches, which provided welfare services to urban blacks. Jones makes the following observation of ghetto churches. "Ghetto churches in general showed a pronounced lack of interest in social-welfare issues during this period; they offered heavenly, not earthly salvation."[9] Lincoln, one of the foremost sociologists of African American religion, also cites the example of institutional and "larger" churches that engaged in outreach to the community, but sadly concludes:

> The social outreach of these larger churches, however, appeared to be the exception rather than the rule. The majority of the black churches were small in size and numerous in quantity. The main function of these churches from World

War I until the mid-1950s was to act as a "cultural broker", a mediating institution, to help acculturate rural migrants to the urban environment. To some
outside observers it appeared that most of the black urban churches during this
period had withdrawn into a revivalistic Christianity and defensive
accommodationism. It is still a matter of scholarly debate whether the black
churches during this period had been completely "deradicalized" as Gayraud
Wilmore has contended, or whether the sudden expansion brought on by the
migrations followed by a catastrophic worldwide economic depression simply
overwhelmed black preachers and their churches. In either case the consequences
appeared to be the same, a relative quietism and an apparent vacuum of church
leadership. . . .[10]

This study examines the role of the African American church community in
Rochester as an institutional agent of social reform and protest activities from
the Progressive Era to the beginning of World War II. The historical portrayal
of Rochester's African American church community questions the image of
the church as inwardly focused and other-worldly and provides a different
perspective on accommodation, one which focuses more on the lives of the
people who occupied the pews of Rochester's African American churches than
upon the stance of clergy, either locally or nationally.

THE IMPORTANCE OF LOCAL HISTORY TO UNDERSTANDING THE WORKINGS OF THE AFRICAN AMERICAN CHURCH COMMUNITY

To gain a more comprehensive understanding of the role of the church in both
the lives of its members and the social, economic and political life of the African American community as a whole (a role consistently acknowledged as
central), scholars need to gather more data concerning how the church functioned at the local, community level. The study of communities, their commonalities and differences, breaks down the tendency to treat the African
American community, or its churches, as monochromatic entities lacking complexity or diversity. An analysis of local situations, especially during times of
historical transition, adds depth and perspective to the landscape of the African American experience.

Recent scholarship has begun to take more seriously the religious avenues
of social reform and protest that occupied African Americans as they addressed
conditions in their own communities in the early decades of the twentieth
century. Ralph Luker, Elisabeth Dan Lasch, Evelynn Brooks Higginbotham,
Robert Gregg, and Clarence Taylor have made contributions that permit a
shift in the historical focus from secular to religious organizations and institu-

tions. Luker's discussion of white and black involvement in the social gospel movement from 1885-1912 underscores the religious roots of African American social reform efforts. He observes,

> If missionary methods were pioneered on the Southern frontier in Reconstruction, they were implemented in Northern and Midwestern cities to reweave a social fabric badly frayed by the stress of industrialization, immigration, migration, and social conflict. There, missions as proto-settlement houses were an important part of the black urban experience. There were settlement houses in black New York, Philadelphia, Indianapolis, Louisville, and Topeka by 1900. The origins of these settlement houses underscore their close relation to religious missions.[11]

Luker is describing efforts led by either white or black religiously motivated reformers, but his discussion of Reverdy Ransom's Institutional Church and Social Settlement in Chicago emphasizes the basically religious nature of the most successful African American efforts. "Owned by the African Methodist Episcopal Church, it ministered to a constituency more than a membership and worship was at the heart of its life."[12] Elisabeth Dan Lasch, while properly focusing on the racism of white reformers during the Progressive Era as the greatest deterrent to the extension of programs into the black community, also cites the blindness of secular professionals then and now as a major reason for the historical neglect of the African American community's own efforts at community reform, through missions and institutional churches.[13]

Evelynn Brooks Higginbotham, Robert Gregg, and Clarence Taylor focus specifically on the African American mainline church experience in reform during the time period under discussion. Higginbotham focuses on the women's movement within the Black Baptist Church on the national level, while Gregg examines the experience of African Methodists and southern migrants in Philadelphia. Taylor focuses on the development of both mainline and holiness-pentecostal churches in Brooklyn.

Higginbotham assumes the centrality of the church during this time period as "the most effective vehicle by which men and women alike, pushed down by racism and poverty, regrouped and rallied against emotional and physical defeat."[14] Gregg, whose thesis contends that the divisiveness within the African Methodist community severely prescribed its ability to alleviate the conditions of the migrants, still maintains the central role of the church as an agent for social reform. Despite internal conflict and the power politics of clergy and lay church leaders (predominantly male), Gregg notes that most churches continued outreach work to migrants and were concerned for their welfare.

> While individual members of the established Philadelphia black community of-
> ten expressed a great deal of dislike for the migrants, whom they saw as a threat to
> their positions, black churches on the whole stretched forth a helping hand. The
> churches were very receptive to the arrival of new members. Throughout the pe-
> riod of heaviest migration, many churches continued to invite new members into
> their congregations through the religion pages of the *Tribune*, and many reported
> large increases in membership both during the war and in the early 1920s.[15]

He also notes that this went beyond practical or political considerations. "The
pastor clearly felt that by encouraging black people to move and by offering
them assistance on their arrival in Philadelphia he was performing a service
both for his people and for God, just as Moses had done in earlier times."[16]

Taylor focuses on the social, political, and cultural significance of the African American churches across denominations in Brooklyn, New York. He contends that both mainline and pentecostal churches resisted the racism of the
wider society by offering alternative values and contesting popular racist images of blacks. While Taylor asserts that the African American churches of
Brooklyn "were forging a positive identity of African Americans in a racist
environment," he faults African American clergy for failing to successfully
challenge the unresponsive white body politic and allowing for the ghettoization
of black neighborhoods in Brooklyn.

> More than any other members of these institutions, pastors and ministers were
> in positions of great influence in their communities. Several black ministers and
> their churches were in a strong position to create an independent movement and
> wage a war against the ghettoization of Bed-Stuy (Bedford-Stuyvesant). How-
> ever, the black clergy of Brooklyn did not take advantage of their strength and
> resources to challenge an unresponsive city government. Instead many tried to
> work with the two-party system but were unable to use it for the benefit of the
> black community. These men took on the role of mediators between the com-
> munity and the state.[17]

Instructive in his discussion of accommodation and political strategies, Taylor
does not address the role of faith and is explicit in his focus on cultural and
political priorities within the churches. He therefore misses an opportunity to
connect the two, or to take into account the role of lay people in the development of either.

Social historians who focus on African American history have developed
scholarship that highlights the role of African Americans in social reform and
political protest in the early decades of the twentieth century. For the most
part, these studies acknowledge the importance of the church to the African
American community, but focus their attention elsewhere.[18] Consequently,

they do not make central to their analyses the possible religious motivations of African Americans engaged in reform efforts.

The work of both Gregg and Taylor especially highlights the need for more study of local African American church communities. The experiences of the congregations within Methodism in Philadelphia, while sharing some broad themes (for example, viewing the extension of church resources to those in need as a service to both the community and God), differ markedly from the experiences of the churches across denominations in Rochester (for example, the size of the African American community, level of economic stratification within it, and the particular conditions it faced). Taylor's book offers an additional contrast in its focus on a large African American community whose diversity among the churches reflected theological, economic, and political stratification. In Rochester, the community's small size certainly contained diversity, but expressed it quite differently. Did the African American church members in Rochester employ Christian sensibilities and mandates to their specific individual and communal situations? If so, how did they do this? How did the church play a role in their daily lives? It is only through analyzing the operation of local communities that such questions can be addressed. The answers to such questions will not only broaden our capacity to understand the possible manifestations of a broad African American church tradition,[19] it will provide a basis for comparing Rochester with other communities whose situations differ, and whose employment of Christian mandates and understandings may also differ accordingly.

The study of local African American church communities also enhances the possibility of incorporating the voices of people who led ordinary lives, but for whom the church meant something important. The church and its membership provided a continuity within communities that survived and succeeded the tenure of particular pastors and it is their voices and evidence which may shed the most light on the enduring values and practices upon which the community chose to rely. This study relies upon interviews with lay people, women and men, who were local leaders of the African American church community but, with one or two exceptions, did not achieve prominence outside the Rochester setting. While I include clergy in my discussion, the emphasis remains with the laity. Only the study of local communities could permit this focus.

Local communities do not reside in a vacuum, however. There are several contexts that shaped the functioning of the African American church community. The theological stance of the African American church as a whole imbued congregations with Christian concepts and mandates particular to (though not necessarily unique for) the African American experience between 1900 and 1940. Both inside and outside the church, African American leaders nationally developed strategies to aid the progress of their race. Rochester's African American population discussed and reflected their understanding of these historically particular strategies. Wider social movements within the white community nationally, especially involving progressive social and political reform, affected the Rochester white community and the way it related to its African American minority.

THE IMPORTANCE OF AFRICAN AMERICAN WOMEN TO THE DEVELOPMENT OF LOCAL COMMUNITIES

The third point of emphasis in this study is the role of African American women within the local church. African American women made it possible for the membership to flourish, for the building to stand, and for the community as a whole to survive. The chapter on the women of the church examines the ways in which women in Rochester held the church together. The importance of women to the development of the African American church community in Rochester extends beyond the explicit consideration of their individual contributions. All of the people interviewed in this study, male and female, noted the importance of mothers, wives, sisters, aunts, and daughters to the development of their faith and to the survival of the church. Women provided inspiration, motivation, role-modeling, and spiritual and material support to men and other women on a daily basis.

Rochester's African American women reflected understandings of their gender roles common to African American women within the nation. African American women in the United States adhered to the conventional notions of gender which maintained the primacy of their roles as wives and mothers. They also devised an argument similar to that advanced by white women reformers and feminists which maintained the moral superiority of women, the extension of their household responsibilities into the community, especially to help reform women and nurture children, and their ultimate responsibility for the future of society.

Despite these surface similarities, the African American women's commitment to both home life and social reform rested upon a far different base than that which buttressed white women's increasingly active social roles. Jacqueline Jones's ground-breaking work on black women, work, and the family, *Labor of Love, Labor of Sorrow*, traces the interconnections between women's work within the home and the wage-labor that African American women performed to help their families survive. Black women and men have never experienced the luxury of developing "separate spheres" with concomitant roles, which stemmed

from the man engaging in the public realm and insuring the economic viability of the household while the woman stayed at home and made that household a serene and wholesome place for both husband and children. For African
American women, the right to stay home and take care of their children cost
dearly, and the desire on the part of black women to fulfill domestic roles
proceeded at least in part from a desire to protect their homes from the prying
supervision of white employers and public officials. While black women might
have preferred to look after their own homes and children for a change, they
could not avoid the economic necessity of working outside the home, and this
historical experience strengthened their perceptions of the fluidity of the boundaries between private and public, domestic and social realms.

African American women reformers' zeal also reflected their understanding
of the unique vulnerability of black people and the destructive potential of
racism, which called them to do whatever they could to strengthen their homes
and communities against its effects. The racist assumptions prevalent concerning the character of black women created a social atmosphere where both
the persons and the homes of black women were not safe. White men could
and did rape black women with impunity, and black women's supposed moral
laxity could serve as an excuse for continued white supervision and control
over African American lives. The notions of black sexual immorality continually served as an excuse to deny African Americans political and economic
power over their own lives. Paula Giddings traces the social and moral imperatives that thus compelled African American women to defend their own
characters in order to both protect and improve their communities.

> Black women activists believed that their efforts were essential for reform and
> progress, and that their moral standing was a steady rock upon which the race
> could lean. They believed that the Black community was at a crossroads. Aban-
> doned by the federal government, subjected to increasing violence, and shorn of
> political power, it would either be pushed into oblivion or would mobilize its
> resources and survive. Standing on the brink of this racial precipice, convinced
> that they could save the race, Black women saw their role in almost ecclesiastical
> terms. They were "the fundamental agency under God in the regeneration . . . of
> the race, as well as the groundwork and starting point of its progress upward,"
> wrote Anna Julia Cooper. . . . It was the Black woman, continued Cooper, who
> "must stamp weal or woe on the coming history of this people." [20]

The secular focus of most work on African American women, including that cited
above, emphasizes the economic, social, and political activity of African American women and their elaboration of a womanist critique of American society.[21]
Womanist scholars recognize that African American women incorporated into

their pride in motherhood their ability to work to support their families. Sharon Harley describes the development of these connections:

> It is clear that a woman's employment was not a detriment to her family's well-being and stability as some race leaders and black middle-class reformers argued. How else were children to be fed, clothed, housed, and educated if mothers did not contribute to the family income? Recognition by family and friends as a good mother, cook, and housekeeper gave many black women a sense of accomplishment and satisfaction not possible in their paid work lives. Testifying to the fruits of her labor, Orra Fisher (a former Washington domestic) remarked: "I worked hard to serve God and to see that my three girls didn't have to serve nobody else like I did except God . . . My girl's in an office, and the baby—my son—over twenty years in the Army. I get full thinking about it. I had it bad, but look at them."[22]

Missing in most of the historical scholarship of the African American community and women's role in its development is serious consideration of the church. Even those works that consider the centrality of the church, either in itself, or as a vehicle for the development of other institutions, treat religious organization as a conduit for social and political aims and treat expressions of faith as theoretical arguments justifying social and political reform, couched in the vernacular.

In their explications of African American organizational efforts, feminist and womanist historians catch the religious flavor, without fully grasping the importance of faith, to African American women's organized activity. Both Linda Gordon and Lillian Williams observe that "black welfare activity, especially before the New Deal, consisted to a great extent of building private institutions" and "the private sphere for these women was inextricably intertwined with the public sphere. Indeed, they felt that their activism was 'ordained' by God. They thus held offices in their churches, as well as in political and social clubs."[23] Other historians who wish to chronicle African American women's contributions to reform find themselves falling back on religious metaphors. In tracing the origins of Lugenia Burns Hope's community organization in Atlanta, the Neigborhood Union, Jacqueline A. Rouse relates, "The women then voted to name their group the Neighborhood Union, to adopt 'Thy Neighbor as Thyself' for their motto, and to raise 'the standard of living in the community and to make the West Side of Atlanta a better place to rear our children'.[24] Ann Firor Scott excoriates the neglect of African American women in women's history and records with astonishment that

> I read, over and over, carefully worded (and some not so carefully worded) expressions of frustration as African American women confronted both disparag-

ing stereotypes of themselves and the uncomprehending detachment of white women; I watched as they gathered up the loaves and fishes and somehow, miraculously it almost seemed, paid off church mortgages, took care of the minister's family, provided for the orphans and the aged—many of them all the while working at the domestic jobs that were virtually the only kind they were permitted to hold, in order to keep their own families afloat.[25]

Yet for all the sometimes unconscious use of religious metaphors and acknowledgement of religious activity, these scholars still miss the primacy of faith as a foundation for activity and source of strength for African American women.

Evelyn Brooks Higginbotham attempts to restore the church to its central place in the development of African American women's organizations and reform efforts. She offers a cogent argument for the role of the Baptist Convention and the separate women's organizations within it as the ground on which African American Baptist women defined both their roles within their own society, sometimes in support of and sometimes in opposition to their men, and their roles within American society as a whole. She challenges the separation of secular and sacred, which historians and sociologists have employed to assert the primacy of public and secular institutions as vehicles for social transformation, by explicating the public nature of the African American church.

> By the law, blacks were denied access to public space, such as parks, libraries, restaurants, meeting halls, and other public accommodations. In time the black church—open to both secular and religious groups in the community—came to signify public space. It housed a diversity of programs including schools, circulating libraries, concerts, restaurants, insurance companies, vocational training, athletic clubs—all catering to a population much broader than the membership of individual churches. The church served as meeting hall for virtually every large gathering. It held political rallies, clubwomen's conferences and school graduations. It was the one space truly accessible to the black community, and it was this characteristic that led W.E.B. Du Bois, long before E. Franklin Frazier, to identify the black church as a multiple site—at once being a place of worship, theater, publishing house, school, and lodge. The church also functioned as a discursive, critical arena—a public sphere in which values and issues were aired, debated, and disseminated throughout the larger black community.[26]

Higginbotham also comes the closest of any contemporary historian to crediting women's faith as a primary force in shaping their social and political action. "The church connected black women's spirituality integrally with social activism".[27]

In her elaboration of a theory of social space, a third domain which mediates between the public and the private, Karen Hansen views the church as the institutional shaper and interpreter of private religious beliefs. While focusing on community formation in antebellum New England, Hansen's work offers theoretical insights for the present discussion.

> Organized religion offered people much more than spiritual salvation. Because it affected spiritual, emotional, educational, philosophical, and economic parts of people's lives, the church must be conceptualized as social, in addition to public and private. . . . If we recognize it as social, church activities and religiously inspired activism are thrown into relief, making it easier to discern their importance in mediating between individual concerns (private beliefs) and political life (public processes). . . .And especially in black communities . . . , the church provided an essential organizing base and spiritual inspiration for social-reform activities. [28]

The present study emphasizes Higginbotham's concept of "dialogue" to make Hanson's model more fluid. The individual beliefs of the people in the pews both shaped and received shape from the local conditions, religious discussions, sermons, activities, and social realities surrounding them. While Hanson focuses on the social functions of the church, separating behavior from individual belief, this study seeks to establish a bridge between what people believed and how they expressed that belief. For African Americans, the social was the religious. How one behaved, while never perfect, measured one's Christian commitment.

With the church as the central, and in many places, only institutional base for community life, Higginbotham explores the participation of women in defining their roles and acting accordingly. Women provided the bulk of the fund-raising efforts in support of the church and its programs. They cooperated with men in these efforts but also challenged their leadership and insisted on their own organizational base to pursue activities in what they considered their appropriate realm. They cooperated with white women, elaborated a theological defense of their social activism, and codified standards of moral behavior and respectability which would serve as the foundation for women's redemptive role in the world. African American Baptist women condensed their profound sense of mission into the following motto: "The world for Christ. Women arise. He calleth for thee."[29]

The most recent work on African American women of faith goes far in establishing the connection between personal faith, contributions to the African American community, and a commitment to social change. *This Far By Faith*, edited by Judith Weisenfeld and Richard Newman, profiles the religious biography of illustrious African American women. Weisenfeld notes:

Very real danger lay in religious protests against the dominant racial order from the period of slavery on. . . . [R]eligiously motivated activism emerges as perhaps the single most prevalent theme in the essays collected here. This activism took many forms, and through those forms African American women confronted a range of enemies. By mounting challenges to the very structures of white supremacy in America, and by contesting gender constraints within black communities that denied them access to leadership and other opportunities, these religious women made contributions that place them among the most significant figures in American history.[30]

The authors in this volume all place these extraordinary women within the context of their own communities and offer insights concerning how context influences the power of religious experience.

These important contributions to the history of African American church women in social and political life provide a basis for contrast and comparison with the lives of the African American women at work in the African American church community in Rochester, N.Y. from 1900 to 1940. The present work locates faith as the fundamental motivating and shaping force guiding women's (and men's) efforts on behalf of their community.

This study draws especially on Higginbotham's constructions of the organizations, activities, and efforts of Baptist women on the national level to provide insights for what women were doing on the local scene across denominations. How did women organize themselves in the black churches in Rochester? What were their goals? How did they perceive themselves as different from their men in their duties and responsibilities? The activities of the women who helped create and maintain the churches provides a template for other chapters dealing with African American efforts on behalf of education, economic self-development and political and civil rights.

Taken together then, the story that unfolds within these pages illustrates that African American women, in partnership with men, within local communities, laid the faith foundations that infused their common struggle against oppression during one of the most difficult eras of African American history.

ORGANIZATIONAL STRUCTURE

Part I: Context

This book is organized into two interrelated parts. The first part provides broad historical and social contexts which frame the workings of the African American church community in Rochester. It includes the Introduction and

Chapter One. Chapter One begins by placing the African American community within the contexts of the times, with special emphasis on the social thought and movements related to reform. It traces the contemporary attitudes toward race, and the then current efforts to reform especially urban environments.

Next, Chapter One explores the contemporary efforts on the part of African Americans engaged in reform movements nationally. It deals with the political and social strategies African American leaders espoused and defines the positions African Americans adhered to as they addressed the deteriorating conditions under which African Americans then lived.

This broad backdrop provides a context for the functioning of the African American church as a primary institution for the betterment of African Americans. The historical role, theological tenets, and social reform efforts specific to the African American mainstream church receive attention here.

Lastly, the first chapter of the book provides an in-depth sketch of the African Americans who lived in Rochester, New York. Rochester is briefly described, with major attention focusing on the characteristics of the African Americans living and attempting to better their condition within this local setting.

Part II: The African American Church Community in Rochester

Part II relates the history of the African American church community in Rochester, New York, during the first four decades of the twentieth century. It includes chapters two through six, with chapter six being the conclusion. Each chapter follows the same internal organization and begins with biographical sketches of individuals who belong to the African American church community and whose lives reflect the focus of the chapter. The personal testimonies and life stories of individuals provide the opportunity for a discussion of the role of religious faith as a motivating factor in the lives of church members. Next, each chapter deals with the particular conditions in Rochester (pertaining to the topic of that chapter) that had an impact upon African American efforts. Finally, each chapter illustrates the role of the African American church, its internal organizations and practices, and any theological stances relevant to the topic of the chapter. Each chapter, then, imbeds the lives of individuals, the programs and mandates of the African American church, within a particular local setting. This process illuminates the relationship between the African American community and the wider white community. Personal faith, and the vehicle for its expression, the church, become grounded in the specific struggles of African Americans in Rochester.

Chapter Two—Women of Faith and Service

The chapter on African American women within the mainstream church community of Rochester, New York, is the anchoring chapter of this book. Women elaborated the system of formal and informal support for people on material, emotional, and spiritual levels. At the level of human service, the basic humanity of African American people received acknowledgment and respect, providing a grounding for individual and community efforts in other areas of personal and social endeavor. This chapter also introduces the theme of gender and illustrates how the African American women in Rochester viewed themselves and their role in support of their community. Women developed the avenues of support upon which all other endeavors within the church rested. The importance of women to the church and community explains the primary position and length of this chapter.

Chapter Three—Education

This chapter examines the role of the church and its membership in the promotion of educational achievement for African Americans in Rochester. During this time period, the African American community and its leaders across the nation, while disagreeing about degree, quality, and kind, viewed education as essential for racial survival and prosperity. The African American church community in Rochester promoted educational achievement in a variety of ways, celebrated accomplishment and challenged restrictions placed upon its educational aspirations within Rochester.

Chapter Four—Economic Self-Development

The fourth chapter examines the role of the churches in the struggles of its members for economic self-development. The chapter describes the economic status of African Americans in Rochester and places their search for economic stability and advancement within the context of the economic environment in Rochester. The African American church in Rochester was deeply involved in the efforts for economic advancement, and provided an institutional framework of material and spiritual support.

Chapter Five—Political and Civil Rights

The fifth chapter examines the challenges to racial proscription that the African American churches and their leaders launched throughout the early decades of the twentieth century, when the African American community across the nation was experiencing continued set-backs in their efforts to protect not only their civil and political rights, but their very lives. This chapter reveals the courage and determination of African American individuals in Rochester and the role of the church as a support for their efforts.

Chapter Six: Conclusion

The last chapter draws conclusions that argue that the African American church community in Rochester was deeply involved in the struggles of African Americans for a better life for themselves and their children in Rochester, New York. The conclusions discuss faith as the motivating force for the members of the churches as they devised strategies for protection and generational advancement. The conclusion also explores the concept of accommodation and what it may have meant for African Americans living in Rochester who drew spiritual and practical sustenance from the African American church.

NOTES

1. I have chosen to employ the term "African American church community" for a number of reasons. The African American church is not a monolithic entity and has, since its birth in slavery and the free church movement in the north during the nineteenth century, displayed diversity both within and across denominations. While common, it is inaccurate to refer to *the* African American church. African Americans express a variety of doctrines, forms of worship, rituals, etc. In addition to having created African American congregations within the mainline denominations, African Americans have formed denominations of their own, and have eschewed denominational formation altogether to congregate in storefront churches, and in a number of sects. (See Hans A. Baer and Merrill Singer, *African-American Religion in the Twentieth Century: Varieties of Protest and Accommodation* (Knoxville: University of Tennessee Press, 1992.)

Coupled with this jubilant diversity is the reality that, as Arthur Huff Fausett points out, writing in 1944, "It is quite remarkable, therefore, that less than one out of every hundred of the millions of Negroes in the United States today who adheres to a religious faith subscribes to any but a Christian belief, although practically all the Negroes living in American at this time are direct descendants of these African slaves whose religious background certainly was African and neither European nor Christian." Arthur Huff Fausett, *Black Gods of the Metropolis: Negro Religious Cults of the Urban North* (University of Pennsylvania Press, 1944), 2.

The Christian religion, in all its formulations, has taken deep root within African American culture, and the church, across denominations, is the institutional body in which African American Christians congregate. One of the goals of this book is to illuminate as much as possible for the Rochester African American community what Peter Paris has termed the "black Christian tradition" which, he maintains, forms the "basis for [African American] collective experience of racial solidarity." Peter Paris, *The Social Teaching of the Black Churches* (Philadelphia: Fortress Press, 1985), xiii.

African Americans in Rochester held basic Christian theological understandings in common, and despite a variety of forms and structures, elaborated practices and behaviors with similar goals of mutual support, self-help, and social engagement. Therefore, the term "African American church community" respects both the diversity of separate congregations and denominations, with their particular contributions and attributes, as well as the unifying Christian sensibilities across congregations that informed their common life.

2. In abstract terms, faith is the human capacity to remain passionately involved in life through the exercise of transcendent understanding. Faith proved to be, therefore, a motivating force for African American Christians living in Rochester during the time period under discussion. This book makes no claims for the exclusive role of faith to motivate behavior, nor that all Christians employ their faith in the way that African Americans in Rochester did. It does claim an essential role for faith in this particular community.

This faith found expression in a specific Judeo-Christian context. Therefore, members of the African American church community in Rochester expressed a faith in God as the transcendent being upon whom they relied, and articulated Christian frameworks and biblical mandates through which to practice that faith.

3. Scholarship on the African American church is extensive, but in essential agreement concerning the church as a bastion of the community. See, for example, *The Negro Church*, ed. W.E.B. Du Bois, (Georgia: Atlanta University Press, 1903). In his introduction, Du Bois states, "The Negro Church is the only social institution of the Negroes which started in the African forest and survived slavery; under the leadership of priest or medicine man, afterward of the Christian pastor, the Church preserved in itself the remnants of African tribal life and became after emancipation the center of Negro social life. So that today the Negro population of the United States is virtually divided into church congregations which are the real units of race life." See also Carter Woodson, *The History of the Negro Church*, 3rd ed. (Washington, D.C.: The Associated Publishers, Association for Study of Negro Life and History, 1972, first pub. 1921); Benjamin Elijah Mays and Joseph William Nicholson, *The Negro's Church* (New York: Arno Press, 1969); Joseph R. Washington, Jr., *Black Religion: The Negro and Christianity in the United States* (Boston: Beacon Press, 1964); E. Franklin Frazier *The Negro Church in America* and C. Eric Lincoln *The Black Church Since Frazier* (New York: Schocken Books, 1974); Milton C. Sernett, ed., *Afro-American Religious History: A Documentary Witness* (Durham, N.C.: Duke University Press, 1985); C. Eric Lincoln and Lawrence H. Mamiya, *The Black Church in the African American Experience* (Durham: Duke University Press, 1990); Hart M. Nelsen, Raytha L. Yokley, Anne K. Nelsen, eds., *The Black Church in America* (New York: Basic Books, Inc., 1971); Evelyn Brooks Higginbotham, *Righteous Discontent: The Women's Movement in the Black Baptist Church 1880-1920* (Cambridge: Harvard University Press, 1993); and Robert Gregg, *Sparks*

From the Anvil of Oppression: Philadelphia's African Methodists and Southern Migrants, 1890-1940 (Philadelphia: Temple University Press, 1993).

4. See note 2, above.

5. Washington, *Black Religion: The Negro and Christianity in the United States*, 35.

6. Gayraud Wilmore, *Black Religion and Black Radicalism* (Doubleday and Co., Inc., 1972), 221.

7. Ernest Morial, "Black Religion and Civil Rights," in Joseph R. Washington, Jr., ed., *Black Religion and Public Policy: Ethical and Historical Perspectives* (n.p., 1978), 25.

8. John Hope Franklin and Alfred A. Moss, Jr., *From Slavery to Freedom: A History of Negro Americans*, 6th ed. (New York: Alfred A. Knopf, 1988), 258.

9. Jacqueline Jones, *Labor of Love, Labor of Sorrow: Black Women, Work and the Family from Slavery to the Present* (New York: Vintage Books, 1985), 192.

10. Lincoln and Mamiya, *The Black Church in the African American Experience*, 121.

11. Ralph Luker, *The Social Gospel in Black and White: American Racial Reform, 1885-1912* (Chapel Hill: The University of North Carolina Press, 1991), 166-167.

12. Ibid., 176.

13. Elisabeth Dan Lasch, "Black Neighbors: Race and the Limits of Reform in the American Settlement House Movement, 1890-1945" (Ph.D. diss., University of Massachusetts, 1990), Chapter Two.

14. Higginbotham, *Righteous Discontent*, 1.

15. Gregg, *Sparks from the Anvil of Oppression*, 199.

16. Ibid.

17. Clarence Taylor, *The Black Churches of Brooklyn* (New York: Columbia University Press, 1994), xvii.

18. Historians of the Great Migration and the development of northern urban African American communities note the importance of the church and its clergy in either discouraging or encouraging migrants. Additionally, these scholars acknowledge the role of the church in urban centers as institutions of self-help, with various degrees of success, and as institutions that reflected class and cultural antagonisms within the migrant population and between the migrants and established African Americans. See the following:

Gilbert Osofsky, *Harlem: The Making of a Ghetto: Negro New York, 1890-1930* (New York: Harper and Row, 1963), 113-117. Osofsky states, "After the collapse of the Afro-American Realty Company, Negro churches played a more important role in the development of Harlem than all other institutions in the Negro community" (113);

James R. Grossman, *Land of Hope: Chicago, Black Southerners, and the Great Migration* (Chicago: University of Chicago Press, 1989), 60, 62, 92, 94, 156-160. Grossman points out that "the most important institutions founded by the migrants were their churches" (156);

Peter Gottlieb, *Making Their Own Way: Southern Blacks' Migration to Pittsburgh, 1916-30*, (Urbana: University of Illinois Press, 1987), 197-205. Gottlieb notes, "churches were important in the settlement of many blacks, because they were key institutions in the black community–the foci of social, political, and cultural as well as spiritual activities" (197);

Kenneth L. Kusmer, *A Ghetto Takes Shape: Black Cleveland, 1870-1930* (Urbana: University of Illinois Press, 1976), 92-96, 207-209; and

Joe William Trotter, *Black Milwaukee: The Making of an Industrial Proletariat, 1915-45* (Urbana: University of Illinois Press, 1985), 128-132. Trotter acknowledges the importance of the church on page 31: "Similar to the pattern in other black urban communities, the church was the oldest and most stable black institution in pre-World War I Milwaukee."

Social historians who focus on reform, reform organizations, and particularly the role of African American women in reform note the presence of the church as an undergirding institution for these efforts. See the following:

Judy Weiss, *The National Urban League, 1910-1940* (New York: Oxford University Press, 1974), 12;

Jesse Moore "Resolving Urban Racial Problems: The New York Urban League, 1919-1959," *Afro-Americans in New York Life and History* 4 (January 1980), 27-44. Moore observes that "the NYUL had not been beholden to the whims and dictates of the Community Chest's Board of Directors, for independent memberships and contributions from churches and foundations accounted for more than 90 percent of its annual operating budget" (32);

Alvin B. Kogut, "The Negro and the Charity Organization Society in the Progressive Era," *Social Service Review* 44 (March 1970), 17. Kogut claims that "first in order of importance in communal life were the Negro churches which had become increasingly liberal and more involved in social-welfare efforts in Chicago";

Steve Diner, "Chicago Social Workers and Blacks in the Progressive Era," *Social Service Review* 44 (December 1970), 393-410.

The legacy of African American women in reform movements during the early decades of the twentieth century is replete with references to the importance of the church. See, for example:

Jacqueline Rouse, "The Legacy of Community Organizing: Lugenia Burns Hope and the Neighborhood Union," *The Journal of Negro History* 69, nos. 3-4 (1984), 114;

Linda Gordon, "Black and White Visions of Welfare: Women's Welfare Activism, 1890-1945," *Journal of American History* (September 1991), 567;

Floris Barnett Cash, "Radicals or Realists: African American Women and the Settlement House Spirit in New York City," *Afro-Americans in New York Life and History* 15 (January 1991), 9; Lillian Williams, "And Still I Rise: Black Women and Reform, Buffalo, New York, 1900-1940," *Afro-Americans in New York Life and History* 14 (July 1990), 17.

19. Peter Paris, *Social Teaching*. See Chapter 1. Paris describes the development of a black Christian tradition in the following way. "Those basic communal values culminate in a distinctive principle of coherence which forms the bedrock of black American religious existence. . . . 'The black Christian tradition' . . . designates the unique

contribution of the black churches to the nation and the world . . . [and is the] principal criterion for their assessment of everything affecting their common life" (xiii).

20. Paula Giddings, *When and Where I Enter: The Impact of Black Women on Race and Sex in America* (New York: Bantam Books, 1984), 81.

21. This critique differs from the white feminist critique in important respects. Womanist arguments assert the primacy of racism over sexism as the source of African American women's oppression and disclose the class and ethnic divisions among women which hinder the development of any common "sisterhood." Womanist scholars stress the historical importance and current vitality of cooperation between black men and women and the relative fluidity of gender roles, while at the same time deploring the sexism and power-mongering of black men in African American homes and institutions. A critical disjunction between feminist and womanist scholars is their understanding and appreciation of the role of motherhood. Feminists traditionally look upon motherhood as a source of gender oppression while womanists acknowledge motherhood as a source of pride and accomplishment for black women. This difference echoes the historical experience of white women whose confinement in the home depended upon their role as mothers while minority women experienced the denial of their role as mothers through the economic imperative to work outside the home.

22. Sharon Harley, "For the Good of Family and Race: Gender, Work, and Domestic Roles in the Black Community, 1880-1930," in Micheline R. Malson, Elisabeth Mudimbe-Boyi, Jean F. O'Barr, and Mary Wyer, eds., *Black Women in America: Social Science Perspectives* (Chicago: University of Chicago Press, 1988), 171.

23. Gordon, "Black and White Visions of Welfare," 560-561, and Williams, "And Still I Rise," 7.

24. Rouse, "The Legacy of Community Organizing," 118.

25. Anne Firor Scott, "Most Invisible of All: Black Women's Voluntary Associations," *The Journal of Southern History* 56 (February 1990), 5.

26. Higgenbotham, *Righteous Discontent*, 7.

27. Ibid., 16.

28. Karen V. Hansen, *A Very Social Time: Crafting Community in Antebellum New England* (Berkeley: University of California Press, 1994), 138.

29. Higgenbotham, *Righteous Discontent*, 157.

30. Judith Weisenfeld and Richard Newman, eds., *This Far by Faith: Readings in African American Women's Religious Biography* (New York: Routledge, 1996), 15.

∼ ONE ∼
HISTORICAL CONTEXT

Justice derives from a keen sense of fairness and equality, it is the aroma and the sweet fragrance of a consciousness of God.[1]

On June 9, 1899, J.W. Thompson and Hester Jerome Jeffreys shared the podium at the ceremony for the unveiling of the statue memorializing Frederick Douglass, abolitionist and orator, journalist and statesman, proponent of women's suffrage and most famous former resident of Rochester, New York. They had every right to feel proud of this accomplishment symbolizing the culmination and passing of an age. Slavery had been abolished and African Americans had responded to emancipation by reconstituting families, making institutions more visible, becoming political actors, and demonstrating economic and social achievement. In paying homage to the greatest proponent of African American rights, the African American residents of Rochester were both commemorating the struggle of the past and pledging themselves to the struggles to come. As Mr. Thompson unfurled the flag and Mrs. Jeffreys led the chorus of forty voices in "His Name Shall Live Forever," the hope and vision for the future of the African American community in Rochester began to take shape. These two leaders would build upon Douglass's legacy and interpret their role in their own communities in light of what they knew from where they stood on that podium. The primary vehicle for the expression of their hope and vision would continue to be, as it had been in the days of Frederick Douglass, the African American church. The movement to create the monument to Frederick Douglass and the ceremonies surrounding its completion and unveiling reveal the historical context in which African Americans in Rochester lived.[2]

What J.W. Thompson and Hester Jerome Jeffreys saw from their podium in Rochester that June afternoon in 1899 reflected both the hope and despair of African Americans. It had taken four long years of protracted struggle by Mr. Thompson, as head of the Committee to Commemorate Frederick Douglass, to raise the requisite ten thousand dollars. In this effort he obtained able assistance from Hester Jeffreys, secretary of that committee, Rev. James E. Mason, D.D., the pastor of A.M.E. Zion (at the time the only African American congregation in Rochester), and prominent African Americans from around the state and nation. The three members of the monument committee who resided in Rochester were all leaders in the church, and Bishop Alexander Walters, of the A.M.E Zion denomination, assisted their work. In raising the money, African Americans and people of color contributed fifteen hundred dollars, (A.M.E. Zion gave one hundred, which was one fifth of the amount raised from African Americans), with the Republic of Haiti donating one thousand. New York State gave four thousand dollars and the rest came from white patrons. J.W. Thompson coordinated the effort, contacting heads of state and prominent citizens in both the white and African American communities. For him, the monument stood as a "witness which will speak long after our tongues are hushed . . . inciting American manhood to love of country; to unconquerable devotion to a great cause, telling our boys that the humbleness of birth is no insurmountable barrier to eminence."[3] Thompson believed that the monument would make it impossible for the world to forget that America had raised such a one as Frederick Douglass, who stood as example and inspiration ideally for all Americans, but especially for "our boys."

Such sentiment reflected the deep concern of African American leaders over the conditions and treatment of African Americans, which became manifest with the close of Reconstruction and the institutionalization of laws and customs circumscribing, marginalizing, and threatening their lives. By the turn of the century, Jim Crow had become law in the South, disenfranchisement of African Americans in the South was complete, the Supreme Court had upheld the doctrine of "separate but equal," and lynching had become a national pastime centered in, but by no means restricted to, the South. Furthermore, the Spanish-American War, in which African Americans had played a key role, had placed a premium on the development of a racist ideology that would justify the domination of people of color in territories now under U.S. control.[4]

As Hester Jeffreys and J.W. Thompson opened their morning papers on "Douglass Day" in 1899 they read of the preparations of the executive committee to coordinate the day's events and welcome the key speaker, Governor Theodore Roosevelt. This executive committee consisted of liberal white philanthropists, ministers, and community leaders who were preparing a banquet to honor Roosevelt, to be held at the Powers Hotel where, as it happens, J.W.

Thompson worked as head waiter. Thompson himself received no mention in the article as the organizer and primary agent behind this event and one can only speculate about the nature of his possible "attendance" at the banquet. During the preceeding week, Rochester's papers had been filled with articles about the event, and while some of these actually considered Douglass's eminent life, few mentioned J.W. Thompson's role, or the efforts of Rochester's African American community to commemorate this great man. The article of the day focused on the arrival of the governor's train, the route he would take to the ceremony, and his subsequent itinerary. The article contained no mention of the other eminent leaders slated to attend, including Victoria Earle Matthews, Ida Wells Barnett, Bishop Alexander Walters, and Elizabeth Cady Stanton. The article also did not discuss the life or contributions of Frederick Douglass.

The following day, the *Democrat and Chronicle* reported on the festivities. It published the governor's speech in full, and included Bishop Walter's prayer (in which appears the only mention of thanksgiving for the work of J.W. Thompson and his committee). Roosevelt's comments are worth quoting at length as they reflect the predominant "progressive" stance on race which he exemplified.

> Let us all strive to pay the respect due his [Frederick Douglass's] memory by living in such a manner as to determine that a man shall be judged for what a man is; without regard to his color, race or creed, or aught else, but his worth as a man. . . .
>
> The worst enemy of the colored race is not the white man who abuses the colored man, but the colored man who fails in his duty as a citizen. The worst enemy of the white race is not some worthless wretch, some colored man who does an infamous act against the white race; it is the white wretch who acts so as to make us ashamed of our people. . . . [S]hameless deeds of infamous hideousness shall be punished speedily; by the act of law let shameful crime be punished, not avenging it by another crime. I would preach to the colored man that the vicious and disorderly elements in his own race are the worst enemies of his race. I would preach to the white man that he who takes part in lawless acts, in such lynchings as we have recently known, is guilty not only of a crime against the colored race, but guilty of a crime against his own race and guilty of a crime against the whole nation. Men who took part in the present lynchings were guilty of such hideous atrocity as should forbid them forever to hold up their heads as American citizens. . . .
>
> I would appeal to every man in this great audience to take to heart the lesson taught by this life; to realize that he must strive to fulfill his duty as an individual citizen, if he wishes to see the state do its duty. The state is only the aggregate of the individual citizens. . . . [H]e has left such a man as Booker T. Washington, a man who is striving to teach his people to raise by toil to be

better citizens, by resolute determination to make themselves worthy of American citizenship; until the whole country is forced to recognize their good citizenship.[5]

Roosevelt was a quintessential progressive and took the middle ground on race, incurring the wrath of Southern congressmen by inviting Booker T. Washington to dine with him at the White House when he became president, and incurring the wrath of the African American community when he dismissed an entire regiment of African Americans and disqualified them from further military or civil service after the Brownsville race riot of 1906, in which some soldiers participated.[6] As a preacher, he leaves much to be desired. His focus on lynching highlights the dominance of this appalling social phenomenon in the minds of race conscious women and men throughout the nation at the time. The next two years would yield 214 of these brutally evil acts of white mob violence, and the next 30 years fruitless attempts to legislate against them. Roosevelt's comments seem particularly inappropriate in the presence of Ida Wells Barnett, who was devoting her life to exposing the underlying causes of lynchings, which had more to do with economic and political priorities than with the rape of white women.

The sentiments on race that Roosevelt espoused reflected the prevailing atmosphere at the turn of the century. African Americans still needed to prove "worthiness" through unremitting toil and the social control of the immoral or worthless elements within their own community. Therein lay the implicit threat; if African Americans did not exert the proper control, white Americans could and would. These sentiments manifested themselves in the general acceptance of the crime allegedly underlying lynching, the rapid advance of Social Darwinist theory in the social sciences, which seeped into efforts for progressive reform, and the ideology of the "white man's burden" which steered foreign policy. The alleged moral inferiority of the Negro both here and abroad justified the social and military dominance of the "fitter" Anglo Saxon race. The progressive penchant for scientific studies led the bulk of social reformers to sop up "the newest teachings of biologists, anthropologists, sociologists, and historians (further popularized by novelists and journalists), who advanced scholarly 'proof' of the inferiority of the darker races."[7] Progressive reformers of the day elaborated many theories for the social ills they were addressing, and those who worked most directly with immigrant and poor populations, especially in the city, often wavered away from the Darwinian position, espousing an understanding of the environmental causes of the conditions they attempted to address. Even those who took this broader view, however, still fell into the habit of blaming the poor for their plight. While many of those engaged in urban reform did not adhere strictly to the Darwinian analysis, even the best of them tended to be uneven on the question of race.

Rochester's white community enthusiastically welcomed Roosevelt. An endorsement of his position is implicit in their blindness to the achievements of the notable African Americans, like J.W. Thompson and Hester Jeffreys, with whom they lived. To white Rochesterians, J.W. Thompson was the head waiter at the Powers Hotel, not the dynamic leader who organized and raised funds for the completion of the first monument to an African American in the nation. They extended this blindness to African American achievement in their willingness to ignore, through a lack of press attention, the presence of nationally renowned African Americans speaking at the event.

Bishop Walter's prayer exemplified the stance African Americans took during those years to address their place in American society. The *Democrat and Chronicle* also printed this text in full. After thanking God for creation and Jesus for redemption, Bishop Walter's thanks

> the Christian church with all its uplifting influences. We praise thee for the many auxiliaries of the church and the great work they are doing for the uplifting of humanity.
>
> We thank thee for our great nation and her splendid institutions. We thank thee for the love of liberty possessed by the Pilgrim Fathers which culminated in the independence of our country and later in the emancipation of the slaves.
>
> We thank thee for the human agencies which thou hast employed in bringing about reforms in all ages of the world, and especially for the life, character, talent and work of him who we have this day assembled to honor. May this monument which has been erected to the memory of the foremost negro of America be the harbinger of the banishment of prejudice from our land, and the dawn of the day when character and intelligence shall be fully realized, regardless of color.[8]

This prayer encapsulates the basic elements Christian African Americans drew on for strength in the decades ahead as their social, economic, and political position in the United States deteriorated. Faith in God and a reliance on the church and its "auxiliaries" to do God's work in the world came first. This work consisted primarily of liberation, effected through human hands, so that all human beings could live into their full potential regardless of color, as God had promised in the foundational tenets of the United States. The emancipation of the slaves was the great symbol of and inspiration for African Americans as they continued to work for liberation.

Neither Walters nor any of the other prominent African Americans attending this important event challenged the perception that their community had to work for its own improvement, and all acknowledged the need. But while African American leaders drew connections between moral character and social condition, their emphasis was on bettering their condition by both uplifting character and eradicating racism. They had faith in the ability of their people to prove themselves worthy and assumed that such worthiness would culminate in the acquisition of social status and civil and political rights. This assumption rested upon the understanding that such social realities established a base line for human beings to fulfill God's will for them as individuals unhindered by social constraints that limited their ability to respond to God's call. Consequently, men and women like J.W. Thompson and Hester Jeffreys engaged in both improvement and protest, combined in the concept of "uplift."

The spirit of protest that permeated the next few decades continually brought to the attention of white Americans the achievements of those who were battling the effects of segregation and discrimination. J.W. Thompson and Hester Jeffreys began this work immediately. Mr. Thompson responded to the slanted and incomplete newspaper accounts by publishing his own "authentic" history of the events leading up to the erection of the monument and published the addresses of the prominent African Americans who had appeared and spoken for the cause of the monument over the preceding four years. These comments serve as a ground for discussion of the ideological tenets and social and political positions African American leaders espoused as they strove against racist slurs and white condescension.

Victoria Earle Matthews, the "speaker of the evening" at a fund-raiser for the monument sponsored by Susan B. Anthony the previous year, expressed her understanding of the need for such a monument. Mrs. Matthews had founded the White Rose Mission in New York City in 1897. This institution began with ten women "from the various churches in the community"[9] who developed a settlement house and social services for young women migrating from the South. A key element in Mrs. Matthews's work consisted of greeting and shepherding young women off the trains in New York to keep them out of the clutches of agents from houses of prostitution. The range of her work included establishing day care, industrial education, and classes in African American history for young women. Mrs. Matthews was also active in the national African American women's club movement and interracial social reform efforts. Her presence at Douglass Day may well have reflected a relationship with Hester Jeffreys who shared the same activities and interests.

Mrs. Matthews's response to Elizabeth Cady Stanton's sincere wish that the monument "might be a school house or a tenement for the poor" is especially instructive in light of her own activities on behalf of those members of her gender and race less fortunate than herself.

Ours is a communion of tears. We know that our children are naked and ignorant and in need of schools; we know that there is great need of rescue and relief
of homes; we do not underestimate the value of education; but as mothers we see
the destiny and ambition of our children hanging in the balance; [and] as to a
monument in memory of Frederick Douglass the colored people have one to
whom they can point as an example, an incentive to their children.[10]

Especially in light of the severe proscriptions of the times, Mrs. Matthews
believed that African Americans needed more than concrete and practical measures, they needed inspiration. As the evidence of the lives of the African
American people in Rochester in the early decades of the twentieth century
will show, African Americans were prepared to make extreme sacrifices and
exert enormous energy to provide such inspiration and strength for their children.

When the monument failed to arrive on time for a scheduled unveiling
ceremony in 1898, the community decided to celebrate Frederick Douglass's
life anyway. Ida Wells Barnett, the fiery and famous founder of the anti-lynching campaign, spoke. She shifted the general tenor of commentary on the life
of Frederick Douglass from the motif of the "self-made" man who brought
himself up from slavery through the cultivation of his own mind and talents,
to the service Douglass provided for his race. African American leaders believed in this combination: individual achievement laid the foundation for
community service. Uplift involved self and others. Mrs. Barnett praised the
"work Douglass has done in espousing the cause of the anti-lynch law, of
women's suffrage and against the hydra-headed monster of prejudice. [He serves
as] inspiration for the present generation to take up those questions with renewed energy until perfect emancipation and freedom were granted to all races
and all sexes in the country".[11] Barnett saw Douglass as more than a brilliant
individual whose brilliance could serve as inspiration for individual achievement. He channeled that brilliance to serve his people and this was the heart
of the inspiration of the monument.

At that same event in 1898, T. Thomas Fortune gathered the attending
African American leadership for a meeting. Both he and Bishop Alexander
Walters had discussed the need to reawaken African Americans to political
protest and employed the celebration of Frederick Douglass to organize. J.W.
Thompson and Hester Jeffreys pledged themselves to political action on be-
half of their people by accepting active roles in the local chapter of the Na-
tional Afro-American Council founded that day. Both Mr. Thompson and Mrs.
Jeffreys served as treasurer of this chapter at different times.

The leadership that J.W. Thompson, Hester Jeffreys, and others like them
exerted on behalf of the African American community in Rochester over the
next few decades centered in the development of the African American church

community, but that community stood within a particular historical epoch and social context.

SOCIAL FRAMEWORK

The extent of the abandonment of blacks to white supremacists was not limited to the North's concession to the Southern states of complete control over domestic affairs and institutions or to Northern tolerance of the epidemic of lynchings and the outrageous activities of the Ku Klux Klan. Of equal significance was that process by which the North took on the Southern view of the black as "an alien, a menial, and a probable reprobate."[12]

The United States, in the first few decades of the twentieth century, became an industrialized, urban nation struggling to incorporate into northern urban centers the combination of immigrating Europeans and migrating African Americans. Urbanization, immigration, and migration touched off such deeply racist and ethnocentric responses as the passage of restrictive immigration laws, the creation of urban residential conclaves (usually called ghettos) for immigrants and African Americans, and the proliferation of race riots. Socially conscious leaders within the cities responded to an increasingly large and needy "foreign" population with attempts to aid the settlers in their adjustment to their new environment. The initial impulse to aid flowed from a religious, charitable, and philanthropic base which combined the Social Gospel with active social reform efforts, most notably present in the settlement house movement. Gradually rejecting a Social Darwinian analysis of society, progressive social reformers, especially those working in city neighborhoods, increasingly shifted their concern from the individual to the environmental causes of poverty. This shift, according to Allen Davis, contained deep religious impulses; "the influence of what Jane Addams describes as 'a certain renaissance of Christianity, a movement toward its early humanitarian aspects,' others called simply, the social gospel. . . . [T]he decision to live in the slums was somehow related to the desire to apply the Christian idea of service to the new challenges and the new problems of the city."[13]

As religiously and compassionately motivated white middle-class men and women set up shop in the slums to aid those less fortunate, they became ever more aware of urban conditions (sanitation, ventilation, education, unemployment, child labor) over which individual immigrants had no control. The change in perception from individual to corporate causes of urban blight led social reformers to engage in the systematic study of urban environments in an attempt to understand, control, and eradicate the social evils attendant upon industrialization and urbanization. This new orientation emphasized objectivity, yet it remained tinged with an elitist, paternalistic attitude. Those with the scientific findings became experts at curing the ills of those less fortunate. Nancy Weiss explains that "Whereas the main qualifications for 'friendly visitors' had been class affiliation, compassion, and a desire to serve, the new profession of social work required technical training."[14] Throughout this time period, social reformers turned increasingly to the scientific study of the city and the application of scientific social work through the active intervention of trained professionals. The development of the professions of sociology, anthropology, and psychology gained ascendancy over charitable and philanthropic personal absorption, while it created institutions and social structures of intervention in the lives of the foreign and poor, with or without their participation and consent. This institutionalization of professionalism over charity still emphasized an assessment of the character of those receiving services: a judgement concerning worthiness.

The transition to professionalization was never complete, however, and especially the paternalism and focus on the worthiness of the poor to receive aid continued to pervade the ostensibly more "scientific" approach. This is nowhere more obvious than in the generally benign but distant attitude of settlement house and social workers toward the plight of African Americans in the city. Historians of the Great Migration and social reform agree that while those efforts to address African American concerns in the cities engaged the participation of social reformers more than any other group, nevertheless, the social reform movement and its participants on the whole still exhibited prevailing racial prejudices.[15] Elisabeth Dan Lasch, a historian of the limits of reform during this time period, observes that for even the best of the era's reformers, the belief that slavery had erased any traces of civilization from African American culture and character led them to espouse self-help and self-improvement and indicated a signal failure in their ability to shift the blame for the causes of poverty from the individual to the environment, as many had been able to do for the lighter-skinned European immigrant.[16] Sometimes this necessitated psychological gymnastics, as in the case of Louise deKoven Bowen's report on the industrial and social status of African Americans in Chicago. Mrs. Bowen provided a comprehensive environmental analysis, citing discrimination against blacks and the effects of such discrimination on family life. Steven Diner points out, however, that her proposed remedies did not follow logically from an environmental analysis. "Instead of proposing changes in the social environment, Mrs. Bowen simply demanded that blacks be judged according to their individual worth. The public . . . should not assume that all Negroes were 'bad' simply because one Negro commits a crime."[17]

When the "scientific" approach ran true to form and purported to be objective, it assumed that once professionals had discovered the nature of basic conditions, professional expertise would help eradicate those conditions through education, and political and social reform. While shifting the focus from individual to corporate responsibility, this assumption contained a paternalistic condescension, claiming expert knowledge that professionals would bestow upon the less fortunate in order that they might learn what they needed to do to improve their lives. Particularly for white middle-class reformers, the inhabitants of urban environments in need of transformation were "other," the immigrant, the alien, the outsider, whose entrance into American society still necessitated adherence to norms of behavior which the social reformers were duty-bound to teach them.

Professional condescension assumed that the ultimate goal for immigrant and ethnic groups was assimilation, the proverbial "melting pot." White reformers presumed that while ethnic groups might retain some aspects of their previous culture, in all the ways that counted, particularly morals and values, immigrants would adopt American norms. This presumption highlights the racism of reformers which allowed for the possibility of civilizing immigrants, who they believed shared the grounding of European civilization, but disallowed the same possibility for African Americans, who they believed either retained the barbarism of Africa or had lost all traces of civilization under slavery.

The ascendancy of the professional, scientific, objective ethic, however flawed, also influenced the attitudes of professional social reformers toward the church, its missionary and religiously motivated work still vitally engaged in the city. Protective of newly acquired professional status, leaders in social scientific fields sought to divorce themselves from institutions and individuals who adhered to a more personal and missionary approach to the eradication of social ills. Competing for social support, not to mention funding, with missions and charitable institutions, social work professionals elaborated a secular approach to social reform that no longer respected religious motivation or agencies.

The desire to differentiate from and elevate professional social reformers above those engaged in "charity" or "missionary" work influenced the history of African American reform efforts. Even though African American sociologists such as W.E.B. Du Bois illustrated the centrality of the church to the African American community, the historical emphasis when studying his and other African American leaders' efforts in the city has remained upon the involvement in and development of secular and political reform. Only passing mention acknowledges that the groundswell of support for organizations such as the National Association for the Advancement of Colored People or the

National Urban League emanated from local church communities (even when the record of clergy involvement was uneven). Additionally, until very recently, very little attention has centered upon the "charity" and "missionary" work that African American churches themselves engaged in, and almost nothing has been done to illustrate how local congregations, as the acknowledged center of African American community life, addressed the social problems of their constituencies. Consequently, the current of religious motivation that energized African American involvement in social scientific investigation and secular programmatic development, as well as the church's own vast array of programs and supportive efforts to address urban problems, remains hidden.

AFRICAN AMERICAN SOCIAL REFORM

> The problem of the Negro in the United States at the opening of the twentieth century was so broad in scope and so deep in implication that only a large-scale, comprehensive attack on it could hope to make more than a dent in solving it. The programs of the National Association for the Advancement of Colored People and the National Urban League were broadly conceived to meet this challenge, but there was no guarantee that these agencies had the right formula. In the difficult task of social reform and regeneration, science and reason together could scarcely keep the door of hope open if passion and prejudice were pressing with all their might to close it.[18]

The single most influential change in the lives of African Americans in the early decades of the twentieth century was the fundamental demographic shift in population from the rural and urban South to the industrialized urban North. The causes and consequences of the Great Migration have captured the attention of historians who have explicated the dynamic tension between deteriorating conditions in the South and the lure of opportunity in the North. The Migration has also provided food for historical analysis of the social processes of African American urban class formation, proletarianization, and the formation of social institutions to address the needs of urban African Americans. This scholarship documents the unique structures and expressions of racism that shaped the oppression and discrimination visited upon African Americans in ways and to degrees that did not form part of the social reality for other immigrant and ethnic groups thronging to burgeoning industrial centers. Additionally, this scholarship records the various strategies and structures African Americans employed and built to challenge discrimination and defend themselves against oppression.[19]

Despite the absence of Jim Crow laws and the superficial civility extended toward African Americans in public, migrating African Americans soon learned that the North had its own structures of discrimination, which, while unwritten, were just as effective in prescribing African American social and economic roles and positions. As migration increased with the advent of World War I, discrimination and racial antagonism heightened. The social and residential discrimination that African Americans faced differed from the immigrants' experience in severity and longevity. Both groups had to deal with harassment, refusal of service, poor service, over-charging, etc., as well as confinement to particular neighborhoods within the city. For immigrants, however, conditions improved with assimilation into the urban scene and the acquisition of economic viability, while for African Americans conditions worsened and economic viability remained elusive. African Americans faced discriminatory measures that immigrants did not. They were first barred from participating in organized labor and then segregated within their own locals, branches, or labor organizations. They continued to live in segregated neighborhoods under worsening conditions, faced the denial of banking and financial assistance (being defined as poor risks), and could not obtain professional positions even with education or training. They continued to find only the lowest and most subservient types of jobs open to them. African Americans also experienced the extremity of racial violence. Lynchings proliferated and became more horrifying throughout the 1920s, and race riots became a common urban phenomenon. African Americans also did not benefit from the social welfare agencies and institutions which reform efforts had spawned for other groups suffering in the cities. The combination and severity of these discriminatory practices led Mary White Ovington to observe that although some white people (the "good" ones) were "glad to assist the poor and ailing Negro [they] are unwilling to help the strong and ambitious colored man to full opportunity." Anne Firor Scott noted that "in contrast to Irish or Russian immigrants for whom business or professional success sometimes overcame ethnic prejudice, African Americans were often more resented when they succeeded than when they failed."[20]

The leaders of the African American community responded to the plight of urban migrants in a variety of ways. The social and political reform efforts that have received the most scholarly attention are those that parallel white social reform efforts and highlight the role of interracial cooperation. Often, for those African American leaders and their liberal white allies in the cities, the tenets and standards of progressive social reform pervaded their own approaches to the problems within the African American community. The "practical application of economic and social intelligence as a tool for reform," galvanized African Americans with the hope that they could prove, objectively, through documentation and scientific evidence, the conditions under which African

Americans existed in the cities, and the social causes for those conditions.[21] Spurred by the possibilities of social scientific investigation, African American professionals broke important ground and advanced the state of their profession with their work. Most notable in these efforts were W.E.B. Du Bois and George Edmund Haynes. Allen Davis described the significance of studies like Du Bois's for the plight of Negroes in the cities:

> These studies . . . provided the first reliable information about the actual status of the Negro in the Northern cities. They showed beyond a doubt that there were large numbers of northern Negroes living under incredibly bad conditions. They demonstrated further that the problems present in any large urban center were magnified for the Negro: in most cases he was unskilled, often unable to join a labor union, and was the first to feel the effects of unemployment; for him the problem of housing and child labor was increased, and the whole situation was complicated by unreasoning prejudice on the part of the white population, as well as by the lack of initiative and leadership among his fellow Negroes. Most of the investigators, including Du Bois and Ovington, rejected the thesis that the Negro's position and slow progress could in any way be blamed on innate racial defect or inferiority.[22]

Such studies produced effects among the liberal white social reformers already sensitive to issues of race. Allen Davis draws a direct connection between the findings of such studies and the formation of the National Association for the Advancement of Colored People (NAACP) which called for the defense of legal rights for the Negro. Nancy Weiss confirms the progressive character and social reformist zeal of the white members of the National Urban League. The Urban League emphasized social scientific studies, the employment of blacks as investigators and social workers, and the development of concrete programs to address the urban needs of African Americans. The emphasis of these efforts was on assimilation, aiding and encouraging the migrants to adjust to the urban environment in ways that would get them jobs, education, and a healthier, safer environment. Assimilationist goals stemmed from a combination of a sincere wish to help the migrants adjust and a fear, which grew as the migration did, that the influx of unassimilated African Americans would threaten the status of African Americans already established in the cities and would upset racial balance and the pattern of race relations.[23]

As the twentieth century progressed, the leadership of the African American community struggled to implement strategies to achieve racial equality. Three leaders have received the most scholarly attention: Booker T. Washington, W.E.B. Du Bois, and Marcus Garvey. The most sophisticated studies point to the differences in ideological stance among these leaders while highlighting their common aim of racial equality with more or less emphasis on political agitation, education, economic accumulation, and the cultivation of morality. The rivalry especially between Washington and Du Bois has stimulated historical interest, but this focus tends, by analyzing the dynamics between male leaders at the national level, to overlook the importance of the development of interrelated strategies that local leaders (women and men) utilized to address specific problems in a particular context. Historians of particular localities, agencies, or programs have begun to give greater attention to the range of activities and intellectual justifications that African Americans developed to respond to urban conditions and shape their own communities. This work illuminates the underlying passionate beliefs that informed African American choices in specific contexts.[24] Such attention to range allows for a broadening of the contours of what constitutes reform efforts and ultimately allows for the investigation of the efforts and activities within the African American church.

Uplift

African American leaders throughout urban communities in the north hashed out positions and strategies that expressed their personal histories, their local social context, and their understanding of what would work best. These leaders all strove for the creation of a society in which African Americans could achieve their greatest individual and communal human potential. Most understood that this goal necessitated achieving racial equality, thus they worked to eradicate discrimination and racism. Some, most especially the followers of Marcus Garvey, were willing to entertain the vision of an African American community free of white domination, but not integrated into white American society, though few Garveyites were committed to moving to Africa or elaborated a sophisticated understanding of African American nationhood. The interplay of varying strategies and the recognition of common aims kept the struggle against continued racial oppression alive.

African American leaders spoke of "uplift" as the method most likely to achieve racial equality in the United States. Uplift included concerted community effort on behalf of individual African American achievement so that more and more African Americans could become exemplars of human excellence. Uplift required an education, economic advancement, and strong moral fiber (the head, the hand, and the heart). With an ever expanding population of intelligent, economically stable, and morally sound African American individuals, the doors to the full responsibilities and opportunities of first class citizenship would open and usher in the complete acceptance and integration of Negroes into American life; or, conversely, provide the framework for a strong and capable African American community impervious to white domination.

Uplift also included attention to the entire individual and the society surrounding that person. Social uplift required not only the strengthening of character, the provision of education and skills, and the public display of accomplishment so that white America might learn the lesson of African American humanity. An essential component of uplift consisted of the political defense of that accomplishment and the continued political protest of any social realities that impinged upon African American efforts for improvement.

The historical record provides the tale of a dichotomy in efforts to achieve uplift; the opposition of strategies of self-help and racial solidarity to strategies of integration and interracial cooperation. Historians usually connect self-help and racial solidarity to the concept of uplift, and emphasize those activities African Americans engaged in on their own behalf. This strategy advocated the development of separate African American institutions, racial economic cooperation, and political protest in the form of the defense of African American social and cultural integrity. This last characteristic grew in strength with the waning of Booker T. Washington's influence and the ascendancy of Garvey; but more importantly it grew out of the urban reality of communal segregation which encouraged African Americans to draw more deeply upon their own strengths, history, and traditions. Conversely, the strategy of integration and interracial cooperation most obviously has utilized the tactics of political and legal protest and the development of interracial or African American institutions that developed programs geared to helping African Americans assimilate into white social structures and institutions. While discussions of uplift generally described self-help and racial solidarity efforts, those engaged in legal and political action on the behalf of integration also were committed passionately to the improvement of the race.

Some historians of African American urban development maintain a rough corollary between these ostensibly opposing strategies and the development of class or social stratification within the African American community. Their thesis posits that the "old elite" espoused an integrationist approach because those leaders within the African American community had succeeded through cooperation with whites and viewed the creation of separate institutions as a surrender to racism. On the other hand, new migrants advocated self-help and racial solidarity, as they struggled to succeed as entrepreneurs catering to a mostly black clientele and took a more realistic view of the progressively more segregated African American community, upon which these "new elite" leaders depended. Integrationists advocated agitation against discrimination, for suffrage, and in support of legislation enforcing equal access. Advocates of separate endeavors for self-help and improvement emphasized racial pride, racial self-consciousness, and racial over interracial cooperation in the formation of separate, African American controlled institutions. According to one historian, even when integrationists conceded the practical necessity of separate institutions, they viewed them as "temporary expedients," not permanent structures.[25]

The dichotomy between supposedly opposing strategic camps collapsed (if it ever held true) under the weight of worsening conditions and as northern urban environments offered African Americans fewer and fewer choices down the road to integration. Discrimination in employment, education, housing, and public services encouraged African American leaders to develop their abilities within racially separate institutions and programs created to meet the needs of African Americans in the city. African American leaders of whatever ideological stamp, male or female, came to believe in the necessity of using any methods available to provide the services their people needed. This blurring of strategic choices highlights the fundamental aims that African American leaders involved in community development espoused. The hope for immediate and full racial equality that emancipation and Reconstruction had engendered gave way throughout the early decades of the twentieth century to a concerted effort to insure African American endurance and survival. Leaders dealt with the issues of the African American community as a whole. Uplift came to signify internal skill development so that people could take advantage of every opportunity to advance the chances of the race. In order to fulfill the ultimate aim of nurturing African American human potential, leaders dipped into various ideological streams and utilized any strategy. Linda Gordon emphasized that "race uplift was usually welfare work by definition, and it was always conceived as a path to racial equality" and recognized that those women engaged in uplift challenged racism from early in their careers. Gordon defined political protest as integral to the notion of black "philanthropy," and while she connected the concept of uplift primarily with the building of separate institutions she also highlighted the political awareness of African American women working within and building such institutions.[26]

As a result, while not eschewing interracial cooperation or abandoning the hope of racial equality through integration of white social institutions, urban African American leaders began to view separatism as distinct from segregation and as a positive strategy for achieving uplift. Class or social status tensions notwithstanding, the growth of positive racial consciousness allowed for the creation of coalitions among various segments of local African American leadership, between the "elite" and the working mass, and between African Americans and those whites who shared their goals.[27] The identification of commonalities across lines of social stratification gained strength from the practical realities of African American urban life. Professional African Americans committed to working for racial uplift found themselves denied those very opportunities they were working to create for more of their brothers and sisters. African American teachers and social workers especially had difficulty finding work outside of segregated facilities or African American institutions. Confronting discrimination that limited the fulfillment of their own potential, African American leaders grew aware of and more concerned about issues of basic survival for African Americans who did not have their educational, economic, or social advantages. The desire to construct institutions and programs that would insure basic survival and provide a framework for the internal cohesiveness and strength to endure the evils of the times took precedence over particular strategic approaches. W.E.B. Du Bois personifies this transformation. By 1935, Paula Giddings notes, Du Bois

> in his *Crisis* editorials . . . had counseled that racial segregation and racial discrimination were two different issues. Integration for its own sake was both meaningless and demeaning. "Never in the world should we fight against association with ourselves," he exhorted. Undoubtedly referring to the patronizing nature of interracial cooperation, Du Bois requested that Blacks not "submit to discrimination simply because it does not involve actual and open segregation". He felt that Blacks should be devoting their efforts to building their own institutions instead of integrating White ones.[28]

Certainly the controversy among the leadership was not over; however, those actively engaged in program development within the African American community, especially at the local level, no longer hesitated to both do it themselves and to cooperate with those whites with whom they had mutual goals.

Historians of African American urban community formation and social reform tend to emphasize the role of segregation and discrimination in forcing the development of racial consciousness and pride. This emphasis suggests that if Northern urban environments had welcomed African Americans, or at least afforded them the same level of opportunity to assimilate into mainstream society that European immigrants experienced, the integrationist approach to racial equality would have held sway over the development of separate institutions. This argument leans on one side of a dialectic while not taking seriously enough the other; the agency of African Americans in creating the community environment most appropriate for the exercise of African American life. Since racism and discrimination played a dominant role in restricting the potential of African Americans, clearly the measures they took to protect themselves were, to a great degree, a response to a hostile environment. Ironically, social analysts and liberation theologians of the 1960s and 1970s have offered a negative interpretation of the African American churches's choice in those years to foster the development of their own institutions and promote individual growth primarily within their own communities through designing and implementing their own services and programs for education and economic advancement. These critics have hurled epithets such as "accomodationist," "betraying," and "inwardly-focused" at the church during this period.[29] Supposedly, African Americans gave in and gave up until after World War II and the beginning of the Civil Rights Movement. Yet that is exactly what African Americans and their churches did not do, despite the waffling and silence seemingly more typical of the majority of African American clergy leadership at the national level.

African Americans chose not to give up in the face of extremely destructive forces arrayed against them. In this choice they turned to each other across social stratification and gender lines for the support, encouragement, and creative energy not only to survive and endure but to prosper and pass on the possibility of success to their children. As they embraced each other's efforts, they saw and took pride in who they were as African Americans. This recognition took place within their own communities and institutions and laid the foundations for on-going as well as future political protest that spoke of the existence and accomplishments of African Americans, and demanded recognition from white America. When Jacqueline Jones speaks of the inward focus of African Americans after World War I, she describes the ways in which they "transformed southern folkways of self-help into northern voluntary and commercial institutions."[30] Such an inward focus strengthened and rejuvenated communities, and ultimately created the root-system for future growth. As such, the institutional and programmatic efforts that African Americans created became collective avenues of self-expression, thus fulfilling the aim of exercising human potentiality and laying groundwork for the future visions of racial equality. As Evelyn Brooks Higginbotham points out, the goal of uplift was "at once progressive and conservative." Progressive, even subversive, in that it claimed equal capacity for African Americans in the attainment of education and accomplishment according to the standards of the white middle class. Conservative in that it adhered to those very standards. Exploring the justification for a liberal arts education for young aspiring African American Baptist women, Higginbotham notes:

> The northern Baptists envisioned their colleges as assimilating apparatuses that would render the black elite "thoroughly homogeneous" with white middle-class culture. Herein lay the dialectic between the conservative and progressive implications of their educational philosophy. When they compared their southern schools to the University of Chicago or to Vassar and Wellesley, as they often did, they signaled a progressive challenge to both racism and sexism and thereby

encouraged their male and female students to take pride in their intellectual capabilities. For example, Hartshorn maintained noble aspirations for its students, stating that it did not prepare young women to be servants.[31]

Elitism

Ostensibly, African American leaders of efforts to address the urban problems of their community shared the values and goals, if not the economic status, of their white middle-class counterparts. Scholars of African American reform efforts are clear that both the "talented tenth" (male and female) and those advocating different routes to advancement shared a set of behavioral mandates indicative of positive character, which communicated human worth. Leaders also shared the attitude that they themselves best personified these values and behaviors and, by virtue of their social position and knowledge, had the responsibility of passing them on to those still striving to become what they themselves were already. Scholars also agree that "this effort of the middle class to mould the behavior of the migrants after its own image was clearly a one-way process. There was never any hint that the black bourgeoisie had anything to learn from its newly arrived neighbors. Nor was there much tolerance for diversity in value systems or lifestyles".[32] Members of urban elites clearly disdained the "lower element" of their own communities and strove to both disassociate themselves from it and transform it in its own image. Behind this disdain lay the fear of the loss of status and position based upon the racial stereotypes, touched off by the behavior of the migrants, that could too easily rub off on "respectable" members of African American communities. Articulate African American men and women understood that their racial identity made them vulnerable to wholesale condemnation based upon the unruly or "criminal" behavior of their unassimilated brothers and sisters. August Meier interprets the sociological work of W.E.B. Du Bois as conveying this message: "Negroes ought to constantly register strong protests against prejudice and injustice, but they should do so because these things hindered them in their own attempt to elevate the race. And this attempt, Du Bois held, must be marked by vigorous and persistent efforts directed toward lessening crime and toward inculcating self-respect, the dignity of labor, and the virtues of truth, honesty, and charity."[33]

The list of values constantly stressed in messages from clergy, teachers, social workers, settlement house workers, and neighborhood advocates in the African American community certainly reads like a Protestant Work Ethic litany. The moral development of the black masses rested upon attaining the virtues of cleanliness, duty, punctuality, efficiency, proper deportment, thrift, industry, fidelity, accuracy, honesty, persistence, intelligence, patience, perseverance, good manners, sobriety, sexual discipline (couched in the phrase "elementary decency"), truth, charity, and self-respect. African Americans bought the promise of American society to reward those individuals who worked hard to get ahead, proving, through hard work, that they deserved that success.

Social analysts interpret any modifications or deviations from the white elitist model as an African American response to white racist hostility which forced a recognition of commonality based upon race. This recognition especially influenced the extent and form of paternalistic condescension African American leaders displayed toward those lower down the social scale. Specifically, African Americans had no trouble identifying the root causes of poverty as environmental, not personal, however much they condemned individual transgressions. Historians of African American women's reform efforts are clearest on this point. Paula Giddings and Lillian Williams concur in their analysis that African American women viewed the harshness of the environment and the lack of opportunity as the basic cause of the social distance between the elite and the masses. Consequently, Linda Gordon explains, one of the important differences between white and African American women reformers was the tendency for African Americans to support universal rather than "means-tested" programs (that could readily separate the "worthy" from the "unworthy" poor). African Americans understood that "unreasoning racial prejudice" played the decisive role in keeping them all in the position of second-class citizenship and the elitism they practiced contained the desire to protect people with whom they identified from the harshest indictments the wider society would confer upon those individuals caught in acts of human weakness or behaving contrary to social norms. Thus, those providing services to the members of their own communities believed in widening and deepening the scope of opportunity rather than restricting access based on behavior. Leaders believed that others of their people would behave as they themselves had if given the opportunity.[34]

Racial discrimination had the more subtle effect of forcing a sense of common identity between the elite and the masses based on a shared sense of economic precariousness. African American leaders seldom had accumulated or inherited wealth and even the most prosperous had to inculcate their children with a thirst for knowledge and a respect for the skills necessary to find stable employment in order to maintain prosperity across generations. Most of the African American men and women engaged in professional work in their communities *had* to work, unlike many of the socially conscious volunteers who thronged the ranks of white middle class reform. Additionally, the occupations that encompassed the middle-class for African Americans consisted of a broad range of professional and skilled employment: job categories that would not necessarily elicit middle-class standing in the white community. African American women and men who did not work under close supervision—seamstresses, small-business owners, and independent skilled laborers—garnered community respect that placed them among the elite. The constant threat to the economic viability of African Americans that the structures of discrimination imposed casts a subtle but important distinction upon the value African Americans placed on characteristics such as punctuality, thrift, industry, persistence, and sobriety. These behaviors not only represented a need for social control but exemplified the rules for economic survival, for the elite as well as the masses. Paula Giddings points out that "whatever their [black women reformers'] views about social sanctions, one reason for the emphasis on morality was that the lack of it could be impoverishing." So it was that Ida Wells Barnett's mother made sure her children "understood discipline and the need for education, both secular and religious. 'Our job,' Ida . . . wrote, 'was to learn all we could.'" Similarly, the daughters of Henry Beard Delany, the first African American Bishop of the Episcopal Church, U.S.A, understood from an early age that they would leave home, earn their own money to pay for their education, go to college, and enter a profession that would serve their people.[35]

The subtle and pervasive effects of racial discrimination played an important role in the service orientation of the African American elite—an orientation which distinguished this body from its white middle-class counterpart in its close identification with the people it attempted to serve, even as it condemned behaviors that fell outside the norms it attempted to lay down. Racism created the conditions in need of redress to which African Americans responded, and shaped the strategies which the African American elite articulated. Yet racism did not dictate the choices and strategies. The litany of morals and behaviors recited above fall in with white middle-class expectations for the social control of the African American masses. However, these values served additional purposes, and they were not the only values that shaped the African American response. African American people drew upon African American cultural values and traditions in order to temper and shape their attempts to support one another under dire circumstances, thus imbuing their community with their own moral imperatives.

African American Cultural Values

The community orientation and stress upon relations of mutual reciprocity that had defined social relations of African tribal life played crucial roles in the ability of African Americans to build a community life that sustained them as a people during slavery. For free African Americans, the social obligation to

collectively support each other through the practice of generosity, cooperation, sacrifice, and flexibility across boundaries of gender and social status
permeated the attitudes of African American leaders and shaped their otherwise elitist pretensions.

The obligation to help those less well off, which engendered condescension
among the elite, was only one expression of a traditional understanding that
permeated the entire community. The African American community ethic
assumed that everybody would help everybody else, regardless of social station
or material resources. The ability to help increased responsibility, but did not
make someone "better," since everyone gave what he could. The moral worth
of an individual depended more upon her generosity of spirit than the size of
her bank account. African American women reformers pointed to the contributions that women from all walks of life made. In her tour of the South in the
1870s Frances Ellen Harper extolled the efforts of humble women. "One of
the most efficient helpers," she said, "is a Mrs. Madison, who, although living
in a humble and unpretending home, had succeeded in getting up a home for
aged coloured women."[36]

The practice of mutuality occurred within the context of personal relationships and local communities and extended into wider social institutions.
Jacqueline Jones described the informal networks of support that created per-
meable boundaries between men and women as they worked to support each
other, between and among households of kin which could expand or contract
as the occasion demanded, and between spheres of private and public activity.
The people creating these networks taught and practiced sacrifice and generosity, cooperation, and the long-term sublimation of personal goals to the
aspirations of a better future for one's children.[37]

Individual attainment represented the potential buried within the community and disproved stereotypes. Therefore, the community supported individual accomplishment and the social accoutrements that went along with it,
including conspicuous consumption and upward mobility. However, African
American communities often stressed cooperative over competitive modes of
behavior in the support of individual success. Susan Greenbaum describes the
importance of group cooperation in the economic development of the African
American community. She challenges the precept that minorities only succeed
"by overcoming the handicaps of group membership, and by learning how to
compete effectively in the market economy." Greenbaum examines the development of mutual aid societies. She describes them both as providing a training ground for the development of managerial and financial expertise and as
shielding their membership from the "competitive exploitation inherent in
market systems." African American mutual aid societies created terms of ex-

change "designed to be generous, not exploitative," and to protect members, not "teach them how to be more efficient exploiters." Greenbaum concludes that "the tangible financial benefits provided at affordable rates were at least as important as the indirect effects of human resource development," at least at the individual level. The risks of not belonging outweighed the sacrifices individuals with meager resources made to support mutual aid societies. Mutual aid societies contributed to the development of human capital at the community level through channeling funds into programs and services benefiting the wider community such as old age homes, orphanages, hospitals, schools, and housing. Greenbaum maintains that the grass-roots development of mutual aid societies grew into stable insurance companies and banks, some of which still operate, forming a viable financial infrastructure for the African American community—something that cannot be said for many of the white financial institutions founded in the nineteenth century that were based upon the principles of individual competition.[38]

Jacqueline Jones describes the stress that African men and women placed upon maintaining appropriate gender roles at the same time that they expected that those roles would be flexible in the service of the greater good of the family and community. Jones describes a "rural folk culture based upon group cooperation rather than male competition and the accumulation of goods" which African American migrants brought with them to the urban North. The sense of gender, family, and group cooperation eased the transition for African American women into the northern labor market and opened channels of support among kin, friends and neighbors.[39]

African Americans respected gender distinctions, admired and aspired to individual achievement, and sought social status both within and outside the African American community, but they sought to create and sustain social roles and social status through cooperation, mutuality, reciprocity, generosity, and sacrifice. The combination of these values led to a particularly porous process of community and institutional formation. Jane, one of the professional women whose life Gwendolyn Etter-Lewis narrates in *My Soul is My Own*, describes the development of the all-black community in which she grew. Jane claims that while hard work was characteristic of every day life, as was the constant striving for self-improvement, striving and hard work were not based on the concept of beating someone else. The community practiced cooperation throughout its institutions. When the school choir learned *The Messiah*, for example, everyone learned all the parts, not just the ones that a person's individual range could reach. Parents were in and out of the school room, dropping in and helping children with their work. The baseball teams played to excel in the sport, but they had the same pitcher and catcher playing for all the teams. Explains Jane, "you couldn't very well have competition if you were gonna use the same pitcher all the time and the same catcher all the time." Jane understands that the cooperative ethic did not extend as far in other communities as it did in hers. She notes that in her town "we had one large church building and one smaller chapel and the different denominations took turns on having service in that one church. You see, where else could you get cooperation like that." She believes that the breakdown of cooperation in other communities has to do with outside pressures; that because African Americans both founded and governed her home town, they had the freedom to develop their own way of doing things.[40]

Cooperating with and taking on obligations for helping others allowed African Americans to work hard and make present sacrifices for the eventual betterment of the community. The strength of this ethic shines forth in the respect members of the African American community showed to individuals who may not have attained material advantage but who used their resources, especially what they acquired through education, for the welfare of the community as a whole. This ethic also declares itself in the willing sacrifices parents made to advance the chances of their children, and in the expectations incorporated by the children to succeed not only for themselves but in order to give back to their communities. The stress upon many of the "disciplining" precepts that formed the more widely touted elitist admonitions to the lower sort takes on a different meaning when placed within the context of practicing generosity and sacrifice for the good of the community. Such qualities as thrift, sobriety, sexual discipline, proper deportment, etc., realigned the avenues for the allocation of resources away from self-aggrandizement and toward community maintenance and prosperity.

African American social reform efforts during the first few decades of the twentieth century took place within a social context of extreme racism which worsened the discrimination and oppression that African Americans experienced. In confronting this environment and in developing their own communities, African Americans drew upon the intellectual streams of thought which informed wider social reform efforts and the traditions and moral precepts that had shaped and sustained them in the past. Their efforts therefore combined in practice strategies and beliefs that would ultimately serve the best interests of the community as a whole and further the opportunity for the achievement of human potential for African American people. The African American church community and its teachings drove this process by providing the institutional setting, theological understanding, and spiritual support necessary to create and sustain it.

THE AFRICAN AMERICAN CHURCH

"Every time the door was open, we went in."
Elsie Kilpatrick[41]

The history of the African American church community in Rochester has its roots in the abolition movement and independent African American church movements of the nineteenth century.

Until 1902, with the founding of Trinity Presbyterian Church, A.M.E. Zion was the only African American church in Rochester. It was founded in 1827, the same year slavery was abolished in New York State. Thomas James, a staunch abolitionist committed to the organization and education of his people, began A.M.E. Zion as a joint church and school, in order to teach illiterate African Americans to read the Bible. James was a friend of Frederick Douglass, and it was at his suggestion that Douglass made his home in Rochester. A.M.E. Zion housed the printing press for the *North Star*, Douglass's abolitionist paper, and became a site on the underground railroad. Frederick Douglass, Harriet Tubman, and Susan B. Anthony addressed African Americans from its pulpit.[42]

Like A.M.E. Zion, the other African American churches included in this study had founders or their ancestors who had been slaves. For example, the father of Jesse Stevens, one of the founders of Trinity Presbyterian, was a slave preacher. James Young's family, which belonged to St. Simon's Episcopal, had been recruited from the south by George Eastman, to become servants. Mt. Olivet's founding band also included people who had come North after emancipation.[43] The members of Rochester's early African American churches had history or experience with the struggle against slavery and resided in a community with a long legacy of abolition and protest.

African American church leaders during the first four decades of the twentieth century extended a Christian understanding of God's protection of the oppressed, and God's success as the liberator of the slaves, into their own struggles. Faced with continued racial discrimination, African American Christians in Rochester, and elsewhere, drew upon Christian ideas and Biblical interpretations, formed during slavery and the abolitionist struggle, to support them. Among the most compelling concepts that informed theological premises were *equality and freedom, justice, sin* and *salvation*.

Equality and Freedom

African American church leaders in the early twentieth century understood that in order to obtain justice, which laid the groundwork for salvation, human beings had to live in a condition of equality under God and with the freedom to respond immediately to God's call. As slaves sought to practice their faith and as free African Americans sought to establish their own indepedent churches, they justified their efforts with the understanding that nothing must interfere with their relationship with God. Albert Raboteau described the struggle for African American Baptist preachers under slavery.

> Our religion is a matter between us and our God, with which no power on earth has a right to interfere. Soul-liberty is the rightful heritage of all God's moral creatures. Not over the religion of the slave has civil authority any power, nor yet has it over that of the citizen.[44]

Robert Ross Johnson reiterated this theme in his consideration of the history of Baptists in Rochester. He claimed that in order for African Americans to respond to God, they must be free. "God's people must be ready for service when God calls. They must never place themselves where they cannot respond immediately."[45] African American Christian theology continues to articulate this theme. For African Americans, equality and freedom do not function as abstract principles but as necessary human experience. Their faith in God claims as evidence of the possibility of equality and freedom the abolition of slavery and the exercise of civil and political rights attendant upon emancipation from a condition of human servitude. The goal of racial equality is a prerequisite for the exercise of freedom in the pursuit of the full actualization of human potential that places human beings in a position to respond to God. For African American Christians, God's love for humanity requires that human beings be free and equal: equal in God's love and equally responsible to God as parent; free to fulfill God's particular will for each person. "If God calls you to discipleship, God calls you to freedom."[46] Freedom thus entails socio-political freedom and economic independence.

African American Christians understood God as deliverer and emancipator. God delivered Christ from death as God delivers all of God's children from oppression. At that time, and into the present, African Americans viewed Jesus's resurrection as God's victory over oppression.[47] African American Christianity emphasizes the Mosaic theme of the Old Testament and conceives of Christ as the liberator who exemplified solidarity with and ministry to the poor and oppressed. Liberation and deliverance both depended upon the activity of Christians in the existential world. Bishop Alexander Walters, in describing the genesis of the Afro-American Council founded in Rochester, New York after the unveiling of the Douglass monument, called for a shift in political action on the part of concerned African Americans. He claimed that in order to be *saved* African Americans must educate themselves, develop their moral fiber, get money, and stop leaving their political fate in the hands of the Republican party. They must organize themselves. As inspiration for these efforts, Bishop Walters identified the hand of God in clearing the path for African Americans to fight for their own emancipation during the Civil War and in electing African Americans to Congress and enacting legislation to further their liberation. He called upon the example of Moses and the Hebrews, whose oppression seemed to them to be increased in the desert, and advocated that African Americans not be discouraged. "Let us improve our morals, educate ourselves, work, agitate, and wait on the Lord." It should be clear that "waiting on the Lord" was not a passive activity, it was a declaration of faith.[48] Monroe Fordham concludes that "in a sense, black religious arguments against slavery and racial prejudice represented an attempt by early nineteenth century blacks to conceptualize a theology for liberation. Through the propagation of such a gospel they hoped that slavery and racial oppression would ultimately be ended, and liberty and justice would prevail for all."[49]

Freedom was a necessary condition for African Americans to act as their own moral agents, perfecting their relationship with God. Freedom also entailed responsibility to act according to God's will, through serving the needs of one's neighbor, and protesting conditions of inequality and injustice. According to Fordham, this understanding reflected the African American Christian commitment to "the proposition that righteous men and the church had a responsibility to work for the improvement or regeneration of society."[50] Such improvement entailed attention to one's personal moral state as well as to the conditions in society.

Justice

Justice involves the redress of existential conditions that limit the ability of human beings to respond to God's call. Bishop J.S. Caldwell, of the A.M.E Zion denomination, speaking at the dedication ceremony of the new Memorial church erected in 1906 in Rochester, preached to those assembled:

> The lash of discouragement cracks continually over the heads of some of the poor of our own kith and kin. It is very easy to fail: some of the greatest characters who have figured in history have failed. We have looked for a long time to legislative enactments for relief in certain directions when our franchise and other rights have been abridged. Many or our efforts have failed and many of us have become discouraged. My text looms amid this awful darkness and brings forward His character and says of Him: "He shall not fail or be discouraged until judgment is set in the earth, and the isles shall wait for His law." He shall not fail as the emancipator.[51]

African American Christian leaders believed that before an individual can respond to the call of God, certain existential conditions must obtain. Spiritual acuity involves the recognition and application of the gifts, talents, and resources that comprise the unique personality fashioned for a specific purpose in God's creation. The realities of the world can impinge on an individual's opportunity to realize those gifts either in preventing a recognition of what they are or in circumscribing their application. Consequently, justice demands that reality bend in service to the realization of human potential.

Sin

African American scholars have described an understanding of sin that differentiates between personal transgression and a broken relationship with God.[52] This distinction allowed African American religious leaders to pinpoint the greatest sin in American society as racism, which prevented African Americans from actualizing their relationship with God. A commitment to this relationship demands that they address and eradicate the sin of racism both for themselves and for the world. Peter Paris explains that "the thought of black churches distinguishes the 'sins' of black people from the 'sin' of white racism, which is considered by far the most wretched. White racism . . . is considered the greater evil and possibly the source of all sin. . . . Consequently, all action (religious or political) that is aimed at correcting the social injustice of racism is viewed as moral action."[53] In their struggles for justice, African Americans often identified the sin of racism as primarily responsible for those struggles and for any setbacks they might experience. From slavery to the present, many African Americans have understood their challenge to white society as a test of the Christianity of white America and of the ability of this society to live out the gospel. Viewing racism as the greatest of evils and facing its permutations throughout a society built upon the promise of equality and justice for all, many African Americans have believed their mission to include not only their own freedom but the salvation of the entire nation. The resistance to racism "affirmed their humanity, since that activity alone imbued them with self-respect and human dignity. In fact, the existence of black churches themselves evidenced their humanity in the most basic way, because in those places they experienced a public racial forum for addressing the fundamental issues pertaining to racial freedom, independence, and justice."[54] In 1932, Reverend James Rose of Mt. Olivet Baptist Church, Rochester, New York experienced racial discrimination within the Baptist denomination. His response reflects the African American emphasis on the practice of racism as the ultimate test for genuine Christianity.

Jesus is our way to brotherhood, but that way hardly runs through the Christian church as it is today constituted. . . . The Caucasian race which embraces Christianity in its organized form, cannot practice real brotherhood with the colored races of the earth as long as it feels itself superior to them. You cannot have brotherhood when one brother is admitted to certain places and the other is excluded, but organized Christianity sanctions it.[55]

In an editorial appearing in *The Baptist*, the author, probably Rose, continues:

It is high time that Christian people, North and South, made up their minds just what their religion does require of them as to racial prejudice and discrimination, whether directed toward Jew, Asiatic or Negro. Without any question the Master of men is judging our Christian professions at this moment not in terms of a formal orthodoxy of theological statement but in terms of our attitudes and conduct toward his brethren of different race or color from our own. If the New Testament does not teach that it teaches nothing. It will be no defense for any man when he comes before the judgment seat of God that he practiced believer's baptism and subscribed to the New Hampshire confession. The verdict at that bar will depend upon what we did or did not to one of the least of those whom Christ calls brother.[56]

Salvation

African Americans' faith in the immediate presence of God in history provides the grounding for their understanding of the historical events of rescue that constitute salvation for their people. Jesus's resurrection and the emancipation of the slaves constitute historical evidence of God's salvific power. Salvation is communal in form and the commitment to salvation informs the obligation of African American individuals to the community. Not until all African Americans experience equality and freedom will justice prevail and God's will be done. Bishop Alexander Walters draws a direct connection between the participation of African Americans in the Civil War with their responsibility to carry on that struggle in the present. His resulting mandate is explicit.

Shall we remain silent when the President of the United States, who could not have been elected without our votes, is utterly silent in his last message to Congress concerning the outrages in North and South Carolina and other parts of the country? Remain silent when the Governor of Illinois threatens to blow Negroes to pieces with Gatling guns if they dare to take the places of white strikers who have refused to work? Silent while the officials of the States of

North and South Carolina admit they are powerless to protect us in our rights? Silent while Mississippi, Louisiana and South Carolina by statutory enactments have practically disfranchised their Negro population, and other States are preparing to do the same? Shall we not speak out when innocent men and women of our race are burned at the stake, hung to the limbs of trees and shot down like dogs? Shall we look on indifferently while our women are insulted and outraged by Negro-hating white men? Shall we say nothing while thousands in the rural districts in the South are robbed of their meager earnings? Were we to remain silent under such circumstances we would be unworthy of the name freemen. While I advise action, I at the same time advise prudent action. There can be no real peace in America until this problem is solved, and solved according to the rules of equity. . . . This nation with all its faults is pre-eminently a Christian nation. The leaven of Christianity (humanity) is at work, and will not cease its work until this whole country is premeated with the humanitarian spirit.[57]

Bishop Walters is advocating concerted political and social action to protect the rights of African Americans. Human beings are the leaven for Christ's work to be accomplished, and that work is primarily obtaining justice for people so that they can live according to God's will. While he eschews the use of violence in his call for prudence, his call is not passive or accommodationist in spirit, but rather active, diligent, and relentless. While African Americans witnessed the whittling away of their rights during the early decades of this century, they elaborated strategies for obtaining justice for their community that grew out of Christian mandates, took place within and expanded from the church, and reflected African American culture. Christian African Americans relied on a personal and communal faith in God, as expressed most cogently through church participation, to inspire the utilization of the meager material and prescribed social resources at their disposal. The church centered the life of the community because it housed that faith and provided the institutional framework for its expression. The secular interpretation of the African American church as the only institution open to African American control and therefore the seat of African American community development misses this crucial point. The social, political, and economic aims of Christian African Americans stood upon their understanding of a loving, liberating, redemptive, and salvific God who worked with them in history to fulfill their potential as God's children.

Strategies for Justice

African American scholars have consistently noted that African Americans do not draw the rigid distinction between sacred and secular that seems to obtain in white America. C. Eric Lincoln built upon this observation to develop a "dialectical model" of the black church which holds a series of dialectic polarities (like priestly versus prophetic functions or accommodation versus resistance) in "dynamic tension." Evelyn Brooks Higginbotham critiques this model and offers her own much more complex "dialogic model." Such a model holds in tension a "multiplicity of protean and concurrent meanings and intentions. . . . Such multiplicity transcends polarity—thus tending to blur the spiritual and secular, the eschatological and political, and the private and public."[58] For African American churches, then, a fundamental strategy, based upon the theological understanding of the existential nature of life and God's personal presence within it, consisted of a daily refusal to separate the material from the spiritual life. African Americans approached the struggle for justice by attending to the context of specific situations and the practical realities with which they had to contend. They brought their religious commitment to every aspect of their lives and integrated their understanding of what justice entailed by seeking as much as possible to reverse the processes of individual and communal alienation. This meant engaging in building a church that was actively involved in the intimate details of personal and family life as well as the social and political activity usually proscribed as secular. Such a church, as Peter Paris describes it, has "a profound concern for the bitter and painful realities of black existence in American as well as an abiding hope in a bright and radiant future . . . free from any form of racial injustice."[59]

African American strategies for justice included a focus on survival (both individual and communal) as a prerequisite for eventual equality and freedom. Survival included maintaining physical life and protecting the political potential of the future. As C. Eric Lincoln and Lawrence H. Mamiya explain, "survival was the requisite first step toward actualizing the political potential among black people in either protest or electoral politics."[60] Communal survival strategies developed community relationships that nurtured political expression which included strengthening the ability of individuals to enter into debate, express themselves publicly, take part in organizational life, and exercise the franchise.

Individual survival strategies serve the radical purpose of sustaining life in hope of a better future. The African American conception of the future becomes a strategy in its own right. The "future" here does not refer to a future after death or in some other world, but a future in one's own life-time or in the life-times of one's children. Justice would come in God's own time, but it would surely come. The reward that one sought did not reside in heaven, but in the existential future. African Americans approached their mission by building churches where they could elaborate their strategies for survival, growth, and eventual justice. The development of the African American church in Rochester, during the first four decades of the twentieth century illustrates how the African American church operated during this time to create the necesary resources to carry on these tasks. The understanding and interpretation of how Rochester churches went about their work relies upon the scholarship concerning African American church development.

THE OPERATION OF THE AFRICAN AMERICAN CHURCH 1900-1940

At the most rudimentary level, the construction of a church building proved something. It proved that African Americans had the resources to build something of meaning, that they could apply those resources and accomplish something for themselves. The existence of an African American church structure in the city demonstrated African American presence. It was visible. It was a beacon for the community. African Americans knew where to go to find each other. It provided the fundamental grounding for self-determination in marshalling the cooperative energies of differing individuals making their own decisions about how to proceed in carrying out God's work in the city. It was, as historians emphasize over and over, the Negro's own institution. They owned it. They owned the land, the building itself, and often the houses around it. Building a church and burning the mortgage were highly symbolic acts which declared that African Americans were no longer property themselves and that as a community they could own and take care of their own resources. It proved that African Americans could work hard to build something for themselves and not be beholden to white people. The church structure spoke to the existence of human beings gathered to do God's will in a society which sought to deny that humanity and to ignore that existence. Bishop Caldwell's sermon to those celebrating the construction of the new Memorial church in Rochester included an affirmation of its ability to serve God by serving each other.

> In this house so commodious, so convenient for the worship of God, let us dedicate ourselves anew. The Gospel teaches those truths without which life would not be worth living. This is that for which we have been laboring. The church is to teach not only how to serve God by worship, but the best methods of benefiting our fellowmen in body and soul.[61]

The act of building a church put into effect the preliminary Christian mandates upon which African Americans relied to inform all of their additional efforts: cooperating with one another, sacrificing for the common good through generous sharing of resources, and declaring hope in the future.[62]

The church building provided the physical context for the exercise of freedom within the institutional structure itself. African Americans developed their own organizational framework, occupied positions of authority, and created opportunities for the exercise of adult responsibilities often unavailable to African Americans outside the walls of the church. African Americans served as their own ministers, trustees, stewards, deacons, and teachers. They developed their own artistic and musical abilities and fostered the development of individual talent and skill. William Warfield testified not only to his own early and consistent nurturance in Mt. Olivet in Rochester, but to the same thread of development woven into the lives of other African Americans. He describes Marian Anderson's beginnings in church recitals, and Dorothy Maynor's roots in her father's church.[63] The institutional nurturance of individual abilities proclaimed a social model of respect for human potential. The successful nurture of individual growth depended upon a complex interplay of psychological and emotional supports that the church deliberately developed.

The church fostered the personal development of its members by attending to all aspects of human need in order to be consistently open to responding with concrete aid and psychological, emotional, and spiritual support. Most basically, it provided a forum for the exchange of information and free conversation. African Americans could go to church to talk to one another without having to pitch their thoughts to a hostile audience. The church offered the primary setting for recreation and entertainment, belonging and fellowship. The simple creation of a safe place for African Americans to be with each other provided the foundation for individual and community development.

Membership in a church community automatically linked people to informal networks of mutual solace and support through the participation in Sunday School, clubs, and other church organizations. People looked out for each other's needs, followed up on those who were absent, opened their homes, kitchens, closets, and pockets to the needy on a personal basis and directed people to more formalized networks of material and emotional support through clergy, stewards, and deacons.[64] These informal and face-to-face exchanges offered the opportunity to develop individual and communal expressions of mutuality, generosity, and cooperation as well as the decision to share resources for the common good. While these efforts were personal and informal, they were not private and they easily overlapped with more formal, visible, and structured programs for self-help.

More formally organized efforts were diverse and coalesced into what Higginbotham describes as "the flagship of black dignity [espousing] strong race-conscious views concerning the preservation of the black community, and, just as important [seeking] to shape the community so that preservation could become progress."[65] While diverse, interconnected, and overlapping, programmatic efforts within African American churches addressed four domains which the dominant culture defines as secular. These are: human services, education, economic self-development, and civil and political rights. While structuring programs within these domains, African Americans continued to practice the Christian mandates of supporting one another in the realization of human potential. In Rochester, the development of programs across these domains also reflected basic socialization patterns operating within the community. For example, women were almost totally responsible for providing basic services, were as active as men in the realms of education and economic self-development, but remained in an almost exclusively supportive role when addressing civil and political rights.

Human Services

African American churches provided human services in order to meet basic individual and communal needs for material existence as a prerequisite for realizing human potential. Such efforts and programs occurred primarily at the local level and were primarily the responsibility of church women. It is within the domain of providing the basics of food, shelter, clothing, care for the elderly, child-care, and work that the porous boundaries between private and public, personal and institutional, informal and formal structures readily blend and blur depending upon the nature of the congregation, the nature of the need, and the nature of the relations between those offering and those seeking help. As African American women served the basic needs of their neighbors, they exemplified and inculcated the Christian ethic of service to others as the basic mortar in the foundations of the African American community. No other efforts could stand without these activities. If basic needs went unmet, human beings could not prosper.

Most congregations offered immediate relief to migrants seeking aid and many collected Sunday offerings explicitly for this purpose. This system continued to help those made destitute during the Depression. Many congregations formed deacon and deaconess boards to address just such needs both within their own congregations and within the wider community. Pastors routinely provided information and assistance with employment. Church families took in foster children and church clubs took care of the elderly. When these more or less informal, ad hoc, or personal forms of assistance proved inadequate to the demand, more formalized programs grew within the churches.

The historical record describes a plethora of programs either designed by or housed within local African American churches. Churches provided kindergartens and day-care for African American mothers who worked. They ran employment bureaus, boys and girls clubs, housing directories, industrial classes, libraries, and recreation and youth centers. What the church structure could not itself house, it raised money to support. Local churches operated and funded orphanages, old-age homes, and mutual benefit societies.

The efforts of local African American churches to alleviate the severe material conditions that proscribed the lives of African Americans in the city led to the creation of more formalized missions and institutional churches as well as links to more secular agencies engaged in the provision of social services. Victoria Earle Matthews's White Rose Mission and Reverdy Ransom's Institutional Church are two of the most famous of the first type of these endeavors. Local congregations provided the bulk of support for the creation of African American YM- and YWCAs, as well as for local branches of the Urban League. The African American church, then, provided the training ground for social action on behalf of the community, bringing children up to "do for others" and teaching the organizational and managerial skills necessary for the cooperative allocation of resources in ways that would benefit the entire community. The Christian mandates that permeated their church life led African American women and men to engage in wide programmatic efforts to alleviate suffering and redress the conditions that kept the majority of their community in poverty.

Education

Throughout the first four decades of the twentieth century, African American churches and communities focused on educating their people. Nothing was more valuable than an education in the efforts to redress the prevailing conditions that limited the ability of African Americans to live out their human potential. African Americans saw education as necessary for survival, as the route to social and material advancement, and as a tool for a more enlightened response to God. Only the educated would be equipped to adequately provide human services, acquire economic advancement, and articulate the battle for civil and political rights.

The historical record is clear that the African American church founded, supported, and promoted educational institutions of every description. Teaching, next to the ministry, was the most revered profession within the African American community and the education of the masses of African Americans throughout the nation was a primary goal of the African American church at the national level.

Efforts to educate African Americans began within the local congregation. Many churches began as combined churches and schools, as did A.M.E. Zion in Rochester, New York. Churches formed Sunday Schools, Christian Endeavor organizations, literary societies, debating clubs, libraries, and formal classes both to supplement and to meet the educational needs of African Americans. Women and men sacrificed to teach, attend, and support educational programs within their own congregations and in other churches, and funded denominational institutions of higher education. Churches not only focused on the process of education for enlightenment and learning, but provided the content most necessary for individuals within their congregations and communities. Thus churches often provided the first classes in industrial education, teaching young women sewing and domestic science or child-care, so that they would be able to earn a living.

The various weekly round of educational programs inculcated the value of learning and the necessity of an education for individual and community advancement. It also afforded the opportunity of getting to know intimately the abilities and talents of the individuals who comprised particular congregations. Providing a forum for educational programs of every description exemplified African American efforts to encourage the development of their own people.

Economic Self-Development

The promotion of education and the direct provision of basic human needs supported the aim of economic self-development by providing individuals within the community with the basics for achievement. Additionally, the most important activities that local churches engaged in to support the economic development of the African community were the creation of mutual benefit associations and cooperative business alliances. W.E.B. Du Bois astutely described the African American church as the "first form of economic cooperation" among black people.[66] Local congregations urged members to frequent black businesses, and at least in Rochester the church housed the first formal cooperative business associations of African American entrepreneurs.

The church created the first African American mutual benefit association which grew into the African Methodist Episcopal denomination. Susan Greenbaum's treatment of these associations, which appears in the discussion of African American cultural values earlier in this chapter, adequately describes their relevance to community prosperity, and notes the ways in which these societies incorporated and expressed cooperation, sacrifice, generosity and the sublimation of individual material gain for the future good of the community.

Civil and Political Rights

The historical record is cloudiest on the activity of the African American church, during the first four decades of the twentieth century, to promote the civil and political rights of African Americans in the face of extremely hostile conditions. This record requires re-examination. Certainly the support for the NAACP proceeded primarily from the membership of African American churches, whatever divisions obtained within the clergy leadership. African American churches provided space for lodge, fraternal, and political meetings, opened the pulpit to political announcements and involvement, took political stands on the issues of the day, like organized labor and women's suffrage, and fostered the political development of its own membership through participation in internal organization. Local churches protested lynchings and ministers led entire congregations out of the South and re-constituted congregations in the North during the Great Migration. The form of political activity and protest depended upon local conditions and practical considerations, but the record of Rochester suggests that the African American church did not forget its obligation to challenge the sin of racism or work for the redemption of human society through open, political activity.

The contextual evidence suggests that African American leaders during the early part of the twentieth century found the strength to do their work primarily through the faith they learned in the African American church, whether or not the church itself directly performed a particular activity that an individual viewed as her or his "mission." The African American ministers and teachers educated in the African American Christian tradition within institutions supported by the African American church and raised within local African American congregations exemplified the theological tenets outlined above. The importance of the faith and its institutional expression to the contours of both African American and the wider American society has not received enough attention. The study of the African American church in Rochester, New York, during this time period contributes to this effort.

AFRICAN AMERICANS IN THE CONTEXT OF ROCHESTER, NEW YORK—A SKETCH

The situation of African Americans in Rochester during the first four decades of the twentieth century blends with and differs from wider social contexts in important ways. First of all, the Great Migration, while almost doubling Rochester's African American population, had very little effect on the social and political situation of African Americans here. This is true for several reasons. The African American population in Rochester remained extremely small throughout this time period. At the turn of the century, there were 601 African Americans in a city of less than 170,000 residents, or approximately .4% of the total population. By 1920, the population of African Americans had doubled, but still represented only .5% of Rochester's 295,750 residents. While World War I slowed the immigrant flow into Rochester, foreign immigrants accounted for most of Rochester's growth. By 1940, Rochester had acquired

3,262 African Americans in a city of 324,975, representing 1% of the population.[67] These figures contrast with the comparably sized midwestern cities of Indianapolis, Indiana and Cincinnati, Ohio, which showed, respectively, African American populations of 13.2% and 12.2% of their totals by 1940.[68] Compared to other cities, Rochester's migration is atypical for its small size, its gradual increment, and its small proportion relative to the white population. Unlike other places, Rochester experienced a migration which allowed African American migrants to assimilate into the existing community and allowed established African Americans to retain informal, face-to-face methods of dealing with each other's needs. Assimilation occured more easily here also because of the origin of most of the migrants. Despite the fact that leaders and church founders had familial experience with southern slavery, over half of the people I interviewed migrated to Rochester from other northern communities, 6 from other places in New York State. Those who came from the South, came from a combination of urban and rural environments and represented seven different states, with only 2 coming from the same state, Virginia. This evidence, obtained from a small sample (19), is replicated by the 1940 Census. The Census records a total of 339 African American migrants to Rochester that year. Of these, 287 came from cities; 116 came from other places (rural and urban) within New York State. The largest numbers of migrants came from New York State, Ohio, and Illinois. Twenty-three came from Southern rural environments.

What this tells us about conditions in Rochester which make the African American community here distinctive is that the migrants did not for the most part bring with them an ignorance of northern urban expectations. The migrants here did not express cultural norms and behaviors that caused consternation among established African American and white communities in places like Chicago, Detroit, and Philadelphia. In sum, there weren't very many of them, they came gradually, from diverse communities (mostly urban northern), and they weren't that different from the African Americans who were already here.

Additionally, the economic context of Rochester created an environment of little class stratification among African Americans. In addition to the fact that many of the African Americans who came from the south were recruited specifically for private domestic service, domestic service remained the largest employer of African Americans throughout this time period. Those who did not work in domestic service found their living in unskilled or semi-skilled labor, largely outside the industrial labor force in which most white workers found jobs. Consequently, most migrants worked both in labor categories which did not call them to alter their habits and in the same kind of jobs that their

African American neighbors did. This meant two things for the African American community here: there was little social distance between the "elite" and the bulk of the African American community, and the leadership of the churches came from the ranks of working-class people. J.W. Thompson, the President of the Board of Trustees of Memorial A.M.E. Zion, and the political leader and advocate for the African American community for close to twenty years, made his living as the head waiter at the Powers Hotel.

Historians have cited large size, internal cultural diversity, and economic stratification as the deleterious forces which created dissension within large African American communities in other urban contexts, and weakened the ability of African American churches and community organizations to effectively counteract the effects of discrimination. Elitism and competition divided the community.

Size had a different effect in Rochester. While allowing for the development of interpersonal networks of support, when encountering barriers from the white community, African Americans had little political clout. The white liberal reformists and economic leaders in Rochester hardly paid attention to what they considered a mere handful, and remained undismayed by the oppressive realities circumscribing the lives of their African American neighbors. Rochester's African American community was atypical in its size and economic coherence, but it faced rigid racial barriers nonetheless.

African Americans in Rochester were able to practice charitable networks of aid based upon mutuality and reciprocity with new-comers who they came to know personally and who joined families and churches, thus becoming in turn contributing members of the community as a whole. This situation helps explain why African Americans did not make scientific, professionally expert analyses of social conditions. Even if they had seen a need to undertake such investigations on their own behalf, their small numbers made it possible for the wider Rochester community to deny them the educational and professional opportunities necessary to create such expertise. Consequently, while Rochester's reformers and public-spirited women and men joined the trend for professional investigation and management, their ranks were closed to African American participation.

The small size of Rochester's African American population had an even more direct effect on how the white community in Rochester treated its African American contingent. Throughout this time period, Rochester confined African American employment primarily to the service sector, hiring African American women and men as domestic servants, red-caps, caterers, porters, and messengers. Even those migrants who came to Rochester with skills or education, or those who managed to attain them here, could not find jobs in which they could practice those skills. The evidence from the interviews is borne out by the employment patterns described in the 1900 through 1940 federal census. For African American men and women, domestic service was the largest category of employment throughout these forty years, with manufacturing claiming the largest numbers of white workers, both male and female, followed by employment in the trades. Professional employment claimed the fewest numbers of African American men and women in the city, while gaining ground among white men. There is an interesting difference evident between African American women and men. In 1920 and 1930, African American men were employed in more manufacturing and trade categories than in domestic service, while for African American women, domestic service always held the dominant position. This indicates the entrepreneurial nature and drive of African American men, who were most likely opening their own small independent shops, not taking part in the transformation of Rochester into a manufacturing and white collar city. The difference between African American and white workers shows this transformation most clearly. White workers, both men and women, held almost exclusive right to manufacturing, trade and professional employment. Domestic service was last for white men, and second to the last for white women, who it seems, were also fairly successfully barred from professional employment.

Rochester changed its industrial base during these years from a city based upon the manufacture of quality clothing and shoes (employing mostly skilled foreign labor) to one based upon the manufacture of high-quality technical products demanding high levels of education and scientific skill. The avenues for acquiring education and skills remained closed to African Americans who, therefore, did not take part in or benefit directly from Rochester's increasingly prosperous industries. Consequently the labor conditions and political questions which consumed the energy of liberal white Rochesterians did not address African American issues or engage substantial African American interest.

Nevertheless, Rochester's African Americans remained socially, economically, and politically active. In response to the employment ceiling, for example, African Americans branched out in the only way they could; they established enterpreneurial endeavors based on meeting the needs of their own community. These small businesses had to rely on both African American and white clientele. By 1926, the African American community could boast over thirty businesses in Rochester in which "practically every service and product from head to foot was owned and offered by black Americans."[69] It seems unlikely that thirty small businesses could support themselves solely from the custom of less than 3,000 African Americans. The testimony of people whose parents and grandparents ran these businesses bears this out. The small business endeavors of African American women and men in Rochester displayed a pattern reflective of economic precariousness. These businesses were often short-lived and served to supplement, not replace, service-sector employment. Some people operated several businesses over their lifetime; when one went under, they tried something else. J.W. Thompson operated a catering business for a while, and then opened a concession stand at the Powers Hotel. George Burks ran a tonsorial parlor and owned and operated a hotel, both for limited times. Neither of these endeavors caused Burks to leave his job as messenger for a Rochester bank. The record indicates that those businesses that were most successful relied upon white as well as black clients.

That Rochester's African American community was small, did not compete with white labor, dealt with its own circumstances of need through tradition-ally informal African American communal efforts, and sought achievement through individual efforts and accomplishment, all had political ramifications for both the African American and wider Rochester community. For example, racial violence was virtually unknown in Rochester. There were no race riots or lynchings here, and while African Americans in Rochester protested these conditions elsewhere, they understood the environment in Rochester to be safer for themselves and their children. The absence of the most extreme forms of racial hostility, coupled with rigid economic and educational racial barriers, as well as economic dependence upon white employers and patrons, created a situation where a small African American community developed strategies of generational advancement, making sure that the next generation of children would have more than the present. From one standpoint, these strategies dis-played a political conservatism in that Rochester's African American leaders challenged white society to live up to its ideals, not change them. Rochester's African Americans did not, then, have sympathy for the socialist leanings of reformers and labor organizers who gained some political influence in Rochester during this time period. On the contrary, African Americans in Rochester were wedded to the goal of cracking racial barriers to traditional avenues of attainment, and they evoked the participation in and contributions to Ameri-can society on the part of African Americans, Rochester natives in particular, as evidence of their right to these avenues.

On the other hand, African American community leaders were tireless in their efforts to challenge restrictions and gain access. They strove diligently to acquire a secure economic base, educational opportunities, and social equality. They utilized the strategies of Booker T. Washington and W.E.B. DuBois to both support their own community efforts and join with others who would help them. Above all, they relied on African American community values to further their aims. These strategies coalesced into a pattern of developing a community institutional infrastructure centered in the church, which created support for individual development based upon an understanding that individual achievers would benefit and contribute to the community. The ensuing chapters, therefore, begin with biographical sketches of individuals who exemplify this pattern, outline the contextual conditions in Rochester with which they had to contend, and then focus on the church's communal role as the primary system of support for African American accomplishment and challenge.

NOTES

1. Samuel D. Proctor, "Black Protestants and Public Policy" in Joseph Washington, Jr., ed., *Black Religion and Public Policy: Ethical and Historical Perspectives* (n.p., 1978), 16.

2. There are differing accounts of the sequence of events surrounding the unveiling of the Douglass monument. The root of this confusion lies in the celebration of different events. The cornerstone ceremony took place in 1897, at which prominent African Americans and liberal whites spoke. Then there was the aborted unveiling ceremony where people gathered and renewed their pledge to get the statue to Rochester, held on September 14, 1898. The unveiling of the actual statue occurred on June 9, 1899, and in this the *Rochester Democrat and Chronicle* and J.W. Thompson's account agree.

3. J.W. Thompson, *An Authentic History of the Douglass Monument: Biographical Facts and Incidents in the Life of Frederick Douglass, His Death at Anacosta, D.C. and Funeral at Washington D.C. and Rochester, N.Y. together with Portraits and Illustrations of Important Incidents of the Four Years' Struggle to Complete the Work.* (Rochester, N. Y.: Rochester Herald Press, 1903), 43.

4. For an in-depth treatment of these historical developments see: C. Vann Woodward, *The Strange Career of Jim Crow* (New York: Oxford University Press, 1966); William B. Gatewood, Jr., *Black Americans and the White Man's Burden 1898-1903* (University of Illinois Press, 1975); David Gordon Nielson, *Black Ethos: Northern Urban Negro Life and Thought, 1890-1930* (Westport: Greenwood Press, 1977); and Franklin and Moss, *From Slavery to Freedom*, especially Chapters 13-17.

5. "Douglass Day," *Democrat and Chronicle*, 10 June 1899.

6. Giddings, *When and Where I Enter*, 106.

7. Weiss, *Urban League*, 4.

8. "Douglass Day," *D&C*, 10 June 1899.

9. Cash, "Radicals or Realists," 9.

10. Thompson, *Authentic History*, 77-78.

11. Ibid., 104.

12. June Axinn and Herman Levin, *Social Welfare: A History of the American Response to Need*, 2nd ed. (New York: Harper and Row, 1982), 131.

13. Allen Davis, *Spearheads for Reform: The Social Settlements and the Progressive Movement 1890-1914* (New York: Oxford University Press, 1967), 27-29.

14. Weiss, *Urban League*, 72.

15. For treatments of progressive social reformers and race, see Weiss, *Urban League*; Davis, *Spearheads for Reform*; Grossman, *Land of Hope*; and Lasch, "Black Neighbors."

16. Lasch, "Black Neighbors," 15. See also Diner, "Chicago Social Workers".

17. Diner, "Chicago Social Workers," 397.

18. Franklin and Moss, *From Slavery to Freedom*, 290.

19. See, for example, James Borchert, *Alley Life in Washington: Family, Community, Religion, and Folklife in the City, 1850-1970* (Urbana: University of Illinois Press, 1980); Gotlieb, *Making Their Own Way*; Grossman, *Land of Hope*; Trotter, *Black Milwaukee*; and Kusmer, *A Ghetto Takes Shape*.

20. Mary White Ovington, *Half A Man: The Status of the Negro in New York* (Norwood: Plimpton Press, 1911), 114; and Scott, "Most Invisible of All," 11.

21. Weiss, *Urban League*, 42.

22. Davis, *Spearheads for Reform*, 98.

23. For a further elaboration on the goals of assimilation by prominent African American and white reformers see Davis, *Spearheads for Reform* and Weiss, *Urban League*.

24. For a consideration of how local African American leaders tailored their strategies to meet local conditions and drew from any sources available to them see: Jesse Moore, "Resolving Urban Racial Problems: The New York Urban League, 1919-1959," *Afro-Americans in New York Life and History* 4 (January 1980); Williams, "And Still I Rise"; Kusmer, *A Ghetto Takes Shape*; Trotter, *Black Milwaukee*; Gordon, "Black and White Visions of Welfare"; Rouse, "Legacy of Community Organizing."

25. Trotter, *Black Milwaukee*, 28. For a more thorough treatment of the connections between strategy and social/class affiliation see also Kusmer, *A Ghetto Takes Shape*.

26. Gordon, "Black and White Visions of Welfare," 580.

27. Several historians discuss the modifications of ideological stance as urban communities developed. For a treatment of the formation of coalitions, see Trotter, *Black Milwaukee*. African American feminist historians (and some white feminist historians) discuss the blending of strategies to address practical conditions. See Gordon, Scott, and Williams already cited above. Historians have also elaborated the connection between segregation and heightened race-consciousness. See Jones and Kusmer already cited and Nielson, *Black Ethos*.

28. Giddings, *When and Where I Enter*, 211.

29. This critique pervades general historical descriptions of the church especially between the two world wars within wider treatments of African American history such as John Hope Franklin's and Jacqueline Jone's. African American theologians also share these perceptions, most especially Gayraud Wilmore in *Black Religion and Black Radicalism*. For particularly virulent attacks see Hart M. Nelson's introduction to *The Black Church in America* and Ernest N. Morial's "Black Religion and Civil Rights."

30. Jones, *Labor of Love, Labor of Sorrow*, 180.

31. Higginbotham, *Righteous Discontent*, 28.

32. Weiss, *Urban League*, 120.

33. August Meier, *Negro Thought in America 1880-1915: Racial Ideologies in the Age of Booker T. Washington* (Ann Arbor: University of Michigan Press, 1963), 193.

34. See Giddings, *When and Where I Enter*, 98; Williams, "And Still I Rise," 14; and Gordon, "Black and White Visions of
Welfare," 576-579.

35. Giddings, *When And Where I Enter*, 102 and 21; Sarah Delany and A. Elizabeth Delany with Amy Hill Hearth, *Having Our Say: The Delany Sisters' First 100 Years* (New York: Kodansha International, 1993).

36. Giddings, *When and Where I Enter*, 73.

37. See Jones, *Labor of Love, Labor of Sorrow*, Chaps. 3-5.

38. Susan Greenbaum, "A Comparison of African American and Euro-American Mutual Aid Societies in 19th Century America," *Journal of Ethnic Studies* 19 (Fall 1991).

39. Jones, *When and Where I Enter*, 100, and Chap. 5.

40. Gwendolyn Etter-Lewis, *My Soul is My Own: Oral Narratives of African American Women in the Professions* (New York: Routledge, 1993), 6-9.

41. Elsie Scott Kilpatrick, Interview with author, 10 July 1993.

42. The history of A.M.E. Zion draws upon: Blake McKelvey, "Lights and Shadows in Local Negro History," *Rochester History* 21 (October, 1959); the author's interview with Charles Frazier and Howard Coles, 21 April 1992; and the records of A.M.E. Zion in the possession of Charles Frazier.

43. Author's interview with Charles Price, 1 October 1993, and with James and Alice Young, November 1993. Information also in Mt. Olivet church records. Many of the early members of Mt. Olivet migrated from the South, settled in rural New York and then moved to Rochester.

44. Albert J. Raboteau, *Slave Religion: The Invisible Institution in the Antebellum South* (New York: Oxford University Press, 1978), 195.

45. Robert Ross Johnson, "The Mountain of Olivet: A Historical Sketch of Negro Baptists in Rochester, New York," (Masters thesis, Colgate Rochester Divinity School, 1946), 4.

46. Lincoln and Mamiya, *The Black Church in the African American Experience*, 4.

47. James Cone, *For My People: Black Theology and the Black Church* (New York: Orbis Books, 1984), 33.

48. Alexander Walters, A.M.,D.D., *My Life and Work* (New York: Fleming H. Revell Co., 1917), 95-140.

49. Monroe Fordham, *Major Themes in Northern Black Religious Thought, 1800-1860* (Exposition Press, 1975), 131, 133-34.

50. Ibid, 34.

51. "Success After Long Struggle," Undated, unidentified newspaper article, found in Memorial A.M.E. Zion archives.

52. Wilmore, *Black Religion and Black Radicalism*, 12.

53. Paris, *Social Teachings*, 16.

54. Ibid., 85.

55. James E. Rose, "Jesus Our Way to Brotherhood," 1932 article (unidentified periodical, found in Mt. Olivet archives.

56. "Race Prejudice in the North," Editorial Notes, *The Baptist*, 13 February 1932.

57. Walters, *Life and Work*, 126-127.

58. Higginbotham, *Righteous Discontent*, 16.

59. Paris, *Social Teachings*, 85.

60. Lincoln and Mamiya, *The Black Church in the African American Experience*, 202.

61. "Success After a Long Struggle."

62. As African Americans took pride in the visibility of their churches, so they tended to expand their physical plant as a strategy to meet the needs of growing congregations when the Great Migration brought African Americans up from the South to northern urban centers. Critics cite the inability of these churches to address migrant needs and by this lack contributing to the proliferation of storefront, holiness, and alternative religious movements. Some mainline churches departed from this response early to create programs, not more space, to meet the concrete practical needs of the migrants, but these seemed to be the exception, not the rule, and were only able to sustain themselves in very large urban environments. Such criticism buys into a linear and progressive view of African American church development which claims a more "prophetic" role for programmatically inclined congregations, thus obscuring how those who chose to expand may have been viewing and using that space. The institution of formal programs on the part of some churches did not replace traditional informal, face-to-face networks of mutuality and reciprocity. Research in Rochester suggests that initial church expansion may have reflected a very concrete response to the need to incorporate more people into networks of support that operated within such internal structures as Sunday School classes and clubs, all of which needed meeting times and space. The proliferation of new congregations, rather than reflecting a failure on the part of large congregations to address the people's needs, may instead reflect the realities of economies of scale. The development of structured programs such as employment bureaus were viable concurrent alternatives that leave discernable records, but did not necessarily replace the informal grape-vine and clergy recommendations based on personal knowledge of both those searching for work and those supplying jobs.

63. William Warfield with Alton Miller, *William Warfield: My Music and My Life* (Chicago: Sagamore Publishing, 1991), 3, 45.

64. Often couched in pejorative terms, the evidence of these informal and organizational systems of support remain implicit in historical accounts of people "indulging" in church services, benevolent society meetings, and visits with friends (Jones), in the dissatisfaction with the impersonal tone of large congregations that new migrants evidenced (Grossman), in passing mention of the "relief" work that deaconesses did, with the caveat that such charity was usually confined to the church membership (as if there was something wrong with that) (Du Bois), and occasionally in a list of activities and internal programs churches developed, such as sick-benefit societies, Christian Endeavor Societies, youth groups, sewing circles, etc. (Wright).

65. Higginbotham, *Righteous Discontent*, 5-6.

66. Lincoln and Mamiya, *Black Church in the African American Experience*, 8.

67. These statistics are taken from: Blake McKelvey, *Rochester: The Quest for Quality 1890-1925* (Cambridge: Harvard University Press, 1956); Blake McKelvey, *Rochester: An Emerging Metropolis 1925-1961* (Rochester: Christopher Press, 1961); and *Rochester Metropolitan Area Studies* (Spring 1957).

68. These figures, and subsequent statistics in this section, are compiled from the federal census tables of the Twelfth through the Sixteenth federal census.

69. LiAni Lewis, "African American Sites of Significance in Rochester, New York 1900-1940," prepared for the Landmark Society of Western New York (Rochester, 1992), 12; and Adolph Dupree, "Rochester Roots/Routes," *about . . . time* (August 1984), 19.

PART II

The African American Church Community in Rochester

⮑ TWO ⮐

WOMEN OF FAITH AND SERVICE

"To promote peace and unity, to bear one another's burdens and prevent each other's stumbling"[1]

EUNICE BULLOCK[2]

If you ask, Eunice Bullock can show you a stack of awards and commendations she has received for her life of service to her church and community. Her church has honored her for participation and leadership in both adult and youth choirs, for over 40 years (in 1975) of dedication and service, and for her "Witness of Christian Service, Christian Character, and Faithful Membership." She has been recognized by the Urban League for community service and leadership, has received appreciation from Reuben K. Davis on behalf of the judges of our courts, and has been recognized as an African American role model for her tutoring activities and as a volunteer in the Senior Volunteer Program.

Mrs. Bullock has belonged to Memorial A.M.E. Zion church all her life, which began in 1915. Her grandparents were members of Memorial. Her grandmother was born in Canada, came to Rochester as a child after the Civil War, and here married Eunice's grandfather, who made his living as a white washer (painter) while she worked as a domestic. Eunice's grandmother took responsibility for and raised Eunice, giving her her own last name, Richardson. Mrs. Richardson saw to it that Eunice went to church every Sunday. "We never decided who was going to church at home and who wasn't. Sunday was the day you went to church. There was no discussion about it." Eunice was baptized, confirmed, and married there. Mrs. Richardson was active at Memorial, working consistently with the Women's Missionary Society as a conference worker and as a member of the Crescent Club. Eunice's mother was also active, though not as consistently. She worked with the Junior Christian Endeavor, Eunice recalls. Eunice attended Sunday School, sang in the choir, and went to Christian Endeavor as she grew up.

Christian Endeavor combined Bible study, social time, and supplemental education. "We used to have a meeting at five o'clock every Sunday afternoon, of teenagers, at which time we wrote essays and gave talks on various things and Negro history as we called it then . . . and we'd have different leaders who would come in and speak. . . . We did Bible studies and reading and then once a month you wrote a paper on some part of what you had learned during the time." Mrs. Bullock believes it is good to teach Negro history in the schools, but some things have to start at home and in the church.

Once Eunice graduated from high school in 1932, the church gave her her first job. "When I came out of high school, the young lady who had been the financial secretary was leaving and I became the financial secretary for $4.50 a month. They would require that I would make a statement every month of the individual financial givings." Eunice attended college through a program of the Works Progress Administration and did course work in business at the University of Rochester and Rochester Business Institute. She became the church secretary at Memorial before taking a job with Graflex as a secretary, where she had more formal education than any of the men she worked for during her twenty-one years as their employee. When she retired, Memorial A.M.E. Zion's Board of Christian Education honored her. She got that job originally through the church.

> I had made friends with members of the old Corn Hill Church and our church had a mission study with them and the Rev. A.C. Bell was our minister and was a part of our missionaries going over there so when Graflex was seeking someone, one of the men from that group said, "Rev. Bell can you recommend to us a young woman from your congregation?" and with hesitancy he said yes because at that time I was his secretary and the church secretary and he did not want to withhold the opportunity of my getting a job but he still didn't want to lose me.

Eunice Bullock recalls that ministers often acted as brokers in getting jobs for members of their congregation and community. It was common for people to come to the ministers for recommendations, and ministers would go to employment agencies to get information about job openings. They would also have regular meetings among themselves to exchange employment information. Ministers were not the only ones who involved themselves in this informal network. Eunice's mother worked as a sandwich maker at Walgreen's. How did she get the job? "There was a man at our church doing janitorial service at Walgreen's and he found out through the grapevine that they were looking for a sandwich girl so he said to them 'I think I know someone.'"

Eunice Bullock continued to be active in her church and community. She taught Sunday School and Education Bible School, and became involved in Youth Programs at the conference level. She raised her children in the church and has enjoyed attending and contributing. She explains:

> It helps me to help others, to impart to others some of what had been given to me. It was like a giving back program, you give to someone else, they give to you and you give back to the community. You don't keep it all just within yourself, you expose other people to some of the things to which you have been exposed, hoping it will benefit them.

Such a philosophy is born in church practice. Eunice Bullock explains that when she was growing up, Memorial had no formalized program or fund to support the educational aspirations of the members, but "we've had some individual church clubs who had a member who had someone in school and they would give something in the name of the club." Similarly, as club members grew older, "whatever club organization you belonged to" became responsible for checking on and meeting the needs of that member. If people in the community were in need, the first place they would come would be the church, because the church would be the first place to help anyone. With limited resources, the church would use whatever personal networks it had to try to help. In addition the church would periodically take a collection during Sunday worship for the "Ministry of Kindness Fund," for use at the pastor's discretion. The pastor was also responsible for assisting in other kinds of difficulties that might involve the white community. Mrs. Bullock reflects, "I think they depended upon their ministers making the waves for them."

In 1921, the black community opened its own YWCA on Clarissa Street, followed in 1927 by a YMCA on Adams Street Eunice Bullock spent Sunday evenings there, along with the youth of other African American churches, especially Mt. Olivet. She described these Sunday evening forums as a kind of extension of Christian Endeavor, with a focus on Black History, but without the Bible Study. Later, in keeping with the spirit of giving back what you have received, she worked at the YWCA through WPA. She taught recreation and handcrafts and escorted "our girls" as they walked to Genesee Valley Park for picnics.

Eunice Bullock spends her life in service and continues to focus on education and racial pride. She tutors children at #6 school, teaching them "reading, math, and manners." She is the organizer of the Bullock Memorial Scholarship Fund, in memory of her husband, a former trustee, which raises money for high school graduates of Memorial to continue their education. She is raising money for a calendar which will commemorate all the people who have contributed to the fund, because, she says, "Your name is worth something, isn't it?"

Mrs. Bullock has practiced and promoted the values of self-development, mutual self-help, racial pride, and community service typical of the African American church women of her day. Her life exemplifies the connections between individual achievement and community service. Her church nurtured her personal development, celebrated and supported her accomplishments, and imbued her with a sense of responsibility and mission to "give back to the community." Her belief that she is doing God's work reverberates in the words that her church uses to commend her and which she honors by displaying in her home: a woman of "exceptional loyalty and devotion to God."

GLADYS SCOTT[3]

Gladys Scott began her devoted service to Mt. Olivet Baptist Church when she came to Rochester as an adult in 1939. Mrs. Scott was raised a Baptist in Virginia and brought to her involvement at Mt. Olivet a definite and strong set of values concerning Christian behavior and church work. When she moved to Rochester, she got a job as a domestic and joined Mt. Olivet on December 9th, 1939.

She joined the usher board the first of the year, 1940. "The Usher Board is supposed to greet the people. You meet the ushers in the church before you meet anybody else and they should always be courtesy to everybody because you're greeting the people before they see anybody else." Ushers also collect the money from the offerings and deliver it to the trustees. The ushers are responsible for the behavior of the people in the seats, and for dealing with anyone who might need something coming into the church on Sunday morning. Ushers also perform similar services for funerals, shepherding the movement of the people and seeing to individual needs.

In addition to these distinctive duties, ushers share common responsibilities with other church boards. Ushers pay dues, which contribute to the operating fund of the church, and sponsor projects to raise money for specific needs that the church may have. Mrs. Scott gave an example.

> The ushers equipped the kitchen, bought the dishwasher, we bought all the dishes and the cupboards in the kitchen. We raised the money. They had the dishes sitting on the floor, so we didn't want it, so we worked and at that time they had a lot of dinners and things and we got tired of washing dishes so that's

why we bought a dishwasher. People wanted to do something else with the money but Dr. Whitaker said no, if that's what they want to work for then that's what we do.

Mrs. Scott understands the value of working for something. Dishes from the kitchen have been broken in recent years, and other equipment has disappeared. She observes, "You all didn't work to buy this stuff. Come easy, go easy. I said, we worked. Well that's how we decided to get the dishwasher. We'd be washing dishes to twelve o'clock at night and we had to go to work [in the morning]. So that's how we all decided we'd work [and get the kitchen equipped]." The church boards and clubs used to have a lot of projects in the 1940s and 1950s and Mrs. Scott worked on most of them, one way or another. Even if it wasn't your board organizing the dinner or event, you might help set up, or buy a ticket. Gladys Scott earned $8.00 a week when she moved to Rochester, doing domestic work like most black women in the city. She gave a week's salary to the church every month until "we got the church out of debt."

Gladys Scott and her husband became concerned about the need for organized activity for the youth of Mt. Olivet. They began a Junior Usher Board. To this organization, Gladys Scott brought the faith and values and sense of responsibility with which she had been raised in an earlier era. She was consecrated to the task, taking an oath under her pastor to "lead these children." She believes she is doing God's work, living out her Christian responsibility and building a foundation into the lives of both the children and the church. She began by recruiting youth thirteen years old or older, to give them something to do. "We started to train them how to walk these people to their seats," but these early attempts were not successful, the kids wouldn't do it. Mrs. Scott thought the children did not have the proper attitude, did not understand the importance, the significance, and the multifaceted nature of what they were doing. They weren't taking it seriously. "We came here to serve the Lord," she said, and she began installing the young people as junior ushers and building an organization that included more than meeting to rehearse what happened on Sunday morning. She described the installation process:

> We ask them why they want to come. [They say] well, we'd like to work in the church . . . get involved in the church or get closer to the minister or we would like to do something with the people. That brings a kid, then we know they want to work, but if we all just take them in because they said they want to join . . . they got to tell us why they want to join. . . . If you can't tell me why then you coming in with empty hands and when I ask you to do something you may not want to do it so you must tell us why if you want to work in the church or get closer in the church, something that they want to do in the church then we

know, we feel that they want to work. . . . They had to tell us in a Christian way that they wanted to come in and work.

Junior ushers made the same commitments to the church that senior ushers did. They paid dues, organized projects to raise money for specific needs of the church, spent social time together at picnics or parties, and sat around and talked things over with Gladys Scott and her husband. Gladys Scott took it upon herself to shape these children for higher things through serving the Lord and their community. She says, "I led them for forty years and there came to be everything in it. The kids, when they would go off to college, those kids went away and some would be doctors, lawyers, there came to be everything in it in forty years." For Gladys Scott, church service has a direct relationship to individual achievement because the work of the church instills the Christian character and faith necessary to accomplish anything. If children can see their own efforts equipping the church, they can see with their own eyes what they might accomplish. Also, they understand their relationship and responsibility to the community, to Mt. Olivet. Once you are a member of the Junior Usher Board, your individual behavior reflects upon the total community. It can take pride in your accomplishments or suffer with you should you "get in trouble."

Gladys Scott bends her considerable energy toward making sure none of her charges gets into trouble. She remembers an incident when the Junior Usher Board planned an outing that she did not supervise. This was supposed to be just for the young ladies, but boys showed up. There was confusion over where they were supposed to go, who was driving, what they were going to serve to eat. When they got back to the church, everyone was tired and disgruntled. The kids went out as a group and got drunk. Mrs. Scott's response was swift and unequivocal. "We don't drink if we go to church, and you people that drink, then, you didn't serve the Lord." Mrs. Scott holds a deep concern for the future leadership of the church and the role the church plays in protecting its children.

> Those kids cannot lead that church in the name of Mt. Olivet and go out and get in something 'cause Mt. Olivet's got to back it. They go out here and get in trouble then you got to go back to Mt. Olivet and Mt. Olivet's got to come to your rescue. . . . When these kids go out and get in something it belongs to the church then the church is going to have to back them. Whether it's good or bad they're . . . representing Mt. Olivet. They're taking the name of the church. If somebody get in something you call Rev. Cook. He's supposed to come . . . goes for anybody in the church.

Mrs. Scott's concern is in molding the individual behavior of the youth with whom she works. It is his or her responsibility to stay out of trouble and to make Mt. Olivet proud. Toward this end she has created channels of influence into every area of the youths' lives through the vehicle of the Junior Usher Board. She is both role model and surrogate parent. Her tone softens as she expresses her affection for the youths who have spent time in her backyard or kitchen, after or before meetings, to talk over what is happening in their lives. She is very clear that the attachments she has created between the children, herself, and the church make it imperative that "for good or bad" the church is there for these kids if they need it. Of course, they're going to have to explain to her why they need it.

The life of Gladys Scott exemplifies the connections between self-sacrifice and the channeling of resources for the greater good of the community. Her strict moral precepts rest upon the understanding that courtesy, self-respect, hard work, frugality, temperance, and self-discipline create the foundations for community survival and advancement. For her, the health of the community depends upon producing individuals of strong moral fibre whose achievements the community can not only be proud of but is obligated to support. That she rests her work upon a faith foundation is clear. She is there to "serve the Lord."

PAULINE MOORE AND ELIZABETH LOGAN[4]

Elizabeth Logan remembers walking three miles to church services twice every Sunday with her mother and, eventually, nine brothers and sisters, to attend Episcopal services with the only black Episcopal congregation in Rochester, St. Simon's Cyrene. St. Simon's began as a mission church, first meeting in people's homes in 1921 and then sharing space in local white Episcopal churches from 1922 to 1934, when the congregation built the church structure on Oregon St. The African American congregation did not worship with the white members of these loaner churches, but had access to their sanctuaries when services for the white members were over. Pauline Moore, Elizabeth Logan's mother, was involved with St. Simon's from the beginning.

Pauline Moore, born in 1893, was the daughter of J.W. Thompson, the illustrious president of the Board of Trustees of Memorial A.M.E. Zion and the most influential black man in Rochester. She graduated from college in 1912, trained to teach, but did not find work as a teacher when she came home. The teaching profession, along with all other professions, was closed to African Americans in this city until the 1930s. Elizabeth Logan recalls that her mother had not enjoyed her student teaching experience and did not attempt to use her education degree until St. Simon's opened the Carver House in 1943. "The war years came and the need for nursery schools for mothers who

were working arose and so the church formed the Carver House Nursery School."
Harry Bray, the director, heard that Mrs. Moore had a teacher's degree and
brought her in to teach. She had been hired originally to cook for the school.

In 1912, however, Pauline Moore (at that time still Thompson) came home
from school and started working with her father. She got married in 1917,
raised ten children, and worked part-time, so she could be there when her
children got home from school, as a waitress at the University of Rochester
Faculty Club at the Women's College (then on University Avenue). She devoted her free time to her church and community.

Pauline Moore was the Director of the Choir and the Organist at St. Simon's.
She taught Sunday School, headed the Altar Guild, and was a member of the
Daughters of the King, an episcopal women's club that saw to the needs of the
sick, the shut-in, and the needy. She raised her children with a strict and
loving hand, made sure they were in church every Sunday, and kept them in
line. In this she counted on the help of the adults in her community. "My
mother drummed into our house: you respect a person who is older than you.
If someone older than you told you to stop doing something, or something
like that, it was the same as if your parents spoke to you." Both of the Moores
nurtured the individual development and creativity of their children, supplying the materials and acting as audience when the band of twelve (including
two cousins), wrote and performed plays and musicals at home. But it was
primarily Mrs. Moore's influence that instilled in Elizabeth the certainty that
"it's through [God] that we learn how to love everybody else. That's a very
strong thing but it's a very private thing."

How can loving "everybody else" be private? Pauline Moore, as a member
of the Daughters of the King, took her responsibilities for visiting the sick
and needy seriously. She did not limit her efforts to that organization or to the
members of St. Simon's, however. Elizabeth remembers running into people
she knew on the street who would tell her that they were doing better, and
when she expressed concern they would ask, "Well, hadn't her mother told
her?" Elizabeth remembers her embarrassment but also her sense of wonder
that her mother seemed to know, and to take care of, everyone, without talking about it.

Pauline Moore may have been visiting and responding to people's needs
every week, without her children or anyone else knowing all that she was
doing, but she also made sure that her daughters learned how to express this
kind of Christian love and responsibility.

> My mother . . . my mother always visited the sick and the shut-in and we would
> go with her and I think from that each one of us who were fortunate enough to

go with her—the boys not so much as the girls—we had a sense of sharing with other people and even if it was a little bag of potato chips to someone who's shut in and loves potato chips . . . I think that it was the basis for each of us as we became adults being involved in the community in various ways.

Elizabeth Logan saw her mother as a woman who lived her religion in her everyday behavior. Becoming involved in the community did not mean primarily trudging around the city calling on people to see what you could do. It meant knowing someone well enough to know that she loves potato chips and can't get out to buy any.

It was important to Mrs. Moore that her children grew up within the church. It was the only place where they met other black people, and where they learned the elements of faith. Elizabeth says that attending church every week gave you

a feeling of belonging, a feeling of continuity because you have friends and associates at work, and you go home. You have neighbors or people you might see once in a while [when] you go out to a bar or a picnic or something like that, but the church gives you continuity and I think that's a part of it. . . . [A]nd I think a feeling of there is someone out there . . . that you can talk to, lean on, get strength from so that you can go ahead and make the decisions you have to make or do the things you have to do . . . It isn't that you're depending on God. It's that you're feeling his presence and then you can go ahead and do what you have to do.

For Elizabeth, the worship service was also a time of peace, "a separation from the day-to-day problems, traumas, whatever. [It was] a peaceful time to me." The solid faith that God is someone you can talk to, who is personally involved in the events and decisions of your life, and who is committed to helping you sort out what to do both for yourself, your loved ones, and your community permeates the lives of Pauline Moore and her children.

Elizabeth Logan graduated from high school at the age of sixteen (her mother graduated from college at nineteen) and could not get into nursing school despite the advocacy of Father Brown because she was too young, although her grades were excellent. It should also be noted here that none of the hospitals in Rochester that trained nurses accepted African American applicants before World War II. She did housework, worked at Kodak, and moved to the Telephone Company where she began as an operator and retired as a supervisor in the Public Administration department. She married and had a son while her husband was serving in World War II. He came home ill, became paralyzed, and Elizabeth took care of him, and worked and raised her son. She too is continuing to live her faith.

The lives of Elizabeth Logan and Pauline Moore illustrate the importance of the church for structuring personal relationships based upon respect, mutuality, and a face-to-face informal response to human need. Pauline Moore instilled in her children a respect for elders and an attendance to the needs of others. The church provided a core community, and relations of respect and service. From this core, people could then extend relations of trust and mutuality to the entire community. Faith played an instrumental role in this process since it is through "God that we learn to love everybody else." Faith, for Elizabeth Logan, also provided the spiritual stamina necessary for individual and community survival. Worship every week steeped her in the knowledge of God's "presence and then you can go ahead and do what you need to do."

The lives of these women illustrate the importance of gender in defining the avenues African Americans created to provide for the basic needs of the people in their community in Rochester during the first four decades of the twentieth century. African American women, like their white colleagues in the wider Rochester community, were the primary actors in developing networks and programs to alleviate the hardships found in an urban environment. African American women cooperated actively with African American men to provide education and economic self-development opportunities for themselves and their children. They also organized and agitated politically, while leaving the leadership in the defense of their rights primarily in the hands of African American men. It is within the realm of service, creating the institutional infrastructure and providing for basic human needs, that women took the lead and did most of the work. And it is this domain of service, providing for and working with each other, that built the spiritual and material foundations for all other efforts within the church and community.

All of these women have different backgrounds and roots. They represent different denominational affiliations and have different levels of involvement in their congregations and communities. Their individual personalities speak from their stories. The commonalities of their lives took shape during what historians call the "nadir" of African American social progress, exemplified in the legalization of segregation, the revocation of the civil rights gained during Reconstruction, the denial of access to the massive social reform efforts aimed at immigrant and poor white communities during the Progressive Era, and the implementation of such violently coercive measures as lynching to keep black people at the bottom of American society. Their lives also took shape during an era of social reform which expressed itself in the development of the Social Gospel, the growth of the settlement house movement, urban reform, and the advent of social work as a profession. All of these historical trends shaped the wider context of Rochester in specific ways that had an impact upon how these women understood themselves as African Americans, as church and community members, and as women. Rochester provided a vital context as a historical leader in the development of women's activisim, the social gospel and social reform.

THE CONTEXT OF SOCIAL REFORM AND THE PROVISION OF HUMAN SERVICES IN ROCHESTER

It is not the intention of this study to explicate the history of the social gospel movement in Rochester, or to detail the diverse institutions and programs that the social reform movement of the early twentieth century promulgated here. The following discussion seeks to establish that the Rochester community engaged enthusiastically in progressive reform. The leadership of that movement included nationally renowned figures and created an unusually liberal contingent of religiously and ethnically diverse people. The diversity within the social reform movement in Rochester excluded African Americans.

> The most important part of a city is not the houses or the stores, but the people; their race and national descent, their physical and intellectual vigor, their skill in work, their moral soundness. . . . Fortunately, we are hardly touched by the race question. With the exception of 601 persons of African blood and thirteen of the yellow race, we are all white men.[5]

As this quote indicates, the crisis which engaged the attention of Rochester's most famous leader of the social gospel movement at the turn of the century, Walter Rauschenbusch, was its burgeoning European immigrant population. Rochester's population swelled from 89,366 in 1880 to 218,149 by 1910. Predominantly Western European, there were 17,330 German immigrants by 1890. Throughout the first four decades of the twentieth century, while the African American community grew, it never represented more than one percent of the total population. By 1910 immigrants from Eastern Europe, especially Russian and Polish Jews, were beginning to tax Rochester's magnanimous spirit. The Italians posed the most difficult challenge, as they increased rapidly, bringing a volubility and volatility that seemed to unnerve the Yankee and Western European core of the community, and greatly increased the Catholic population. Rochester also attracted contingents of Hungarians, Finns, Serbs, Rumanians, Bulgarians, Greeks, Turks, and other ethnic groups of varying but not extremely significant size.

What is interesting to note about the plethora of immigrant groups thronging to Rochester during the Progressive Era is the response on the part of civic and religious leaders. Even the smallest foreign element stirred interest among those engaged in reform.

> The number and diversity of these newcomers began after the turn of the century to awaken some older citizens to a realization of the complexity of their European heritage. While the politicians could safely neglect the twelve small ethnic or linguistic groups which numbered fewer than 100 residents each, the social and religious reformers proved less indifferent, as the writings and speeches of Rauschenbusch and Rumball indicated.[6]

The discrepancy between Rauschenbusch's response to immigrants and his response to African Americans is instructive. African Americans did not receive attention because their numbers posed no threat and their assimilation, therefore, was not imperative. They could safely fade into the background in a city of white men. The size of any given immigrant group presented no such barrier to reform attention. This strongly suggests that Rauschenbusch and his colleagues shared the prevailing assumptions dictating that assimilation was an appropriate goal for European immigrants but not African Americans. Rochester's liberal record of reform left a legacy of racial exclusion.

THE SOCIAL GOSPEL

The Depression of 1893 energized a generation of social reformers who self-consciously adhered to the Social Gospel. Walter Rauschenbusch was the most famous and articulate of these, but by no means the most active. He leant his support to and contributed in the efforts of his colleagues to build institutional churches, settlement houses, and social centers. Among the most influential religious leaders and proponents of the Social Gospel in Rochester during this era were: Rev. William C. Gannett of the Unitarian Church, Rev. Dr. Algernon Crapsey of St. Andrew's Episcopal Church, Rev. William Brown of Plymouth Church, Rev. Paul Moore Strayer of Third Presbyterian Church, Rev. James Dennis of St. Michael's Episcopal Church, and Rev. William R. Taylor of Brick Church. In addition to these Protestant clergy, Bishop McQuaid and Dr. Max Landsberg provided vital religious leadership to the social reform movements of the Progressive Era in Rochester. These religiously motivated individuals responded to the economic crisis and the rapidly increasing foreign population that created destitution and unemployment on a grand scale in Rochester for the first time. They attended to the members of their congregations and neighborhoods by creating programs, institutions, and settlements specifically to address the needs of unemployed and unassimilated immigrants. Religious sentiments also influenced other members of Rochester's civic minded elite, most notably business men like Joseph Alling and women reformers like Mary Gannett and Helen Montgomery. A large and diverse band of religiously motivated women and men led Rochester's reform efforts for the first two decades of the twentieth century. Liberal minded and inclusive for the most part, these women and men rarely considered African Americans as anything but potential clients, and not the most desirable of these. Consequently, while Rochester developed a wide variety of reform efforts and programs, African Americans did not directly benefit from most of them.

The initial response to the devastation of the Depression of 1893 was to provide charitable relief. This impetus quickly exhausted traditional sources of aid and revealed the extent of the need to socially conscious leaders. Rev. Gannett demanded the creation of jobs rather than relief, and Rev. Dennis opened a small loan institution which charged reasonable interest for the economic relief of the unemployed. As proponents of the social gospel met political resistance to their efforts, they widened the scope of their activities by creating programs and institutions themselves from their church bases. Gannett opened a Boys' Evening Home which became the Gannett House by 1910 and William Taylor, pastor of Brick Church built the Brick Church Institute that year. Church programs and institutions provided an experiential base for the dialogue between reformers and economic and civic leaders. As the scope of the problems became more evident, reformers entered the political arena. (This development receives in-depth treatment in chapter five.)

African American efforts to alleviate economic and social hardship took a parallel course which, according to the historical record, rarely if ever intersected with the agitation within the white community. Churches rallied to support orphanages (Mt. Olivet was a primary backer of "Mother" Dorsey's home) and foster care, recreation centers, good government clubs, relief efforts, YW and YMCAs, and club houses. Most of their efforts retained an informal, face-to-face character and took place within and between the churches, and were organized and implemented primarily by women.

As Rochester returned to prosperity, reformers did not retreat into the woodwork but used their influence as much as possible to shape the new industrial and economic forces coming to the fore in the city. Reformers coordinated efforts to meet the needs of Rochester's workers and immigrants. McKelvey notes that

> far more significant than the new material burdens, which could be borne in the prosperous times, was the new emphasis on rehabilitation as against relief. The Society for Organized Charity endeavored to place needy and often bewildered people in suitable jobs. The Children's Aid Society, chartered in 1895, sought homes for the public wards under its care and developed a new practice of

making periodic visits to insure their proper treatment. Efforts to assure poor children a better chance for wholesome development characterized several of the other institutions.[7]

Rochester's reform leaders attempted to integrate their efforts across religious affiliations and institutions and focused on developing classes in English, industrial training, and wholesome recreation. Their strategy indicates both an acceptance of the environmental causes for urban social conditions and a desire to provide avenues for education and individual character-building which they believed necessary for working class people to combat such conditions and improve their lives. The acceptance of external factors in the creation of social hardship did not erase the emphasis on promoting individual efforts to alleviate distress and obviate the need for charity. Home visits carried this double-edged purpose: concern for actual conditions, and checking up on individual efforts. The veneer of objective professionalism did not remove the persistent tendency to assign moral culpability among those in need of aid.

Interethnic and religious cooperation and tolerance manifested itself in the admittance of Polish Jews and any kind of Catholics to the YMCA in the 1890s. The YMCA would establish separate branches for some immigrant groups, but this reflected the need for English language development rather than a desire for segregation. While some branches of the Y admitted a few African American members, the African American community developed separate YW- and YMCAs in the 1920s. The numbers of African American members who may have joined the mainline Ys were, in all likelihood, too small to encourage the development of programs to meet the specific needs of the African American community, much less encourage the inclusion of African Americans to decision-making roles within the institutional structure. The Y did both for immigrant groups. The creation of separate institutions for African Americans took over thirty years. This speaks both to the small size and resource base available to the African American community, and to the determination of that community to provide for each other. Separate branches of the Y gave African Americans organizational leadership over what happened within their own community. Eunice Bullock, among others, for example, testified to the African American history lessons received there.

WOMEN'S ORGANIZATIONS

WEIU

One major organization that exhibited interethnic cooperation and religious tolerance was the Woman's Educational and Industrial Union (WEIU), the foremost women's activist organization during the first quarter of the century in Rochester. This organization admitted Jewish and immigrant women, but not African Americans, to its governing board. Susan B. Anthony and Mary Gannet began the Rochester chapter[8] of the WEIU in 1893 as an effort to provide broad organizational reforms that would have an ameliorative influence on the lives of women in all stations of life. The WEIU consciously recruited women of differing religious and ethnic, but not racial, backgrounds to develop its platform of reform. William Reese interprets the motivation and ideology of the women who organized these reforms. "The creation of a new form of domesticity was the heart of the ideological world constructed and inhabited by Progressive women," Reese maintains.[9] Women elaborated a justification for their involvement in social and political action by invoking the power of motherhood and expanding the role of parental duties to include addressing the conditions under which working people had to raise their children. They believed in the moral power of women to transform social conditions and viewed the reform movements they engaged in as ends in themselves, rather than springboards for more radical change. Yet the ethnically and religiously diverse women with whom white middle class women were willing to share leadership also shared with them social standing. African American women who were serving the needs of their community came, by and large, from the ranks of the working class, women whom reform leaders viewed as the very objects of reform.

Blake McKelvey's assessment of the contributions of the WEIU perpetuates the impression of the dominance of the wives of Protestant clergy and Yankee businessmen in the reform efforts and organizations of activist women. The historical record, however, indicates a much more complex interaction between women of diverse religious and ethnic backgrounds. The first successful social settlement in Rochester grew out of the Jewish community and took root on Baden Street. That the Jewish community of Rochester created the quintessential example of the social "gospel" reflects the large population of Jewish immigrants in Rochester, their need, and the Judaic tradition of community aid. McKelvey's interpretation of the Jewish origins of this groundbreaking institution credits the influence of the Gannetts on Max Landsberg and the Jewish women who joined with Mrs. Gannett in the Woman's Educational and Industrial Union.

> Many of Rabbi Landsberg's congregation were close to such Unitarians as the Gannetts, and the women in particular were being drawn into association with other church women by the Ethical Club and the Woman's Educational and Industrial Union, both . . . inspired by Mrs. Gannett. Indeed Mrs. Gannett's success in bringing other ladies to the fore and imbuing them with some of her

inexhaustible humanitarianism was one of the largest single contributions to the movement in Rochester. Mrs. Montgomery, Mrs. Landsberg, Mrs. Alling, and Mrs. Lewis Bigelow were but a few of the women who owed much to Mrs. Gannett's inspiration. [10]

An alternative interpretation might credit Mrs. Landsberg and the Jewish women and men who formed the Baden Street Settlement with inspiring their Christian colleagues to other efforts for social reform. What is most illuminating, however, is the presence of active, collegial relationships among leaders of differing religious persuasions and ethnic backgrounds in leading Rochester's social movements. Such collegiality glaringly emphasizes the absence of any African Americans among the leaders of these movements.

A reading of the history of social reform in Rochester could lead one to conclude that the African American people in Rochester were, at best, the recipients of white largess. In order to study, streamline, standardize, and professionalize the delivery of services, white reformers created the United Charities (1910), the Bureau of Municipal Research (1915), The Community Chest (1918), the Council of Social Agencies (1923/24), and the Industrial Management Council (1926). These agencies accepted and considered African American as well as white clients, but African Americans did not belong to their decision-making bodies, while members of immigrant groups and religious minorities did. Any impression of passivity on the part of African Americans based upon their exclusion from these agencies would be erroneous. The trend in Rochester toward professionalization and standardization of human services reflected larger national trends away from a focus on religious and charitable efforts and toward secular means of reform. The African American community in Rochester, as elsewhere, continued to channel their service efforts through the institution of the church and through primarily informal means. That the religiously motivated leaders of the reform movements in Rochester, like Walter Rauschenbusch and Mary Gannett, did not extend the hand of fellowship to African American men and women illustrates the racial barriers with which African Americans had to contend.

Susan B. Anthony and her relationship with African American women in Rochester constitutes one exception to this rule of exclusion, although her organizational efforts to include African American women are fully treated in the chapter on political and civil rights (chapter five) and receive only passing mention here. As leader of the Political Equality Club, which organized in Rochester for women's suffrage, Susan B. Anthony invited Hester Jeffreys to join. This relationship had an impact on both Mrs. Jeffreys and upon the congregation through which she worked for reform, Memorial A.M.E. Zion. The other exception is the local NAACP (National Association for the Advancement of Colored People), where some white men and women joined and served as officers. (A discussion of this organization also occurs in chapter five). Otherwise, the progressive reformers who held sway during the first two decades of this century in Rochester excluded African Americans from their organizations and activities.

GEORGE EASTMAN AND REFORM

Racial exclusion continued to operate under the leadership of George Eastman as Rochester elaborated more scientific, professional, and managerial approaches to reform during the teens, twenties, and thirties. George Eastman's influence permeated every level of Rochester's social and political development. World War I had prompted Eastman to organize a Patriotic and Community Fund to coordinate the war effort in Rochester and as President, Eastman converted this fund into the Community Chest after the war. The Community Chest became the main distribution center for charitable funds for reform work in Rochester. Its expectation of efficient and professional management prompted the development of the Council of Social Agencies, to direct the overall planning of social services. The Council of Social Agencies often relied on the Bureau of Municipal Research, again founded and funded by George Eastman, to supply it with the necessary data to make informed decisions. The Council tended to promote the growth of agencies already within the Community Chest fold, rather than encourage "new ventures," which solidified the network of experts and professionals who came more and more to shape the raising of funds for and the delivery of services. The exclusive character of this organizational network that placed the power over the distribution of material resources within the hands of a professional white elite made it well nigh impossible for African American church and community programs to gain access.

The onset of the Great Depression taxed the combined resources of this network of social agencies. Despite the combined and centralized efforts to provide relief during the Depression, the crisis deepened. During the first week of January, 1932, eleven thousand people registered for relief work. Rochester's industrial and civic leaders faced a situation where their cooperative, professional, coordinated efforts were not solving the city's problems and their ranks split between those who continued to seek ways to provide relief and those who began to insist on economy and to question the reality of the need for relief, calling into question the moral character of the poor and destitute.

At this point, the Bureau of Municipal Research stepped in to take the initiative away from the Civic Committee on Unemployment. Approaching the situation scientifically, the Bureau conducted research in three cities comparable to Rochester: Dayton, Cincinnati, and Cleveland. The results of this "objective" research noted that these three cities were expending far less for relief. The reply of local welfare administrators reveals the hold that professionalization and expertise had developed on the reform structures of Rochester. "A second survey, assisted by an experienced social worker, revealed that the services and the coverage [in the three other cities] were much less adequate." The religious community and some reformers surviving from an earlier era voiced the only note reminiscent of the social gospel as services and relief programs lost financial backing.

> "What kind of city do we want to live in?" demanded Rabbi Philip Bernstein of both the City Council and the Bureau . . . Superintendent Herbert S. Weet warned that the public school program and the future of thousands of children were alike threatened. Alternate charges of dishonesty and corruption, of sentimentality and heartless penny pinching, of self-interest and cultural stupidity, were bandied about as the trying year [1932] drew to a close. [11]

Throughout these years the Council of Social Agencies conducted surveys to determine its role in cooperation with government programs. In maintaining their efforts to study and meet the needs of the destitute of Rochester, the social agencies began to take note of a body of human beings whose sufferings during the Depression created long-term rehabilitation problems, the first hint of an assumption of the permanence of destitution for some in Rochester. Scientific investigation began to take on the role of delaying measures of amelioration. When even the Bureau of Municipal Research experts were shocked at housing conditions and proposed immediate action, the Chamber of Commerce and the Citizen's Tax League mounted their own investigations and campaigned for alternatives to public housing.[12]

The Depression, unemployment, and the intensified efforts of centralized, professional agencies to meet the need had diverse impacts upon African Americans in Rochester. The Depression and unemployment hit African Americans hard, as they held jobs in service and adjunct sectors of the economy that lost priority quickly as employers tightened their belts. Also, relief efforts did not benefit them evenly, as many programs provided by industrialists in Rochester based eligibility on a history of industrial employment. They did not benefit, for example, from Kodak's innovative unemployment insurance plan.

Both the emphasis on centralized organization and the failure of local efforts paved the way in Rochester as elsewhere for the implementation of federal New Deal programs in Rochester. The social welfare agencies thus created provided avenues for African Americans to obtain relief. They did so within the contours of their culture and community. For example, women like Cora Young applied to social services to get African American foster children placed in her home. Her son, Buddy Young, recalls that while the pay was not that great, it gave his mother a chance to take care of the "worst" cases, the ones no one else would take, because she loved kids. Over the years, Cora Young took in somewhere around twenty foster children. In addition to whatever social services gave in terms of support, Cora Young took in washing and opened a restaurant to make money to provide for the family. Buddy's father worked three jobs. Eunice Bullock took a job at the YWCA through funds provided by WPA. She worked within her own community and for the benefit of that community.[13]

African Americans in Rochester faced both the hardships and promise of the first four decades of the twentieth century by providing for each other within their churches and community and by taking advantage of and celebrating any opportunities the larger community offered them. The concept of service, of taking care of one another, stood upon a faith foundation and became implemented primarily through the hands of African American women who, as their personal testimony shows, viewed it as both duty and joy. Women like Eunice Bullock, Gladys Scott, Pauline Moore, and Elizabeth Logan lived and worked during an historical era that provided particular definitions of gender and models for women's organizational activity.

African American women participated in church life as women and behaved in accordance with what they understood to be their role as African American women of faith. They differentiated their behavior from the men with whom they shared their lives and perceived this differentiation as cooperative and vital. Elizabeth Logan referred to her mother's tireless efforts to take care of community people as well as to the fact that she took her daughters with her consistently so they would learn these same lessons. Pauline Moore required that her sons learn also, but particularly emphasized the rule of care-taking to her daughters. Gladys Scott saw the junior usher board as important for both genders, but it was also important for girls and boys to learn to do their own work, and to cooperate with one another.

African American women understood what they were doing not only as women's work but as God's work. As they shouldered their responsibilities and took delight in their accomplishments, they relied on their faith, their men, and their community. Gladys Scott "worked for the Lord," relied upon her husband, and became surrogate parent for dozens of children. Eunice Bullock was proud of her job, her service, and her faithfulness. She also found great fulfillment in giving back to her community. These women were never blind to the discriminations of race and gender which limited but did not destroy their efforts. Pauline Moore waited twenty-five years to exercise her talents as a teacher, and finally did so within her own community. Eunice Bullock noted that she had more education than any of the white men she worked for.

AFRICAN AMERICAN WOMEN'S ACTIVISM

Upon this faith foundation, African American women shaped their lives within their families, churches, and communities. As Judith Weisenfold describes it, "religious belief systems have assisted African American women in centering themselves and their communities in times of hardship, and they have provided a language for expressing the joy and hope of better times."[14] Both language and action drew from the materials of prevailing social conditions and gender roles. Rochester's women acted out of local conditions, but their efforts formed part of and reflected wider national movements. Across the nation, African American women participated actively in the call for organized activity to confront the setbacks, oppression, and discrimination facing black Americans since the end of Reconstruction. The strategies of their leaders emphasized racial uplift (with its intrinsic connection to "moral uplift") through self-help and mutuality, racial solidarity, and political action. Depending on their own reading of a particular situation, program, or event, African American women and their organizations combined the strategies of self-help promulgated by Booker T. Washington, with the political action advocated by W.E.B. Du Bois and the NAACP. On both national and local levels, African American women moved between these camps and drew lessons to apply to specific situations. Lillian Williams points out that the African American women involved in reform efforts in Buffalo, New York, during the Progressive Era "staunchly adhered to the contemporary black ideology of self-help and racial solidarity as expounded by Booker T. Washington, W.E.B. Du Bois, and T. Thomas Fortune. Yet they succeeded in perfecting a delicate balancing act that permitted them to be independent of these apparently divergent camps."[15]

In Rochester, the heart of African American women's efforts on behalf of their own community resided within the church. They organized and communicated within this structure a far-reaching and complex network that insured the survival and future prosperity of their people. They performed this role with a clear understanding of themselves as women.

Most Excellent Women

You Went to Church

On the most basic level, women saw to it that the people attended church. In virtually all of the families whose descendants I interviewed, Sunday was the day you went to church. Every Sunday. Sometimes twice on Sunday and a couple of times during the week. Overwhelmingly it was the women—grandmothers, mothers, sisters, or aunts—who made sure of this. Most men attended also, though some stayed away, like Oscar Hawkins' father, who made his living as a musician and worked late on Saturday nights. In a few cases, like Ernest DuBois's, his grandfather, one of the founders of Trinity Presbyterian Church, was the one who insisted they go. The prevailing force behind church attendance, however, was the women, and this included women who worked on Sunday, as many domestics did. Alan Adams' mother often worked on Sunday, but his grandmother made sure he was in church. Charles Frazier's mother routinely rounded up the children of friends and neighbors to bring them to church services and events. Ruth Brown recalls picking up seven or eight other children in addition to her own, in the old days, on her way to St. Simon's. The meaning of such regular devotion could not emerge from a consideration of African American women's national church or secular reform activities.

Women strictly enforced church attendance for a number of interrelated reasons, spiritual rejuvenation and "learning about the Lord" being paramount. Praying, listening to the word, and meditating on God's purpose personally fortified people. Mary Thompson, who described her involvement in church as less than enthusiastic ("I was the trouble maker"), credits the long history of church attendance with teaching her how to pray. "If I get in a tight spot, I pray to the Lord and put it in His hands." Elizabeth Logan testified to the spiritual connections so important to clarifying one's problems and course of action. Daniel Garnett spoke eloquently of the power of worship and prayer in allowing him to face the tribulations of the outer world in which he had to work during the 1940s. "When you're in prayer it gives you time in that praying and your mind becomes a little clearer and you can look back at that problem in a different light." When a coworker questioned his religious involvement, Mr. Garnett replied: "I look him in the eye and I said, 'Monday morning when I look you in the eye, I'm better fortified to deal with you cause my faith has carried me through.'" Mr. Garnett also emphasizes that he got his reward—in the pride and joy his parents expressed in his employment and in his own satisfaction at "looking down the third base line" and seeing other African American men and women entering skilled and professional employment in Rochester.[16]

Learning about the Lord entailed more than participating in the spiritual exercises of worship and prayer which connected individuals to God. Regular church attendance drummed into people the lessons of Christian behavior and character. Even Mary Thompson, who claimed her devotion to church was not as strong as that of other women in her family, went to church every week, and insisted that her children attend also. People attended church in order to "come up right" and learn "right from wrong." Expressed in rudimentary strictures, the inculcation of mores called for consistent attendance to monitor and encourage particular behavior. Such strictures included: no lying, no cheating, no stealing. These sanctions formed the foundation for young people's understanding of respect for others, a moral imperative that dictated behavior between individuals. Everyone learned to respect his or her elders (especially children), the family unit, and the church community. Children communicated respect for elders and elders communicated respect for the family and the church community most clearly in the reciprocal child-caring and child-disciplining roles the adults of a particular community exhibited. Across congregations and generations from the turn of the century until the 1950s and 1960s, African American adults cooperated in supervising and admonishing the behavior of children. If an adult caught a child doing something he or she wasn't supposed to do (running around, swearing, talking back, lying, etc.) that adult would either take custody of that child and return him to his parents, or administer punishment on the spot. "And you didn't struggle," remembers Charles Frazier. If you struggled or complained to your parents, things invariably got worse. Mary Thompson recalls that such complaints were useless. If she told her mother somebody had "fanned her behind" her mother would say, "you deserved it." Ruth Brown remembers that parents talked to each other about their children's behavior, to reinforce effective mores and to extend parental influence from the home to the church and into the community. While both men and women performed this communal parental function, women most often took care of, watched over, and disciplined kids.[17]

Regular attendance established the pathways of spiritual sustenance and moral imperatives to connect members in a social network important for sharing news, creating peer groups, introducing potential marriage partners, and providing opportunities for relaxation and recreation. Alan Adams remembers the importance of going to church regularly to find out what was happening in the community. People didn't have telephones, newspapers did not carry the news most significant to African Americans, and few parishioners were wealthy enough to have cars so they could go visiting. For Elizabeth Logan, who lived in a predominantly white neighborhood and went to school with mostly white children, church was the only place she could get to know other African American children. Kay Jordan brought her children to St. Simon's so they could associate with the people within the African American community most able to provide a good example and appropriate values. Ms. Jordan acknowledges that such sentiment could be elitist, but she wanted her children to have "the best." She explains, "It is possible to soar and you can only soar when you're with people who can allow you to soar."[18] Several of the people I interviewed came from marriages that originated in the church. Charles Frazier's parents met on the steps of the church. Eunice Bullock met her future husband in church. Ruth Brown met her husband singing in the choir. Elizabeth Logan met her husband at St. Simon's when they were little, and they grew up together.

Women's insistence that their children and families not only come to church but attend regularly, every week, provided the habitual grounding for the formation of community relationships and interpersonal connections. These relationships grew out of the explicitly African American Christian context which voiced the moral imperatives of respect for and paying attention to each other. Through regular attendance and active participation in worship, church events and activities, and organized group activity, children learned and parents practiced Christian behavior. This behavior had clear social and political implications, but its intrinsic value came from its connection to the will of God. Ruth Brown remembers Father Brown, the first priest at St. Simon's, teaching the young people there, "Whatever you do and wherever you go, it's all right as long as you can take God with you." For her, this is how you told right from wrong.[19]

Regular church attendance established one as a member of the community, one who could both call upon others when in need, and be responsible for providing help when asked. Being present created the possibility of knowing one another well enough to know what the others needed and how best to supply it. For example, when elderly people missed church, someone found out why. If children were absent from Sunday School, the teacher called on the family to see how she or he was doing and if any help was needed.

To Carry Out The Work

The women of the black churches in Rochester cooperated with their men in establishing and working in church organizations that carried out the work of the church. Some of these organizations, like the Deacon(esses), Steward(esses), Ushers, Sunday School and Missionary Societies, were denominational bodies and had traditional functions within the church structure. Early in the century, most of these groups had separate male and female counterparts, while later, some congregations combined the men's and women's groups and either kept the genders separate in terms of tasks or blended the tasks of the entire group across genders. Other organizations, called clubs, emerged within and were particular to specific congregations. Both women and men organized these clubs; some of them had gender specific membership, others did not.

Unless restricted to male membership (for example Trustee Boards were overwhelmingly male during this period, as were governing boards such as the Vestry at St. Simon's), women often led these organizations and clubs. Men claimed the pulpit, and with rare exceptions presided over those church committees that made policy and administrative decisions (Trustees, Deacons) or controlled funds (Stewards). Women organized cooperatively with men at the local level, establishing Deaconesses, Stewardesses, and Women's Usher Boards, for example, but the ultimate decision-making and financial authority resided in the hands of the men of the church. The historical record suggests that women frequently headed church organizations and clubs that functioned to support male efforts or to develop along independent lines in ways that nurtured church and community development.

The church organizations ostensibly took care of the administrative and spiritual needs of the church and its membership, while the club's most obvious purpose was to "raise money" for the church. The involvement of women in church organizations and clubs have led African American women historians to conclude that women raised most of the funds on the local level for national missionary and other church programmatic work. Most organizations and virtually all clubs required the payment of dues which financed group activities, but also contributed to general church funds. Clubs sometimes originated during fund-raising drives with the expressed purpose of sponsoring events or dinners, the money from which would relieve the church's debt. As the instigators, presidents, and members of these church bodies, women provided the bulk of the work behind attaining church solvency. The records of Memorial A.M.E Zion church reported the results of fund-raising efforts to build their new church in 1906.

> The various organizations within the church have given toward the edifice as follows: Stewardess Board, $70.70; Junior Stewardess Board $80; Ladies Auxiliary No 79, $42.25; Paul Lawrence Dunbar Club, $133.68; Dorcas Society, $24.31; L'Overture Club, $55; Independent Club $31; Excelsior Club, $25; Frances E. Harper Club $22.06; Young People's Missionary Society $3.70."[20]

With the exception of the Independent and Excelsior Clubs and the Young People's Missionary Society, all of these groups had women presidents, and the bulk of them were explicitly women's organizations.

While most historians of African American reform efforts acknowledge both that the church played a supportive role in those efforts and that women provided funds and organizational support, Higginbotham goes further in acknowledging the role of women's fund-raising and organizational efforts within the Baptist denomination to support programs of community uplift and social reform. On the national level, for example, the Women's Convention "stated that its objectives were to disseminate knowledge; facilitate the growth and activities of existing women's societies at the church, district, and state levels; work through these societies and organize new ones; and enlist the assistance of women and children in fund raising for educational and missionary purposes." In pursuit of these objectives the convention:

> established its own educational institution, the National Training School for Women and Girls, and it also established a settlement house in Washington, D.C. under the direction of a trained social worker. The black Baptist women also supported secular institutions and organizations that worked for racial and gender advancement, such as the National Association for the Advancement of Colored People (NAACP), the National Association of Colored Women (NACW), and the National League for the Protection of Colored Women.[21]

The fund-raising activities of African American church women at the national level supported numerous missions and outreach efforts. The local congregations and their women's organizations and clubs contributed in this process, but, as the history of organizational units and clubs within the congregations in Rochester reveal, fund-raising supported more than specific programmatic reforms and fund-raising was not the only purpose for which these groups came together.

Fund-raising served as an organizing force and primary purpose for club work but the financial support of church work was the end product, the ultimate expression of the Christian character and practice that these groups promoted. The organized activity of both women and men in Rochester's African American churches created interpersonal relationships of mutual support, and inculcated the concepts of Christian service that fostered their ability to give to each other in many practical and material ways, culminating in financial sacrifice for their common good. Gladys Scott's financial contribution to Mt. Olivet, and her insistence that the Junior Usher Board "work" and pay for their own material contributions to the church as they themselves defined them, exemplifies this connection between fund-raising, Christian service, and the common good.

Both women and men were Sunday School teachers, ushers, youth group leaders, and club members. Their role as adults and officers shared common features and responsibilities. Gladys Scott's husband took charge of the young men on the Junior Usher Board in much the same way that she took charge of the young women. Christian Endeavor at both Memorial A.M.E. Zion and Mt. Olivet took advantage of the adult men and women in the congregation who taught, lectured, spoke, and supervised the activities of their youth. Deacons,

Stewards, and Men and Women's Missionary Societies kept tabs on the requirements of the poor and needy in their congregations and communities, while clubs performed the same functions for their particular members, male and female alike. Whatever their articulated purpose—to teach, socialize, study the Bible, study African American history or literature, assist the pastor, or administer the programs of the church—these various organizations focused on Christian practice in their day-to-day operations. The publication of the duties of a Sunday School teacher at Memorial A.M.E. Zion church illustrates this point:

> The duties of a Sunday School class leader [are: to] meet his class once every week at the appointed place of meeting, and to visit those who may be absent as soon as possible, in order to inquire how their souls prosper; to advise, reprove, comfort or exhort, as occasion may require; to make a collection in his Class once in three months for the poor at the time of giving out the Love-Feast tickets; to make such weekly or monthly collections for the support of the Pastor; to meet each other's classes as often as convenient, and to see that the sick and poor Members have proper attention given them; to apply through the Pastor to the Poor's Steward for means of relief for his needy members; to collect . . . for the support of the Presiding Elder . . . to collect . . . as much as he can of the General Fund Assessment and Special Assessment.[22]

Sunday School did more than teach biblical lessons. All the members of the congregation attended Sunday School, children through adults, and each Sunday School class created an interpersonal network of people concerned about one another's presence, spiritual state, and material well-being. Sunday School connected its individual class members to the wider mission and activities of the church by supporting the pastor and contributing dues to church work. Each Sunday School class was Christianity in practice. Club work did much the same thing. While the focus of the club meetings might be on the poetry of Paul Lawrence Dunbar or the historical contributions of Harriet Tubman, if anyone in the church was in trouble, if they belonged to a club, its members would help them. As they grew older, club members took care of them. The weekly or monthly meetings provided the informal and interpersonal context for promoting such mutuality and respect for each other.

While organizations such as Sunday Schools and clubs had both women and men at their heads, the record indicates that more women than men taught Sunday School and there were more women than men's clubs. Churches also had explicitly female organizations, such as the Women's Auxiliary or Women's Missionary Society. Women's organizations operated according to the mandates of gender. The Deaconess Board of Memorial A.M.E. Zion church, formed in 1910, was "composed of Christian women who have consecrated themselves to the work of the church and the service of God. [They] have started out to help the pastor in his pastoral labors which are daily increasing owing to the constantly growing congregation. These sisters are to wear uniform dress and will spend much of their time visiting the sick and caring for the poor and needy of the church and city."[23] African American women thus expressed their duty to God, their subordinate position under the male pastor, their job as the purveyors of respectability connoted by dress, and their role as the providers of nurture for those in need. The Deaconess fund of Mt. Olivet contributed to the sick committee in 1929 and the largest contribution from the Mt. Olivet Ladies Missionary Society in that year went to local relief work. Alan Adams remembers the activities of the women of Trinity Presbyterian church:

> The women were very devoted to seeing that the membership didn't have a problem. They visited the sick and so on, they were very religious in that regard. [Members and] friends were the same thing. There were times when unfortunate things were presented they'd visit the jail, the hospital, so on and so forth they were very social. The men did not respond as readily as the women did which is not unnatural cause men don't tend to spread themselves out that way. They put in their eight to five and that's it, but on occasions when they were needed [they'd respond].[24]

The women among the various churches in Rochester created Deaconess Boards, Missionary Societies, and a variety of clubs in order to meet the needs of members of their congregations and communities. Their activities paralleled but contrasted with the activities, programs, and agencies of white social reform women in Rochester. First of all, whether as members of their own congregations, or as members of the wider African American community (even newcomers to Rochester), the recipients of aid were people whom the women knew personally. They were serving the needs of family members and friends. Even in the case of meeting people getting off the train, as the Missionary Society at Mt. Olivet did, the women took care to get to know who people were, what they needed, and where they came from. Many migrants came to Rochester as a result of family connections, and the burgeoning population, while creating a strain on resources, did not disrupt the ability of the already established African American community members from getting to know people personally, assessing their needs, and offering aid. The people for whom African American women organized material resources were members of their own community, not strangers, even if they had never met them before. Often the recipients of aid were well known. For example, fostering of children often occurred when the family resources were strained and individual children moved in with relatives or friends.

Additionally, as the example of fosterage illustrates, the economic marginality of the entire African American community, based primarily in service and entrepreneurial employment, obviated against class pretensions in the distribution of aid. The Moore family, for example, lost their home during the Depression. Jesse Stevens, one of the founders of Trinity Presbyterian, lost his grocery store and worked the rest of his life as a boot black. That Pauline Moore and her husband continued to provide for their ten children and two cousins speaks eloquently to the herculean efforts of the most established African American families on their own and others' behalf during times of severe need. That disaster could strike anyone lessened the tendency to assign moral culpability to those in need. The women in Missionary Societies, Deaconess Boards, and clubs exhorted standards of behavior, to be sure. These strictures combined the need for social control with the understanding that moral conduct provided a hedge against disaster by channeling individual resources toward the common good. (A more thorough discussion of the dynamics of elitism follows in the discussion of the justification for and implementation of more formal programs.)

The informal connections arising from common club and organizational activity provided the primary avenue through which church members and African American community residents brought each other's needs to light and worked to meet them. At its largest, the African American community of Rochester numbered 3,262 and represented less than one percent of Rochester's total population until the advent of World War II. Its small size, various congregations, and numerous church organizations facilitated this informal face-to-face mutuality. Despite its size and the frequency of informal communication, Rochester's African American congregations often engaged in more structured programs of social reform and service and supported more obviously secular agencies. These efforts supplemented rather than replaced the predominantly informal networks communicating and serving the African American community's needs.

To Better Our Condition

The African American congregations in Rochester created and supported social service programs and agencies with the explicit intent of bettering their social condition. Spokespeople for the African American church were explicit in connecting God's will to the work of improving the lives of African Americans. Rev. J. W. Brown, pastor of Memorial A.M.E. Zion early in the twentieth century, articulated the connections between the community's faith that God expects African Americans to develop themselves, the role the church plays in that, and the expectations for women in this work.

Many nations have risen, and some have fallen because they have lacked the regenerating power of the Holy Spirit and the refining influence of the Gospel as it is preached in the Christian church. . . . [I]ndustrial education, or any other kind of education alone, will not subdue passion and develop strong moral character. This comes by the teaching of the Holy Spirit manifested in Christ and His church. These lessons should first be taught in the homes. Some one has said that no race rises higher than its women. It is only a few men and women who outlive the impression made upon them in their early home life. Therefore, it is necessary that our homes be good and clean. Those at the head should know of Christ's teachings, and these can best be learned in the Christian Church.[25]

The women of Memorial, while not quoted extensively in the newspapers, acted in ways that gave their assent to Rev. Brown's view of women as the "heads" of the home and the primary influence in redeeming and molding African American character to God's purpose. At the A.M.E. Zion Regional Conference held in Rochester (probably in 1906), Mrs. A.W. Blackwell, corresponding secretary of the women's missionary societies, spoke.

If the American negro is to rise to a higher level in this country, it will only be because the women of our race do their part in lifting it up. And that time will not come until our women are ready to sacrifice. . . . We must rise as a race. There can be no upper classes among the negroes of America. The negro race can not hope to rise above its lowest class. The good negro women can accomplish much in this advance. Let her go into the slums to work for the redemption of fallen brothers and sisters. The women of the other race do it. Why should not we? There is no place so evil it can contaminate a good woman, be she negro or white, and there is no force more potent for good than the sympathy and the help of good women.[26]

The women of Memorial responded enthusiastically to this call. Honoring Mrs. J.W. Hood, President of the National Women's Home and Foreign Missionary Society in 1907, Memorial's women celebrated with presentations. The topics of these were: "The need of special training for successful Missionary work," "The dawning of a brighter day for the Women of Zion," and "The Influence of a noble woman." Mrs. Lula Meadows, affiliated with both Memorial A.M.E. Zion and Mt. Olivet Baptist churhes, personified the efforts expected on the part of "good women." Mrs. Meadows "marched through Rochester's red-light district to save the sinners and all over town to heal the sick with praises from the Good Book." She practiced what she preached and provided a foster home for over 60 children during her lifetime.[27]

Memorial A.M.E. Zion, for generations the only African American church in Rochester, and the most powerful into the second decade of the twentieth century, led the way in African American attempts to institute formal programs. "To demonstrate our belief in the training of the head and hand as well as the heart, the Trustees purpose (*sic*) to open a public reading room in the Church about the middle of September where our young people can spend their leisure time profitably—Sewing classes are to be organized among the young women. There will be lectures given on domestic science, home making and house-keeping and cooking. They will also open an employment bureau."[28] This proposal led first in 1909 to the rental of a house on Favor Street to "provide recreational and social facilities for colored youth" and then to the purchase of property on which to build a parish house "in which we can have a library for the young people, teach domestic science and hold various meetings of the clubs and other church organizations. . . . When this building is established we can arrange better hours for the domestic science classes for our people than is done at the Mechanics Institute."[29] The house on Favor Street operated as a center for social and educational programs and Charles Frazier and Howard Coles remember calling it "the Brotherhood House," perhaps because it also functioned as the meeting house for local African American Elks and Masons on occasion.

In his discussion of the purpose for such a center, J.W. Thompson revealed the deep concern African Americans in Rochester had for the education, training, and employment opportunities for local blacks. The center addressed both the higher education goals of Du Bois (the library) and the manual labor and self-help aims of Washington. Thompson's emphasis on "domestic science" and the Mechanics Institute played upon the wider white community's sense of the appropriate. It also recognized the practical reality of the source of employment for blacks in Rochester and the need for African Americans to be as highly trained as possible in service occupations to compete with European immigrants.

The historical record suggests that Memorial A.M.E. Zion could not muster the material resources to build a permanent structure to house its programmatic efforts on behalf of the community without the cooperation of other congregations in the city. The concern for training and providing educational and social opportunities for young women culminated in the opening of the "colored" YWCA in 1921, six years before the formation of the "colored" YMCA. All three of the African American congregations active during that time, Memorial, Mt. Olivet, and Trinity, supported the Y. The YWCA provided recreation, classes, training, and instruction for young women from any of the African American churches and served as a focal point for the efforts of Christian African American women to influence the character of their daughters. The YWCA supplemented the activities of youth groups and Christian Endeavor organizations, most notably in its religious work (Ernestine Burks was the chair of the Religious Work committee at the Y) and lessons in African American history. Testimony from women who attended functions at the Y suggest that it operated to bring the members of the differing congregations together in common efforts of social and moral development.

Mt. Olivet's early attempts at providing formal programs followed a similar path. Mt. Olivet was successful in building Hubert Hall, which it utilized for worship, recreation, a day-care center, and the first home of the West Side YMCA, which opened in 1927. Mt. Olivet created a church library which contained over two hundred volumes for the use of the community. Mt. Olivet's support for women's efforts to provide services to the community took the form of Dr. James Rose and his wife's assisting Isabella (Mother) Dorsey as she established the first orphanage for African American children in Rochester. The Dorsey orphanage began early in the twentieth century, operated in Mrs. Dorsey's home on Bronson Avenue until 1916, and then moved first to Lake Road, and then to a farm site in Brighton (currently the location of McQuaid High School). Both Dr. Rose and his wife "supervised and taught the children at the Dorsey orphanage in 1920s."[30] Isabella Dorsey was also instrumental in the formation of St. Simon's Episcopal parish. Her appeal to the Diocese for a kindergarten for black children led to the establishment of a mission in 1921, which grew into St. Simon's.

In its attempts to care for homeless African American children Rochester's African American churches combined the traditional methods of informal foster care and support for the more formal institution. Several of the people I interviewed, across denominations, spoke of women in their families who took in literally dozens of homeless children, especially during the Depression. Women were the instigators and organizers of these efforts and the first to recognize the need for additional services. St. Simon's early focus on providing a kindergarten for African American children gave way to building the first African American Episcopal congregation. But in 1943, with many African American men entering the armed forces, St. Simon's opened the Carver House, which housed a day care center for the children of African American women entering the labor force. Carver House provides a cogent illustration of the African American community's acceptance of women in the labor force, and their need for aid in raising children as a result. Carver House united with the Rochester Children's Nursery after the war and continued to operate.[31]

Women's efforts to improve the social, educational, and employment prospects for African Americans and to protect, house, and educate their children in Rochester necessitated cooperation across congregations. These efforts cast into relief their sense of themselves as African American women, in relationship to their men, to white women, and to white society's conception of them.

As Respectable Women

Evelyn Brooks Higginbotham's study of women in the Black Baptist Church argues that the leaders of the Women's Convention and women's related organizations in the church constituted a "Female Talented Tenth" that self-consciously promulgated standards of behavior for women that reflected "Yankee, neo-Puritan, Victorian, or middle-class" values. In so doing, these women claimed leadership for their race, became teachers and missionaries in order to disseminate these standards and values to the masses, and were intolerant of diverse patterns of behavior that deviated from the norms they set down (though exhibiting various degrees of compassion towards transgression).[32] The leaders of the Baptist Women's Convention stood as exhorters and role models, preaching the goals of upward mobility through education, professional training, and economic advancement while at the same time reflecting the successful accomplishment of those goals in their own persons as teachers, the wives of ministers, and women of economic means.

These female race leaders stressed "sexual purity, ladylike behavior, hard work, frugality, temperance, punctuality, neatness, and piety" and an attendance to the home and family, the church and school, as the teachers and missionaries most directly responsible for the future of the race. Most especially as mothers, African American women held the vital position within the home and community for insuring the survival and progress of the race.

At the national level, Baptist women challenged their subordinate role by claiming equally important though gender-specific duties for their people, fought to control their own funds, and advanced theological arguments in support of evangelical womanhood. By so doing, they threatened the male clergy leadership, which extended protective arms around the politics and pulpit of the Baptist church.

Higginbotham argues for a growing elitism among the female Baptist leadership that "increasingly linked the 'new' values with upward mobility and the 'old' with backwardness." They took it upon themselves to express a "representative and authoritative voice" which articulated "their people's collective will." Acknowledging the role played by "those who had very meager economic resources and never attended college or high school" in accepting and disseminating the same values, Higgenbotham views these women as the groundswell of support, but not, ultimately, the shapers of the behavioral ethic that would promote the prosperity of the race.[33]

Usually, such middle-class values and behaviors steer the aims of individuals toward upward mobility in a highly competitive society. Such behaviors and characteristics supposedly give one an edge. Higginbotham rightly stresses the *collective* goals for the advancement *of the race* for which these women worked. The values and behaviors women sought to inculcate among their people served most emphatically to channel meager resources away from the self and into the community. The women in the Baptist convention stressed the leadership of educated, professional women, but, Higginbotham claims, they also acknowledged the worthiness of lesser employments in which the mass of black women engaged and the moral standards to which they adhered. Thus, any individual accomplishment stood upon the contributions of the community and the sacrifices people made to insure an education, a job, or a business for individuals. This distinction becomes important in understanding the elitism and adherence to strict social norms on the part of African American women and men not only at the national level, but within local communities.

The example of the women working in the churches in Rochester, New York, contrasts with the women in the black Baptist church in important ways. The African American community was both old and small. It had a history of abolitionist activity and a bedrock of families escaped from slavery or born in freedom. While freed families migrated to Rochester after the Civil War, their numbers were never overwhelming and their "habits" never presented an urgent social problem beyond the ability of the residents to address. Middle-class, Yankee values had been the norm for the African American community in Rochester for generations before the Civil War and continued to hold hegemonic sway among that population. The women and men in Rochester's pews set and enforced standards they devised, and supported leaders who reflected their own sense of moral behavior. As such, it was the relatively uneducated, working-class members of the congregations who dictated what their leaders more publicly espoused.

With all its abolitionist fervor and advocacy of civil rights, the size of the African American population in Rochester allowed the city to deny its black citizens access to opportunities for higher education or professional employment prior to the 1930s. Thus, the leadership of Rochester's black congregations consisted of porters, bellhops, redcaps, manual laborers, small businessmen and domestics. These leaders articulated and enforced behavioral imperatives consistent with the values voiced on the national level. For them, such values and behaviors held the promise of upward mobility, but more importantly, framed the foundation for the internal survival and well-being of the entire community.

Christian imperatives and African American cultural norms of sacrifice and liberation informed behaviors of hard work, frugality, thrift, and mutual support to create a community whose collective well-being became more important than self-gratification. Individual material accomplishment advanced one's station in life so that additional resources could augment community reserves. How one contributed to the community defined one's prestige and status more than one's station in life. Pauline Moore's status in her church and community depended more upon her generosity and care-taking than on her teacher's degree. Gladys Scott, who worked as a domestic all her life, personified respectable womanhood, and gained a leadership position in her church.

The stress upon community efforts harnessed the roles of men and women at the local level in ways that mitigated against any direct challenge to male leadership in Rochester's congregations. While Baptist women at the national level fought against their subordinate position and challenged male authority, Rochester's black church women cooperated with their men and did not challenge the male prerogatives to preach or govern. Women who served in leadership positions reflected the need to draw upon all the talents within the community and did not transgress gender norms.

This is not to say that the women in Rochester's churches who defined and articulated appropriate roles for women refrained from elitism. They strictly enforced codes of behavior and understood the church as the arena in which they and their children would associate with "the right kind" of people. They extended charity to the less fortunate both within their congregations and to members of the community, attempting to redeem women in Rochester's red-light district, disciplining young women who succumbed to the temptations of drinking, and they created youth groups and recreational outlets to keep their children "out of trouble." The disciplines of respectability were necessary to bring the community together, to insure its survival, and to gain both self-respect and the respect of the white community. Charles Frazier's mother admonished him to do nothing that would "humiliate his family"; Gladys Scott made sure her young ladies understood that they represented the church in their public behavior.

Rochester's African American women did not tolerate deviations from respectable norms and defined the community as consisting of those who practiced these norms. Women and men asserted in their interviews that people who belonged to the churches "didn't get into trouble." Coupled with this assertion came the observation that few African Americans living in Rochester at the time eschewed church membership. Yet if everyone belonged to the churches and no one in the churches transgressed respectable norms, to whose aid did ministers, deacons, missionaries, and club members come in times of need? Who could call on Father Brown or Pauline Moore to visit them in jail or stand up for them in court? Why would the youth group of Trinity Presbyterian church visit Industry, the juvenile detention home, and who produced the orphans fostered and succored by Lula Meadows and Isabella Dorsey?

The African American community is protective of its reputation, stresses its accomplishments, and is reluctant to discuss with white researchers the problems within its own community which church members strove to deal with quietly and effectively on their own. Quite understandable in light of the condescension and bias on the part of white researchers and historians who have traditionally examined African American life, this reluctance hides the compassion with which African Americans treated those whose behavior reflected less than the ideal and makes it more difficult to discern nuances of difference between what the white middle class and the African American community termed respectability.

Examining the implementation of the canons of respectability in the day-to-day lives of church women in a local community emphasizes the internal collective nature of the standards set for regulating mutual, reciprocal relationships. Community survival also depended upon convincing the white community, which controlled employment opportunities as well as civil and political advocacy, that African American standards of respectability did not differ from white standards. When faced with transgressions, especially those which might elicit a different response from African Americans than from whites, the black community chose to deal with them quietly on their own.

The maintenance of sexual purity carried perhaps the most significant implications for African Americans. During the early twentieth century, white racist assumptions concerning the sexual laxity of African Americans permeated even the ranks of staunch liberal white supporters of African American progress. The challenge to the image of black women as sexually promiscuous rallied African American women in their demand for respect and respectability. Evelyn Brooks Higgenbotham traces the development of the racist stereotypes, and black church women's response:

> Their effect was to ascribe pathological uniformity onto black women as a group, such that every black woman regardless of her income, occupation, or education became the embodiment of deviance . . . Guy-Sheftall notes the prevalence of the following racist themes: the immoral black female teacher as cause for the weakness of black schools; the immoral black mother as responsible for the degeneracy of the black family; the acquiescence of the black husband to his wife's infidelity; and the widespread belief that black women were unclean.

> The Baptist women's emphasis on respectable behavior contested the plethora of negative stereotypes by introducing alternate images of black women. . . . Speeches and reports bestowed dignity upon the convention's members—commending the sacrifice of "daily toilers," the faithfulness of "everyday women," as well as the impressive achievements of members such as banker Maggie Lena Walker . . .

and Gertrude Rush. . . . By privileging respectability, and particularly the capacity and worthiness of poor, working-class black women for respect, the WC's public discourse emphasized a critical message to its members, namely, that self-esteem and self-determination were independent of contexts of race and income.[34]

A focus on women's accomplishments and the possibility for sexual propriety on the part of lower-class "everyday" women obscures the way local communities responded to the women in their midst who bore children out of wedlock. These women did not necessarily give up their claim to respectability.

In the white community, women who gave birth outside the sanction of marriage had "lost their virtue" and could find redemption only through an acceptance of their shame and training in domestic occupations so that they could make an honest living, thereby mitigating future temptation. Such women were assumed to be unfit as marriage partners, (unless to the putative father) thus necessitating their entrance into the labor force to support themselves and their children, who carried the stain of illegitimacy.[35] Unwed mothers did not rejoin the ranks of middle-class, respectable womanhood.

The history of Rochester's African American church community suggests a different attitude and pattern of response, significant for what it reveals about the African American construction of the relationship between individual behavior and community life. Three of the women who contributed to this study had personal experience with unwed pregnancy; two were the children of single mothers, and one gave birth to her first child before she was married. Other people interviewed expressed attitudes and described appropriate responses to women who "made mistakes." In an effort to respect confidentiality, I have withheld the names of the women.

Adult members of the African American community kept a vigilant eye on the behavior of young men and women in an effort to regulate sexual behavior. Unwed pregnancy held disastrous implications for the reputation of the community as a whole and the future of the individual women involved. It strained resources and caused sorrow and dismay. The women who became pregnant before marriage were expected to acknowledge their mistake and suffered shame and ostracism from their community, at least initially. The church could publicly discipline them. Their return into the community depended upon how they behaved. One women explained that "Everyone is entitled to one mistake." Another woman, herself the child of a single parent, excoriated young women who "flaunted" their condition, as if they were proud of it, and asserted that women who behaved that way were not welcome in the church. Their children, however, would be because, after all, "it's not the child's fault."

After the initial dismay and shame, however, the community rallied to support unwed mothers and their children. Confined at home during her first pregnancy, occurring a year or so before she married a man who was not the father of her first child, Caroline Little (pseudonym) described the response of the church. "They were wonderful. They helped any way they could." The women brought clothes and furniture and food for the baby. Caroline brought all of her children up in the church, and was married there, as were her children.

Edith Brooks and Sarah Clyde (pseudonyms), whose mothers bore them before they were married, remembered that their mothers got help raising them from other women in their families, and got support from the women in the church. Both of their mothers were active in church work and raised their children in the church. Both Edith and Sarah rose to positions of leadership within their congregations and contributed actively to their communities. Their mothers, grandmothers, and other church women served as role models.

African American women who bore children before marriage could re-establish their reputations and re-enter their churches and communities if they first understood the seriousness of their transgression, did not repeat it, and contributed to the life of their community through good works and material contributions. Their respectability rested upon their moral understanding, future moral conduct, and Christian contribution. Women who had children out of wedlock remained respectable. The African American response to these young women reinforces the perception that their Christian understanding of sin and redemption rested more upon the consequences that individual acts might have upon the community than upon the nature of the personal transgression. Bringing a child into the community, despite potentially disastrous individual circumstances, added life to that community.

Thus, African American women took care of needy women and children through informal and church centered avenues. As economic hardship worsened during the Depression, for example, more women took in foster children, men took on additional work, and church clubs, deacon boards, missionary societies, and ministry of kindness funds, distributed what resources they could. The church expanded to support orphanages, the YW- and YMCA, recreational, educational, and job-training programs, all without material aid from the white community.

The African American women in Rochester's churches claimed respectability for themselves and worked to instill behaviors that would exhibit respectability to the outside world in which they had to live. African American women in Rochester's churches understood their role as women to include serving one another in cooperation with African American men for the ultimate benefit of their children, and thus the future of African American society. That faith provided the foundation of their endeavors is clear not only from what they say about the importance of prayer and worship as fortifications for their day-to-day lives, but most eloquently from the evidence of those day-to-day lives themselves. Gender conventions shaped African American women's activities to reflect the primacy of women in maintaining the church, overseeing the development of children, and taking care of and serving the basic needs of others.[36] Within the realms of education and economic self-development, women worked in tandem with African American men, and within the realm of political and civil activism women organized and agitated, and supported African American men as the primary leaders in that struggle.

NOTES

1. Memorial A.M.E. Zion Church Archives, in the possession of Charles Frazier.

2. The discussion of Eunice Bullock's life is taken from an interview with the author, 21 January 1993.

3. The discussion of Gladys Scott's life is taken from an interview with the author, 12 May 1993.

4. The discussion of Pauline Moore and Elizabeth Logan's life is taken from an interview with the author, 17 August 1993.

5. Walter Rauschenbusch, delivering the report of the year-long YMCA investigation into social conditions in Rochester, 1904, quoted in the *Union and Advertiser*, 30 May 1904. There are no known extant copies of the actual YMCA report. Both the *Union and Advertiser* and the *Rochester Herald* printed condensed versions of the report and Professor Rauschenbush's opening remarks, followed by the introduction to the first section of the report, entitled "Race and Nationality." Looking at both articles is instructive for what it reveals about nuance, emphasis, and "accurate reporting." The *Rochester Herald*'s report differs slightly: "There is no 'race problem' in Rochester with only 601 persons of African blood and 13 of the yellow race. This is emphatically a city of white men."

6. Blake McKelvey, *Quest for Quality*, 152.

7. Ibid., 128.

8. The WEIU was founded in Boston, in May 1877, and soon spread throughout New England. For more information on the nature and scope of this women's organization, see Karen J. Blair, *The Clubwoman as Feminist: True Womanhood Redefined, 1868-1914* (New York: Holmes and Meier, 1980).

9. William J. Reese, *Power and the Promise of School Reform: Grass-roots movements during the Progressive Era* (Boston: Routledge & Kegan Paul, 1986), 50-60.

10. Blake McKelvey, "Historical Origins of Rochester's Social Welfare Agencies," *Rochester History* 9 (April 1947), 30.

11. Blake McKelvey, *Emerging Metropolis*, 64-67.

12. Ibid., 91.

13. James (Buddy) and Alice Young, interview with author, November 1993; and Eunice Bullock, interview with author, 21 January 1993.

14. Weisenfeld and Newman, *This Far by Faith*, 2.

15. Williams, "And Still I Rise," 10.

16. Mary Thompson, interview with author, February 1993; Elizabeth Logan, interview with author, 17 August 1993; and Daniel Garnett, interview with author, 13 May 1993.

17. Charles Frazier, interview with author, 13 May 1993; Mary Thompson, interview with author, February 1993; and Ruth Brown, interview with author, 19 August 1993.

18. Katherine Jordan, interview with author, 10 August 1992.

19. Ruth Brown, interview with author, 19 August 1993.

20. "Success After Long Struggle."

21. Higginbotham, *Righteous Discontent*, 157, 162-163.

22. "Sunday-School Notes," *The Zion Church News* (March 1910), Memorial A.M.E. Zion Archives.

23. "Deaconess," *The Zion Church News* (March 1910).

24. Alan Adams, interview with author, 24 July 1993.

25. "To Meet Need of Zion Church," unidentified newspaper, found in Memorial A.M.E. Zion church archives.

26. "Conference Sessions Continue," unidentified newspaper, found in Memorial A.M.E. Zion church archives.

27. "Red Letter Day in honor of Mrs. J.W. Hood," flyer found in Memorial A.M.E. Zion church archives; and Dupree, "Rochester Roots/Routes" (August 1984), 18.

28. "Our Institution at Work," fund-raising pamphlet, ca. 1908, found in Memorial A.M.E. Zion archives.

29. "Zion Church has New Parsonage," undated, untitled newspaper article, ca. 1910, found in Memorial A.M.E. Zion church archives.

30. Dupree, "Rochester Roots/Routes" (August 1984), 16-71.

31. Elizabeth Logan, interview with author, 17 August 1993.

32. Higginbotham, *Righteous Discontent*, 18-45.

33. Ibid., 56 and 43.

34. Ibid., 190-191.

35. Marian Morton, "'Go and Sin No More': Maternity Homes in Cleveland, 1869-1936," *Ohio History* 93 (1984), 117-146.

36. For a more in-depth treatment of African American women's understanding of gender and women's roles, see the Introduction, the section titled "The Importance of African American Women to the Development of Local Communities," (pp. 10-15).

～ THREE ～
EDUCATION

The watchword of the hour is, Educate*!* Educate*!* Educate*!*
Bishop Alexander Walters[1]

ERNEST DUBOIS[2]

Ernest DuBois's grandparents, Leon and Carrie DuBois, were founders of Trinity Presbyterian Church, which began as a mission in 1898 and was incorporated in 1902. Ernest DuBois was born in 1926 and he and his family lived with his grandparents. From his grandparents, and from his mother, Ernest DuBois learned the importance of religion and education.

Leon DuBois migrated to Rochester from Syracuse in 1890, when he became active at A.M.E. Zion church. He met his wife, Carrie Sprague, at A.M.E. Zion, and they were married in 1895. When a cluster of members split from A.M.E. Zion to create Trinity Presbyterian, the DuBois family was among them. Ernest DuBois remembers that his grandfather was "a great believer in the church" and that his grandmother was always there. They believed not just in attending, but in "working" for the church, and "of course," Ernest remarked, "I inherited that." His grandparents were the kind of people you could look up to, and he did look up to them. His grandfather worked first as a messenger, then as a porter and stockman for Central Trust at 25 East Main Street. Inclined to be formal, Leon DuBois was intelligent and a man of strong opinions, though he didn't push them on anybody. Carrie Sprague DuBois was an interesting person who could do all kinds of things, her grandson recalls, like carpentry and painting. They both attended and participated in Trinity, but his grandfather, who was an Elder and Trustee, was the one who expected and made sure that the family attended and become involved.

Ernest DuBois remembers his grandfather as a "true Christian in all respects" who gave of himself to others who were in need. Members of the African American community who were destitute ("It was the Depression, remember") could come to Leon DuBois and he would do what he could. No one had very much money, but Leon DuBois would invite people over for dinner and try to find them employment when he could, which was seldom. Ernest DuBois remembers the enjoyment he felt as a young child, listening to people clustered around the dinner table telling stories. Some of these people were strangers in need, some friends just over for dinner, but whoever they were they got the same courtesy, respect, and good food.

Leon DuBois thought that church was essential for his grandchildren, and was adamant that they attend and participate at Trinity. Ernest DuBois reflected upon what his grandfather believed religion would give his grandchildren. Certainly, it would make you a "better person," but what did that mean? It meant acquiring the necessary background to be able to take the ups and down of life. "You had a constant that you could turn to when things were not as they should be." Ernest DuBois was quick to qualify. "It wasn't an excuse for anything." His grandfather took a very positive approach. The combined evidence of the interviews suggests that this positive approach consisted of looking above the current situation, drawing upon one's sense of self-respect, and moving beyond the present into a vision of an alternative future.

Ernest DuBois's mother (Leon DuBois's daughter-in-law) concurred about the value of religion, which people received through regular church attendance and participation, for her children. While she herself seldom attended church, she made sure that her children went every Sunday, primarily for the religious background, also for the social contact, and to keep their grandfather happy. Ernest DuBois remembers his mother as a religious person who made sure her children received religious training through the church, but who did not feel the need to be involved at Trinity. It was also his mother who emphasized the value of education for her children. Leon DuBois was proud of his grandchildren's accomplishments and expected them to get an education, but Ernest's mother revered education as the route out of poverty. "Not the way out of being black," but the way out of being poor. For Ernest DuBois's mother, religion provided the mental and spiritual discipline that would sustain a person in their pursuit of an education. Learning how to take a positive approach toward obstacles provided the skills one needed to persevere when the going got rough. Ernest DuBois remembers that it was his mother who instilled in her children the connection between religion and education. She "pulled it together."

Mrs. DuBois was very deliberate and systematic in inculcating the need for education in her children. From the time he was four or five years old, Ernest knew where he was going to go to school because his mother walked him over to the building and showed him that that was where he would begin his education. He knew that he was going to college. There was no question. His mother made sure he understood that he would have to work hard because they had no money to send him to college so he would have to get scholarships. She herself had spent a year and a half at the University of Rochester, but wasn't able to finish.

Mrs. DuBois read to all her children when they were young. She took them to the library, and to concerts, and to plays, especially those cultural events that featured the talents and accomplishments of children. And she made sure they went to church. At church they received discipline and role modeling, as well as the fortification to face social obstacles to their future success. Ernest DuBois reflected that what you learned about appropriate behavior in church, you took to school with you. "You went to school and you behaved in school too." And, of course, Elizabeth Walls taught Sunday School at Trinity. Ernest DuBois remembers the effect she had on the children. Just the fact that she was an African American who taught in the public schools, the only one at the time, made an impression. She also used her training to advantage with the children at Trinity. She and her sister, Jennie Stevens, who Ernest DuBois believes also could have been a teacher, taught the children at Trinity academic skills that reinforced their education in the schools. "We *wrote*, and did things," Mr. DuBois recalled. He observed that this blended with what he was learning in school in "a concomitant way."

Aside from the skills, appropriate behavior, and rolemodeling Ernest DuBois absorbed at Trinity, the church inculcated basic values that were indispensable in the pursuit of any life goal, including an education. You learned "respect for yourself and for other people . . . you went and paid attention to what was said and taught . . . and you carried it on into the rest of your life . . . absolutely."

Ernest DuBois started carrying what he learned from his grandfather, his mother, and Trinity Church into the rest of his life at a very early age. There were several circumstances that led him to explore other churches in his neighborhood. The DuBoises lived on the other side of town from Trinity, which limited his ability or willingness to get totally immersed in the life of that church as a child. There weren't very many other children his age at Trinity. His mother's religious expression offered an alternative to total commitment to one congregation, and there were lively and active churches just around the corner. Insatiably curious, at the age of thirteen Ernest DuBois began to attend Bible School at Bethel Church, an evangelical congregation near his home. By the age of fourteen he was teaching there. "I'd had all this at Trinity, this was all the sort of thing I'd been doing at Trinity anyway. My sister and I were already running the Sunday School at Trinity." So he pitched in at Bethel when they asked. He knew he had an ability to communicate and could deal well with younger children, and he enjoyed it. But he wasn't an evangelical and he didn't stay long enough to join this church. Covenant Church, around the corner from his house, was a different story. Here he also started teaching Bible School, but he found the congregation more congenial, there were more people his age there, and they liked him a lot. He was African American, and he was from the neighborhood, and the primarily white church welcomed him enthusiastically. He went every week. He also still went to and taught Sunday School at Trinity. The timing of the services made it possible for him to contribute in this way to both churches.

Ernest DuBois's commitment to education, and his talent as a teacher, found a natural expression and a welcoming environment within both churches. In both places, the fact that he was African American played a significant role. At Trinity, calling forth and applying the talents of African American young people was a significant, instrumental way that the African American church supported the personal development of its people. The African American church identified, trained, educated, and allowed talented people to practice what they were good at within the church. Covenant provided a frame-work for Ernest DuBois to teach white children, something that was not common or accepted in the wider Rochester community. This, combined with the example of Elizabeth Walls, shaped Ernest DuBois's future as a teacher in the Rochester schools.

Ernest DuBois joined Covenant Church the year his grandfather died, in 1948. By this time he had obtained his Bachelor's Degree from the University of Rochester. As Ernest DuBois's life passed through the period we are addressing and into the postwar decade, it is important to note that he consciously applied the religious training he learned to "put up with whatever nonsense I had to put up with." Oh yes, it was a given that African Americans encountered "nonsense." But putting up with it did not mean giving in to it. Ernest DuBois got his Masters in Education at the University of Rochester and when even some of his relatives told him he'd never get a job in Rochester, he said to himself, "We'll see." In 1951, he became the first African American to teach in the secondary schools in Rochester.

Ernest DuBois's life reflects the importance of the church as a steadying influence upon personal development. For both his grandfather and his mother, religious training provided the spiritual stamina to acquire an education in an environment unfriendly to that goal for African Americans. The church actively inculcated behaviors that would help Ernest DuBois meet his goals, but more than that it provided spiritual fortification. Religious faith was not used as an excuse, neither did it allow one to give in when the going got tough. It did provide the foundation for perceiving and rising above "nonsense" in order to continue to achieve.

ELSIE SCOTT KILPATRICK[3]

Elsie Scott was born in 1907 and came with her parents and five siblings to Rochester in 1909. Her father, who was a professional caterer and electrician, found employment in Rochester doing janitorial and maintenance work in the public schools, and catering. George Eastman was one of his customers. Elsie Scott remembers that her mother's health was not good and the family moved to Rochester where her grandmother, Charlotte Herndon, lived. When Lucinda Herndon Scott, who primarily stayed home to raise the six children, went out to do day-work to supplement her husband's income, Charlotte Herndon took care of Elsie.

Her grandmother was a staunch member of Mt. Olivet Baptist Church from its inception in 1910. Charlotte Herndon, Lucinda Scott, and the six children went to church every Sunday. They went to every service or event during the week, and the children were active in Sunday School and the Baptist Young People's Union (BYPU) from a very early age. Elsie Scott said, "Every time the door was open, we went in." She explained that for one thing, aside from seeing everyone you knew, attending worship, Sunday School, and especially BYPU were important because of the values and morals they taught. The church was the place where both children and adults learned the difference between right and wrong. This occurred through not only hearing and memorizing moral maxims, but also through the counseling and advice you got concerning specific situations or problems. Elsie Scott remembers, for example, that Rev. Rose provided the same kind of guidance and counseling for children as he did for adults. If any child had a question, or got into trouble, he could go to him, in fact he expected it. She says "He really had a great big heart for children. He took a great interest in the children." Rev. Rose was congenial, but strict. "We were all afraid of him," Elsie Scott claimed. The children carried his admonitions around with them and pulled them out to help them decide the right course of action in a given situation.

> We'd say, you know, what Rev. Rose'd said. We'd tell each other, you know what Rev. Rose said . . . we can't do that, you know. He was very good at helping our parents. He cooperated with them to help raise the children. If they got into trouble they went to talk to Rev. Rose . . . and he'd sit us down and we'd find out

what we were supposed to do and what we weren't supposed to do and we took it very seriously, you know.

Elsie Scott sang in the Junior Choir and attended BYPU every week. BYPU combined Bible Study with lessons on appropriate behavior and academic habits. Elsie Scott remembers she used to get dressed up "neat and clean" with starched skirts, and arrive early for the evening program. You "had to be on time. Not allowed to be late. [If you were] more than fifteen minutes late, [you were] not allowed to come in; [we] got there ahead of time, not on time." The students would memorize passages from the Bible, like the Ten Commandments, or the Twenty-third Psalm, and would be expected to interpret Jesus's purpose and teachings. Mt. Olivet had a close relationship with Colgate Rochester Theological Seminary and students there would come to present programs. Elsie Scott remembers these times as opportunities for the youth to talk with the college students, and as a time for the students from Colgate to get to know them.

Having her children participate in this kind of youth development was important to Elsie Scott's mother, and other parents, who "didn't want the children to get misled and go out in the world and do things that they shouldn't do so if they gave them things to do within the church then they would know where they were and who they were with." School was of primary importance to Lucinda Scott. She herself had only a third grade education, but she wanted all of her children to at least graduate from high school so that they would have better opportunities than she and her husband had had. (He had graduated from high school, but had not been able to get professional work.) Both of Elsie Scott's parents believed that if you had an education, "you could do things that *you* wanted to do." Which meant going beyond high school. Of the six children, four graduated from high school, and Elsie Scott went further.

When she was seventeen years old Elsie Scott decided she wanted to be a nurse. In the struggles she experienced in pursuing this goal she drew upon the foundations of her youth and actively sought solace and guidance from the church. She knew that she would need the church to make it through nursing school. "That's why," she said, "when I got to New York to become a student nurse I got affiliated with the Abyssinian Baptist Church."

The road to New York was not easy. Student nursing was not easy. Finding a job as a nurse was not easy. When Elsie Scott was seventeen, she was hurt in an accident. The care she received from her nurse in the hospital inspired her to become one herself. She learned what she would have to do, and took courses that would prepare her for nursing during her remaining two years in high school. Graduating from East High in 1926, Elsie Scott applied to all the hospitals in Rochester for nurse's training. None of them would take her. "They *suggested* to me that I go to a hospital where I could get in, so then I called Harlem in New York City and they said yes so then they sent me applications."

Elsie Scott was severely disappointed. She wanted to stay in Rochester, and she had never encountered such racial hostility before. Her experience as an African American child in the Rochester public school system had not prepared her. From a very young age, until perhaps the issue of dating arose, she remembers being accepted socially on equal terms with the other youngsters in her class. They were all in and out of each other's homes, attending school functions together, walking home together. She was one of only three African Americans in her class during high school.

These observations were typical of the people interviewed for this study. Before the 1950s in Rochester, African American children met with very little overt prejudice, and African Americans in general in Rochester encountered hostility only when they tried to break what were clearly inflexible racial lines. African American women could not be nurses in Rochester, despite the quality and progressive nature of its medical school, nursing school, and hospitals.

"When they said no, I said, well, I'm still gonna be a nurse," Elsie Scott recalls. When one looks at the foundations and role modeling she received, such a response is not surprising. She had been exposed, from a very early age, to the concept that education was the key to a future that involved freedom of choice. She had been exposed to, learned from, and received respect from college students, some of whom were African American. The pastor of her church, Rev. Rose, was himself a graduate of Colgate Rochester Theological Seminary and was actively pursuing graduate studies while he pastored her. When asked what she remembered about Rev. Rose, the first thing Elsie Scott said was that he was a graduate of Colgate. Colgate Rochester Theological Seminary was the first institution of higher education to admit and graduate African Americans in Rochester. It had Baptist foundations, and Mt. Olivet reaped the rewards. The importance of education, a college education, was in front of Elsie Scott every time she entered Mt. Olivet, and was an integral part of her own parents' teachings.

Her time at Harlem Hospital was rigorous. Students had to be accepted into the program, they were on probation for six months, they had to keep their marks up, and they worked seven days a week, with one day off every two weeks if they were lucky. If that day was Sunday, they were especially lucky. After the six months probationary period, they received room and board and fifteen dollars a month. Elsie Scott was accustomed to hard work, and she enjoyed being a nurse so much that the work at Harlem did not seem hard to her. She had worked to bring income in to her family since she was old enough to find a job, baby-sitting, and in high school working at the Powers Hotel. After high school and during summer vacations she worked at the Seneca Hotel in the check room. Harlem Hospital brought enjoyment as well as hard work. She felt a wonderful sense of uplift from helping people, "because they need it. It fulfills a need." And, she was "very proud of that white uniform."

During her ten years in New York as a student nurse and while she strove to find work practicing her profession, Elsie Scott leaned heavily on the spiritual inspiration she found at Abyssinian Baptist Church. Adam Clayton Powell, Sr., was pastor there, and his reputation for active social engagement is well documented. His sermons provided her with the messages she needed to deal with discrimination, and to continue seeing herself as a nurse even when she couldn't find work.

> It meant a lot to me to go. I enjoyed the spiritual uplift that I got from going. The message that I got, you know, and it would help me in my everyday life so that things weren't so difficult, it'd be easier for me. . . .It gives you a lift and helps you carry on because some people are so evil and I had to deal with that, so when you go to church and have that foundation there it gives you help, it helps you, so I appreciated the help that I got.

When Elsie Scott Kilpatrick graduated from Harlem (she had married and had a son by 1930), in the middle of the onslaught of the Great Depression, the only places hiring black nurses were the TB Centers. The working conditions for all fifteen of the black nurses hired were horrible. Though she does not draw this direct connection, it may have been partially the influence of Rev. Powell and the Abyssinian Church that encouraged her to request an investigation from the City into these working conditions, after which the supervising nurse was dismissed and conditions improved.

Elsie Kilpatrick does credit Rev. Powell and the worship services at Abyssinian with reinvigorating her faith, and this faith helped keep her identity intact. Beginning in the late thirties, for more than ten years, Elsie Kilpatrick could not find work as a nurse and instead worked as a domestic. She came back to Rochester in 1938, hoping to find conditions improved here, but couldn't get a job. If she had to work as a domestic, she thought, she might as well do that in New York. She went back to New York City and earned thirty-five cents an hour doing housework throughout World War II. Her faith "took me over." For all of those years, she said, "I believed it would only be temporary. Look at Job, he went down to skin and bones. So that kind of carries you over, beliefs like that. [You may be] down today, but not tomorrow. . . . The foundation is there, see," she says, "and if you're built on a Christian foundation, you're not going to swaver too much. Might swaver a little, but you always get back to that."

While the rest of Elsie Scott's story takes us out of the time period under study, it is important to note two things before going on. Elsie Scott (she had taken back her maiden name after her divorce) returned to Rochester after the war. In 1949, she decided to apply for a nursing job at Highland Hospital. They hired her on the spot. "It was the quickest hiring I ever got. I went up there one day and she told me to come to work the next." (Yeah, I said, it only took them twenty years.) She worked at Highland as a nurse from 1949 to 1969. During that time she put her son through college. He got his doctorate in education from the University of Rochester.

Elsie Scott Kilpatrick's life exemplifies the ultimate triumph of faith over adversity. Her nurturance in the church, the moral precepts and behavioral norms it taught engaged a profound sense of self-respect that allowed her to find avenues around seemingly insurmountable obstacles. The foundations of faith she learned as a child and young adult saw her through the worst years of her life, culminating in the realization of her dreams. From her belief in herself and her calling, she never "swavered."

EDUCATION IN ROCHESTER

The context of education for African Americans in Rochester from the turn of the century through World War II presents a complicated tapestry of progressive and liberal movements infused with a subtle racism that promulgated discrimination. African Americans shaped that context with their own attitudes and activities on their own behalf. The extremely small size of the African American population continued to provide a substantial limiting factor to their efforts, without limiting their energy or conviction.

Nineteenth Century Struggle for Integration

The struggle to integrate Rochester's public schools, which occurred in the 1840s, requires brief attention as it left a legacy that influenced the nature of education available to African Americans in Rochester in the decades before World War II. As Rochester moved toward establishing publicly supported education for its children, the African American population of the city petitioned to have their children admitted. Originally, in the 1830s, African Americans had asked the city to establish a separate school for children of color, reasoning that, with their small numbers, to disperse them among the white students in the regular schools would expose them to prejudicial treatment and discrimination. Now that public funds were available to provide for elementary and secondary education, the African Americans in Rochester wanted their children to benefit along with white children. Abolitionist sentiment brought white allies to the cause for integrated public schools. For several years petitions flew back and forth, resulting in the unsatisfactory arrangement of opening a total of two schools for children of color and *prohibiting* their admittance to any other public school without the expressed consent of the Board of Education.

When, in 1849, Rochester became embroiled in the controversy over the segregation of Rosetta Douglass (the daughter of Frederick Douglass) within Miss Lucilia Tracy's Seward Seminary, a private institution, the resulting controversy led to the partial integration of Rochester's public schools. The combined efforts of Douglass, other African Americans, and white abolitionists in Rochester forced the Board of Education to "designate School No. 13 on the east side as an integrated school for Negro and white children in the southeast district. Some of the younger Douglasses attended there for a time and in 1857 Rochester finally recognized the stupidity of segregation and admitted all Negro children to the regular city schools."[4]

Consequently, Rochester had an integrated public school system before the Civil War. Yet, an ironic result of this progressive move seems to have been the erection of a racial barrier within the teaching profession of Rochester. It appears that Rochestarians were not so liberal as to accept the possibility of African Americans teaching white children in the public schools, and since the schools were integrated, Rochester did not train or hire African Americans in the teaching profession (with the exception during the 1930s of Elizabeth Walls) before World War II. This situation stands in stark contrast to what was occurring elsewhere in the United States throughout this time period. The teaching profession and the ministry provided the most common avenue for both education and professional practice for African Americans coming out of Reconstruction and establishing themselves as free persons in American society. The absence of teaching as a route for advancement for African American women particularly, and the absence of African American teachers in the schools, contributed significantly to a rigid and low ceiling for the participation of African Americans within the professions in Rochester. The African American population throughout the first four decades of the twentieth century in Rochester was not large enough, wealthy enough, or politically prepared to sacrifice integration in order to create their own system of schools, or to train or hire their own teachers. Education, however, remained of critical importance to Rochester's African American parents and they did what they could to incorporate and emphasize education and academic preparation through their churches.

The Progressive Era and Educational Reform in Rochester

The WEIU and Public School Reform

In 1893, Susan B. Anthony and Mary Gannett first suggested the development of "a union of all women for all women, for whatever was helpful in women's mental, moral and social advancement" in an urban environment.[5] Under the leadership of Helen Montgomery and Mary Gannett, the Women's Educational and Industrial Union "started the first kindergarten play groups in school yards, launched the first vacation classes for public school youngsters, sponsored school gardens, established a milk depot, and led a movement to supply lunches to children for a penny."[6] The WEIU emphasized the provision of these services to *all* women and children, primarily through the public school system.

Rochester's educational system benefited from the combination of a strong women's movement in Rochester and a strong progressive movement bent on reform. Rochester had historically emphasized the primacy of education, being in the forefront of providing free public education, and establishing secondary education. When the WEIU and other social reformers in Rochester viewed the schools as the appropriate site to begin sweeping social reforms, the school system went through total change, from pedagogy to curriculum, from architecture to utilization of space and time. The process of reform was meant to be inclusive, its benefits universal, but as William J. Reese, the historian of this movement, points out, "organized women who advocated more intensive state intervention, especially in the lives of the poor . . . viewed the situation from their own class and ideological vantage points."[7] Viewing themselves as "municipal housekeepers," women like Helen Montgomery took proprietary roles over the children of poor and working women. The very inclusivity of their approach made everyone legitimate targets of intervention. While there is no question that the public schools and the children attending them benefited from the programs that the WEIU and other reformers launched, African American mothers had no say in what kind of programs would most benefit their children. The WEIU governing body and committees included middle-class immigrant women, but did not include representatives from the bodies of women whose lives they wanted to affect most.

The proprietary maternalism displayed by the progressive women in Rochester contrasted, then, with the parenting responsibilities that African American women and men extended to one another's children. This practice of all the children belonging to all the adults, described in the interviews, contains a reciprocal theme and mutual respect lacking in the attitudes of white reformers. As Reese comments, "One might have asked such a woman of standing if poor parents had the same jurisdictional rights over her children".[8] The answer is implicit in the public assumptions that white middle-class women articulated toward the children of the poor.

The new programs in the public school system did not discriminate according to race, but they also did not address the racial barriers very much intact and operative in Rochester, nor did they include the voices of African American parents in their design. Consequently, the African American churches took on the responsibility of supplementing what the schools provided, combatting the sometimes overt racism of white teachers through moral and spiritual support, and encouraging young African American women and men to do better, to strive for more, and to overcome whatever obstacles lay in their paths. The testimony of the interviews indicates, for instance, that the combination of church and family teachings and the emphasis they placed on education aided parents in telling the difference between when a child was shirking, not doing his homework, or handing in sloppy work and when teachers were not allowing African American children to do their best. Since parents and other adults were intensely and actively involved in the lives of their children, and since children themselves took on responsibility and moral precepts from a very early age, such discernment was possible. That is not to say that African American children never lied or failed to do their homework or misbehaved in school, only that African American parents could usually figure out what was going on and who they needed to take to task.

White progressive reformers, for all their zeal, did not address the basic structures in the city that supported continued discrimination. Their aim was to expand opportunities for poor and working class people, and insofar as they succeeded, African Americans benefited. Educational reform did not, however, address the rigid racial lines still in force concerning what African Americans might do in Rochester with the benefits of this progressive education. For a time, there was one movement in Rochester aimed at a radical transformation of the educational system, a transformation that, theoretically at least, promoted the inclusion of African Americans in the shaping of educational policy and socio-political decision-making. The fate of the Social Center Movement in Rochester established the limits of reform for the city.

The Social Center Movement

During the first decade of the twentieth century, Rochester's public school system underwent complete transformation, culminating in the social center movement, which drew national attention and acclaim. Reese argues that Edward J. Ward made the social center movement in Rochester unique with his principles of center organization. Ward established the social centers in

Rochester on the basis of self-government. The centers were civic clubs that promoted activities and debate designed to awaken all of Rochester's citizens to the public concerns of the city. Ward demanded that the centers not reflect class, ethnic, or racial bias and left each center alone to decide how it would run its own programs. The only stipulation he insisted upon was that everyone be welcome to attend and everyone have an opportunity to speak and participate. As a result:

> The civic organizations became reasonably all-inclusive, and the adult civic clubs were often highly representative of Rochester's class, ethnic, ideological, and racial interests. Besides Jews, Catholics, Protestants, and atheists, organized labor and business representatives often served on the steering committees of the local clubs. While Kansas City in particular followed the color line in its "community centers," the Rochester clubs were racially integrated and prominently publicized as such in social center publications. The centers gained a reputation locally for radicalism and intense criticism of various municipal policies, and they were reportedly utilized by "people of all creeds, parties, and incomes."[9]

Such goings on sent business and political leaders into a state of apoplexy. The response of many of Rochester's civic leaders reflected more than ideological outrage. During this period, the people of Rochester experienced their most severe labor conflicts in the clothing industry and building trades. Labor unrest led to violence for the first time in Rochester and the socialist leanings of much of the rank and file cooled support for labor. The socialist flavor of the labor disputes influenced the perceptions of the open debates flourishing within the social centers.[10]

The demise of the social centers as a forum for socialist and radical thought occurred on the cusp of Rochester's transformation into a technological and research industrial complex, led by George Eastman, who employed skilled workers, inventors, and white-collar labor. George Eastman was most concerned with the state of labor-industrial relations in Rochester and was extremely leery of socialist elements influencing his work force. Expunging the most radical and socialist elements of the community, while retaining a commitment to liberal reform, became a pattern among Rochester's civic and social leaders, a pattern for which Eastman provided the patent.

While African Americans may have participated in the debates in the social centers, the historical record does not show involvement or association with the social centers on the part of prominent African American women and men. The reasons for this, while speculative, make historical sense. The social center controversies that drew the most fire centered around socialist and labor debates. The unions in Rochester did not include African Americans, and the conditions and circumstances that aroused political frenzy only touched African Americans peripherally. While the social centers accepted the participation of African American women and men, there is no indication that the centers themselves debated the issues and conditions of racial discrimination then extant in Rochester.

Additionally, most of the African American citizenry in Rochester were more politically conservative than the socialists and labor advocates creating such a stir in the centers. Those African Americans who filled the pews and pulpits of the churches were solid working-class women and men, believing in and striving for a better future for themselves and their children within American society and institutions. They did not challenge the basic premises of the society they lived in, while they strove to make those premises more applicable to themselves.

Further, the African American population did not need this public institutional space as a forum for debate concerning issues important to the African American community. African Americans found the freedom and platform for social and political debates within their churches. Therefore, the social centers neither provided white allies with whom African Americans could join to debate or organize movements to improve of conditions for African Americans, nor did the social centers provide a needed institutional space for public debate.

Higher Education—Spanning the Progressive Era, the Depression, and World War II

The progressive nature of educational reform at the elementary and secondary public school level had an effect on institutions of higher education in Rochester. Educational pedagogy and curriculum in Rochester schools emphasized "industrial" education. By this educators meant an ideology of educational training that believed in "training the brain through training the hand," recognizing the importance of motor activity, experimentation, analysis, and demonstration to the learning process. This method, rather than dull memory work and passive acceptance of knowledge poured into students brains by teachers, gained ascendancy throughout the educational institutions of Rochester.

A second meaning to "industrial" education emphasized training students in the technical skills and mechanical arts needed to replenish and advance the increasingly technological industries in Rochester. Thus "industrial education" meant preparing people for a meaningful life of industrial, skilled labor. Such an educational approach expanded the mind and spirit through the training and practice of meaningful work.[11] The Atheneum and Mechanics Institute (known as the Mechanics Institute, the institution that would become the Rochester Institute of Technology) practiced this pedagogy. The Mechanics Institute had the backing and funding of Bausch and Lomb, and eventually Eastman Kodak. The Lomb family founded the Institute and recruited from its graduates for their company, as did other industrialists in Rochester.

This pedagogy echoed a prominent educational ideology adhered to by leading African Americans of the times and within Rochester. Public pronouncements on the part of African American leaders such as J.W. Thompson are replete with the call for education of the "hand, head, and heart," the industrial educational philosophy put forth by Booker T. Washington. Thompson and other African American Rochestarians understood this philosophy to mean something more than insuring that African Americans only worked with their hands. It meant education that touched the total individual and combined all personal resources for self improvement and community service. Such a philosophy stressed a meaningful life which carried no shame for those who *did* work with their hands, but also inspired African Americans to do the most with their varied talents, especially if they could succeed academically and professionally.

In light of such a convergence of educational aims, one might expect to find the classes and graduation exercises of the Mechanics Institute to be filled with the brightest and the best of Rochester's African American youth. The historical record shows a more complicated picture, however, a picture that once again reinforces the rigid racial marginalization operating in Rochester. The Mechanics Institute did indeed admit, and graduate, African Americans. A.M.E. Zion records report that Hester Jerome Jeffreys established a scholarship fund for young women who wanted to attend Mechanics Institute. This indicates both that the institute would accept African Americans and that it was difficult for them to pay for this technical education. Even if students could get in and pay their way, incentives to graduate were much weaker than for the white and immigrant students. For African Americans there were few if any jobs available upon graduation. Neither Bausch and Lomb, nor Eastman Kodak, the major recruiters, hired African Americans, even if qualified. Eunice Bullock's mother received training at the Mechanics Institute and worked as a sandwich maker at Walgreens during the twenties. She got that job through the church.

This same dynamic remained in force throughout the twenties, as Rochester moved completely into its identity as the home of technical, highly skilled industry. The University of Rochester became the paramount institution of higher education in Rochester during this decade, thanks to the generosity of George Eastman and other Rochester industrialists. The organizational and professional management techniques that had coordinated the war effort during

World War I had convinced George Eastman of the value of a college educa-tion for the managerial and white-collar labor upon which he depended to run his by-now international business. Eastman was also committed to providing diverse educational opportunities for the daughters and sons of his managers and inventors. He wanted Rochester to be the kind of city where people would want to live and raise families. Both of these philosophies blended in the var-ied support he gave to the growth of the University of Rochester. The University's move from Prince Street to the River Campus during the twen-ties signaled this expansion. "The Prince Street Campus was not only too small for existing needs, but lacked space for work in civil and electrical engineering or for a contemplated institute of optics or, peering into the longer future, for professional schools of education, business administration, law, and graduate training."[12] This expansion was in addition to the opening of the school of medicine and dentistry in October of 1926, also funded by Eastman. The funding drive for the River Campus move echoed Eastman's avowed philoso-phy: "to provide 'the boys and girls of Rochester' with 'a favorable opportu-nity for a higher education. . . . When the pupils were ready for mature train-ing the colleges for men and women would be ready to welcome them."[13]

George Eastman, one of his directors, George W. Todd, and their friend, the President of the University of Rochester, Rush Rhees, all billed the Uni-versity of Rochester as a community institution, interested in advancing the educational opportunities for all of Rochester's citizens. African Americans, however, found it difficult if not impossible to be admitted to the University of Rochester before World War II. Even when they were admitted, often they didn't finish, like Ernest DuBois's mother, or only took particular courses, like Eunice Bullock. That university administrators understood a direct connec-tion between expanded educational opportunities and expanded professional and economic roles becomes apparent in their policy toward at least one Afri-can American student. Caught between meeting the ideal of education for all and maintaining a denial of access to professional opportunities to African Americans, the University of Rochester graduated an African American woman, probably its first, Beatrice Amaza Howard, in 1931, with the explicit stipula-tion that she not look for a job in Rochester.[14] There is disagreement concern-ing when the University of Rochester graduated its first African American. Blake McKelvey records that this occurred as early as 1891, while according to Adolph Dupree, who researched this topic, the first African American to attend the University of Rochester did so in 1926. When he did not finish, the University "claimed blacks incapable of college studies and did not admit others for some time."[15] Whenever it first occurred, the University did not welcome African American students until after World War II.

George Eastman committed suicide in 1932 and left bequests to the University of Rochester that allowed it not only to survive, but to prosper and expand during the Depression. It was able to offer a haven in those times to students who could not find or had lost their jobs, but could still afford to continue their educations. Few if any African Americans had such resources. Federal aid to education brought the first real opportunities to African Americans who entered extension courses offered by both the Mechanics Institute and the University of Rochester during the thirties. Even with such incentives, African Americans who graduated from the University of Rochester could not get jobs here. Neither Arthur Blake, who graduated with an M.S. in Chemistry in 1938, nor Harry Bray who got his B.S. in Sociology the same year, could find work in the city. When World War II came, the University of Rochester and the Mechanics Institute benefited from war contracts and under federal mandates and public scrutiny from the African Americans in Rochester, the Mechanics Institute at least graduated African Americans who found employment in Rochester.

During the Depression and throughout the thirties, then, the standard practice was to deny educational opportunities beyond high school to African Americans, and to deny employment to those few who did manage to get into college. The record is, of course, uneven. Colgate Rochester Theological Seminary graduated African American students, and the Mechanics Institute at least admitted them. It appears, however, that these were the exception, not the rule, that the cost of higher education was prohibitive, and that the access to employment or professional standing that such an education usually provided was almost non-existent. The interviews back up these conclusions. They record an understanding that wages for African Americans were so low that financing a higher education was almost impossible. Even so, women and men got as much as they could, either here, or elsewhere. African Americans understood that professional employment depended upon getting a Bachelors Degree, but that obtaining one did not guarantee this result. Still, they insisted that their children go to college. They continually pushed against the structured discrimination they faced, trying to widen any cracks.

The history of education in Rochester during the first four decades of the twentieth century reveals a contradiction between its espoused educational philosophy of inclusion, reform, and opportunity and its treatment of African Americans in search of educational opportunities that would advance their economic and professional standing in the city. African Americans in Rochester worked within this context to provide an educational ethic for their children, supplement their public education with classes and programs that would address their needs, send them out of the city to college, and consistently challenge the racial barriers that confronted them. The primary vehicle for these efforts was the African American church.

THE AFRICAN AMERICAN CHURCH'S ROLE IN EDUCATION

The African American church in Rochester provided for the educational needs of the community in a variety of ways. It 1) inculcated the value of education, 2) provided for educational opportunities and training, 3) supported African American institutions of higher education both monetarily and by sending students to attend, and 4) challenged educational restrictions in Rochester.

The Value of Education

The African American churches in Rochester emphasized, taught, and preached the value of education in a variety of ways. They instilled, through Sunday School, youth organizations, and adult programs, the behaviors and character traits that would aid African Americans in their efforts to succeed in school. This included the inculcation of moral precepts and a conscious avowal of the importance of moral character as an accompaniment to intellectual development. The churches honored those individuals who achieved an education, insisted on an educated ministry, celebrated historical figures who had succeeded through intellectual development, and celebrated the educational successes and efforts of their own people in Rochester.

Ernest DuBois recalled the discipline he learned in Sunday School at Trinity Church, and how he and the other children carried this behavior into school. Elsie Kilpatrick spoke of the need to be on time for youth development events and how she and the other youth strove to get there early in order to participate. Gladys Scott recognized a clear connection between the emphasis on hard work and commitment to achieving goals which she instilled in her junior ushers, and their subsequent success in college or careers. Charles Frazier recalled teaching Sunday School to a group of young men at Memorial. He found this to be a challenging and rewarding experience which forced him to delve deeper into his own knowledge and resources in order to be ready for sharp young minds that wanted to both challenge his knowledge and stay after lessons to discuss what it all meant in their lives. He listed the professional accomplishments of these young men, where they are now, and what they are doing. He is especially proud of the training he gave one young lad with a speech impediment who is now a presiding elder in the denomination.

The leaders of the African American church in Rochester viewed the church as an educational institution and debated what **kind** of education they should emphasize. In the early years, the value of "industrial education" received attention, especially in light of the fact that many patrons from the white community were declining to contribute to the church and were, instead, giving their money to Tuskegee Institute. J.W. Brown, pastor of Memorial A.M.E. Zion, appealed to the greater Rochester community.

> We occasionally meet a person who says that he will not give to a church; that whatever he may give for the benefit of the negro will go toward his industrial education, as if the church were not an educational institution. Now we believe in industrial education and would like to see a Tuskegee Institute in every state where negroes are largely represented. But industrial education, or any other kind of education alone, will not subdue passion and develop strong moral character. This comes by the teaching of the Holy Spirit manifested in Christ and His church. . . .
>
> Along with the education, industrial or higher, the negro needs a well-equipped church, with an educated ministry, where lessons of righteousness and morality may be taught. . . . Give the negro an industrial education, give him higher education, with equal privileges in the pursuits of life; but before all and with all give him a moral and religious education.[16]

J.W. Brown delivers in this article a quite shameless appeal to white fears of African Americans, and especially of the African American male's sexuality and criminal tendencies, reflecting the most virulently racist assumptions of the times. What on earth might happen within the African American community if it did not have a church to subdue the passions and refine the moral sense? However, the article ties this concern to a broad definition of *human* character, and expands the understanding of unbridled male lust to include, and, in fact, be exemplified by, white men. The article quite bluntly blames white men for miscegenation and claims that all African Americans want is the society of their own kind in churches where they can "worship God in the front seats if we so desire and where lessons of righteousness and morality may be learned." The church, Brown asserts, is needed in all societies everywhere to provide the kind of education that will call forth the best in human nature and create the finest citizenry and greatest society.

J.W. Brown's main point is echoed by J.W. Thompson, when he writes that "Industrial training alone is not sufficient. For the building up of any people with a complete life there must be moral and religious training. . . . We believe in Industrial education, we preach the Gospel of work and urge every man to make an honest living but before and with a living he must be taught to make a **LIFE**." Alexander Walters puts it quite succinctly, "It is the negro church that has fitted the black man for the higher walks of life and been one of the main agencies in giving him a standing, a place of honor in all lands."[17]

The pedagogical implications these leaders espoused would find coherence with the broader understanding of "industrial" education, the training of the entire human being, which African American leaders (including Booker T. Washington) espoused. Church leaders in Rochester were doing two things with this line of argument, however. First, they were challenging the adequacy of an exclusively vocational education which eschewed higher education, and second, they were maintaining the primacy of the African American church as the vehicle for the education of African Americans as human beings. This kind of education was foundational to any other educational efforts.

In his Masters Thesis, Rev. James Rose of Mt. Olivet Baptist Church echoed these beliefs for the Rochester church during the twenties and thirties. His thesis addressed the development of a Sunday School curriculum. He begins with the premise that to develop any program

> we shall have to arrange our material, our methods, equipment, and messages in accordance with the needs of the growing child. In short, we must know the child. And after knowing the child the next in importance comes the knowledge of what is best for the child.[18]

In his last chapter, Rev. Rose declares that the primary aim of the Sunday School is not to teach the Bible, but through the teachings of the Bible, to develop Christian character. Christian character consists of acting righteously and it is significant that Rev. Rose chose the Old Testament prophets, with their warnings of what befell those who practiced oppression, as the appropriate models of and tutors for Christian character. Rose advocated a Biblical education so that young African Americans could learn to critique American society and model righteous behavior, as had the Old Testament prophets.[19]

J.W. Brown, in earlier years, had made the same argument. White people were primarily responsible for the existence of unrighteous behavior, but African Americans must look to their own character development, both for its own sake, and in order to challenge white perceptions and behavior. Rev. Rose, with an emphasis on child development which speaks to the context of his times, calls for the character development of African Americans as a prerequisite for challenging the behavior of those who oppress them, equating unrighteous behavior with the many manifestations of oppression. In order to work for justice, an education was necessary, an education that blended the moral sensibilities of the church with scholastic achievement or the development of talent. That Rev. Rose took his own mandates seriously is evident in the testimony of people like Elsie Kilpatrick who both feared and adored him. He took time to get to know, and to teach, the children.

The churches placed the value of education within a framework that linked it to more than professional or economic advancement. While these were certainly necessary goals, their necessity reflected the higher aim of the good of the community as a whole. Education was good, in and of itself, only when linked with the development of a greater moral understanding on the part of the individual and used in service to the community. Anyone who used her education, whatever the nature of their employment, to add critical thinking, talent, or skills to the congregation and community, received honor. Passing on what one knew to the younger generation and helping them in their scholastic endeavors also proved the value of educational attainment.

The African American church in Rochester instilled the value of education through setting examples, role modeling, and celebrating the academic successes of their members. These churches insisted upon, and lifted up, an educated ministry. Charles Hubert started out as the treasurer at Mt. Olivet in 1910. He was the first African American to be admitted to Rochester Theological Seminary and by the time he graduated, in 1913, he was the pastor for Mt. Olivet. Rev. James Rose was also a graduate of Colgate, and earned his Masters there in 1930. He went on to receive an honorary doctorate from Howard University. Rev. Frank Brown of St. Simon's Episcopal Church graduated from St. Stephens, became a member of Phi Beta Kappa, and earned his graduate degree in Divinity at the Philadelphia Divinity School. The pastors of Memorial A.M.E Zion and Trinity Presbyterian were college educated. Thus, a primary example of educational attainment occupied the pulpit and preached to the people every week.

Additionally, the educational attainments of the laity received homage. Hester Jerome Jeffreys served as a role model for a generation of African American women and men who spoke of and recorded her accomplishments as the most highly educated African American woman in Rochester. Memorial's records proudly display the newspaper article that announces that one of their teenagers, Stella Gibbs, had become the first African American to be admitted to a prestigious high school. "Stella E. Gibbs, a 16 year old negro girl, won the gold medal presented by Secretary William Kerr of the Hoboken Board of Education for the highest percentage at the midwinter examinations for admission to the Hoboken High School. She is a graduate of public school No. 9 and attained a general average of $99^1/_3$ per cent in six subjects."[20] Elizabeth Walls held a graduation ceremony every year at Trinity Presbyterian Church to honor those African American students who graduated from high school. The students so honored came from different churches and within the community, but Trinity, and Mrs. Walls, held them all up. Elizabeth Walls also taught Sunday School at both Trinity and Memorial. She provided a clear presence, an example of someone who had acquired an education, was employed as a result, and considered education to be of paramount value to African Americans.[21]

The churches also brought in volunteer adults from nearby colleges to make presentations or teach their youth. Memorial brought representatives from Cornell's Agricultural Extension Department to speak on the "civil, social and economic welfare of the Afro-American citizens of the State of New York and what the University is willing to do to help better the condition of colored citizens of Rochester." During this presentation, Hallie Queen, of Cornell University, recited the poetry of Paul Laurence Dunbar. Such events celebrated African American accomplishment, presented by educated African Americans, in the service of furthering the educational opportunities of African Americans in Rochester.[22] During the twenties and thirties, Mt. Olivet enlisted the help of seminarians to run Baptist Young People's Union (BYPU) meetings and testimony from the members of Memorial referring to the same time period recalls accomplished adults from the community coming to do presentations for Christian Endeavor.

Throughout the first four decades of the twentieth century, the African American churches imbued their members with the value and primacy of education. Education was the route out of poverty, as Ernest DuBois's mother believed, the way toward independence, professional attainment, or skilled accomplishment. Every African American who succeeded in school reflected the innate abilities of the entire community. The churches leaders believed, however, that neither higher nor vocational education would meet, by themselves, the needs of African Americans. In order to sustain themselves as human beings, especially in the face of discrimination and the denial of access to professional practice, African Americans needed to combine academic excellence with strong Christian character. Such a character would celebrate the talents and skills of individuals whatever their worldly occupation, and make it possible for individuals to contribute what they had to the community, most often through the church itself. Such character would also give individuals and communities the strength to resist and challenge racist perceptions and assumptions. Church leaders modeled the kind of Christian character they sought to instill by putting their money where their mouths were, and provided material resources, training, classes, and programs to enhance the educational attainments of their members.

Educational Programs

Both A.M.E Zion and St. Simon's Episcopal churches began explicitly as combined churches and schools. Thomas James, the founder of A.M.E. Zion, first gathered the African American population of Rochester to teach them to read the Bible, and to address the question of literacy among their numbers. St. Simon's began as a religious mission and kindergarten. Mt. Olivet Baptist, also from its inception, took seriously its responsibility for both adult education and instruction for children. Only Trinity, which began as a splinter group from A.M.E. Zion, did not contain an explicit reference to the education of the people as a justification for its existence.

Basic academic skill development became a focus for both Sunday School teachers and youth leaders. Club activity, as well as Sunday School classes for adults, gave adults a chance to acquire, enhance, or practice their intellectual abilities. Sunday School, Christian Endeavor, and BYPU all incorporated exercises such as spelling bees, essay contests, poetry recitations, African American history lessons, memorization, oration, and debate. Church clubs would sponsor political or social debates, much like those creating such frenzy at the social centers. For example, A.M.E Zion staged a "Debate and Trotter Supper . . . under the auspices of the Young Men's Guild, for the benefit of the Pastor, J.W. Brown. Subject of Debate: 'Resolved that the Republican Party has been more beneficial to the Negro Race since its infancy than the Democratic Party.'"[23] Such an event combined social interaction, great food, fund-raising, intellectual development, and political acumen. It echoed, with a distinctly African American cast, the efforts then abroad within the social centers. It also provided a comprehensive example of the emphasis upon, and value given, to educational attainment. Such a debate not only reflected intellectual and verbal skills, but applied those skills to the critical analysis of issues important to the entire community.

The churches also provided a welcoming and nurturing platform and stage for the development of talents and skills among the members of the congregation. Churches regularly put on productions and programs that included music, drama, and oration, sometimes consisting of competition between teams which the entire congregation would then judge. Charles Frazier recalls that parents made sure their children learned their parts for pageants, programs, and productions. Mildred Jacque recalls the importance of Trinity Presbyterian church as an "educational setting for young people. People who had talent and skills contributed to the upbringing of children and provided role models." These people did not necessarily have formal training, but the church was a platform where they could express and pass on the fruit of their talents. Mrs. Jacque believes this played a fundamental role in preserving the self-esteem of both adults and children who could exercise their gifts without having to have credentials. Her mother had attended music school in Auburn, her brother attended the Eastman School of Music, and she herself played both the piano and violin. In church her family could relax, expand, enjoy themselves, and receive appreciation for their gifts.

William Warfield, one of Rochester's most famous musical talents, confirms the importance of the church to the recognition and development of his talent. The Warfields had come to Rochester after hearing from relatives that Rochester was a place where "blacks as well as whites could get a free high school education, maybe even dream of going to college."[24] Robert Warfield, William's father, wanted to be a Baptist minister. Rochester could give him that opportunity. After arriving in the early twenties, Robert Warfield enrolled in night school, introduced himself to the Baptist community, and came "under the wing of a mentor, the locally celebrated Dr. James Rose, pastor of the leading black congregation in Rochester, Mount Olivet Baptist Church."[25] William Warfield recalls making his theater debut at five years of age at his father's church, Aenon Baptist. Mt. Olivet gave him his first exposure to the meaning of music in his life.

> Of course, my first "real" music boomed out from Mount Olivet's resounding pipe organ. . . . It was at Mount Olivet, before I was old enough to know what I was hearing, that I first enjoyed some of the classics of western church music— Handel, Bach, and others—alongside the traditional Southern religious songs and Negro spirituals. It was there that classical music first became an easy and familiar part of my daily life. . . . In the spiritual environment of Mt. Olivet, a concept so simple as "the family of man" came perfectly naturally. It was an article of faith. And with it, part and parcel, came an associated concept, "the music of mankind"—the continuity of all music, of harmonies for all people, everywhere.[26]

William Warfield's first music teachers were church members. Despite economic disadvantage, Warfield attended and graduated from Eastman School of Music and went on to perform internationally.

In addition to the nurturance of skill and talent that permeated class, club, and congregational activities, the African American churches created space, classes, and programs to supplement and further educational goals. Both A.M.E. Zion and Mt. Olivet Baptist boasted reading rooms equipped with books and desks where their youth might study. In tandem with Hester Jeffreys' scholarship fund, A.M.E. Zion planned to build a Parish House in which they would teach "domestic science" classes. J.W. Thompson stated that "when this building is established we can arrange better hours for the domestic science classes for our people than is done at the Mechanics Institute." A.M.E. Zion was committed to not only enhancing economic opportunity but also to providing supplemental educational activity that met the explicit needs of African Americans.[27] During World War II, St. Simon's Episcopal Church established Carver

House. One of its primary aims was to provide a nursery school for African American children.

Faced with limited resources, African American churches did what they could to provide formal and informal programs that would encourage their members to excel academically and vocationally. In addition, the churches supported higher education.

Higher Education

Both Memorial A.M.E. Zion and Mt. Olivet Baptist formed and maintained close ties with institutions of higher education throughout this time period. In 1908, the members of Memorial dedicated one of the new windows in their church to the memory of J.C. Price, founder of Livingstone College. They paid homage to his Christian character and academic distinctions. In raising money and dedicating the window, Memorial placed within visual reach the scholastic attainments for which it wanted its membership to strive. Throughout the decades under discussion, and indeed into the present, Memorial A.M.E. Zion raises money for the support of this denominational institution of higher education.[28]

Mt. Olivet enjoyed a special relationship with Howard University throughout the twenties and thirties. Rev. Rose was a colleague and friend of Mordecai Wyatt Johnson, President of Howard and former Colgate Rochester Divinity School graduate. Dr. Johnson visited Mt. Olivet often, and Howard became a welcoming haven for not only Mt. Olivet, but Rochester's aspiring young African American men and women. In his research, Adolph Dupree discovered that Howard University was the institution of higher education which drew the most African American students from Rochester. During the thirties, Dupree cites ten young people graduating from college or obtaining graduate degrees. Of these, eight are from Howard. There were twenty additional young people who attended and received some higher education at Howard.[29] In the face of severe economic constraints, the attitude of African Americans in Rochester was not to let that stop them. They got as much education as they could, even if they couldn't finish. Obtaining higher education gave one the credentials one needed to challenge the barriers against professional practice for African Americans in Rochester.

Challenging Discrimination

The foregoing sections all provide evidence of a continuous challenge delivered by the African American churches and their people in Rochester, a challenge to the basic idea that African Americans could not achieve academically, and therefore could not practice in the professions. At the turn of the century there were very few college educated African Americans living in Rochester. Most of the working-class jobs, service occupations, and entrepreneurial enterprises that African American adults engaged in to provide economic support for themselves and their families required little education at all. These people began working to make sure that their children graduated from high school, and did everything they could to make it possible for them to go to college. The testimony of the interviews is replete with observations that parents assumed their children would graduate from high school. Like attending church, there was no question about it. The DuBois family, the Moore family, the Lees, all viewed a high school education as vital to the future of their children and the African American community.

By the twenties and thirties, African American students were routinely making it through high school graduation. When they couldn't attend college in Rochester, they went elsewhere. A small but vocal population of college-educated African Americans in Rochester set the stage for public challenges to the institutions of higher education in Rochester that continued to deny African Americans opportunities. In addition to graduating more of their own daughters and sons from college, the population and atmosphere of Rochester, especially the welcoming and nurturing reputation of such figures as James Rose, drew professionally trained people to practice in Rochester. This provided direct evidence that African Americans could be nurses, dentists, doctors, and lawyers.

Dr. Van Tuyl Levy, D.D.S., is a case in point. He tried to study specialized surgery at the University of Rochester's medical school, but the dean refused even to look at his letter of recommendation from Columbia.[30] He settled down in Rochester to practice dentistry and became one of the three (along with Dr. Rose and Dr. Lunsford) to publicly challenge the University of Rochester's admission policies in the thirties.

Dr. Lunsford, a graduate of Howard University and its medical school, knew Dr. Rose, and came to Rochester to practice medicine in 1921. He was the first licensed African American physician in the city. In 1939, Drs. Lunsford, Van Levy, and Rose challenged the University of Rochester Medical School to admit African American students. Editorials defending the University policy claimed that society was not ready to allow African American doctors to attend white patients (even though most of Dr. Lunsford's clientele was white) and that there were not enough African American patients to provide adequate training for African American interns. "Society will not tolerate that. White mothers will not think of having Negro medical students present at, or participating in, the delivery of their babies." The public furor resulted in the Medical School admitting African American students, but as Kay Jordan recalled, she thought they took about one a year, and the atmosphere was purported to be "icy." It would take many more years before the University policies would change substantially.[31]

CONCLUSIONS

Rochester placed a premium on quality education, both public and private. Its free public education and universal programs created an environment in which African American children could excel. As William Warfield's autobiography attests, and as many of the people I interviewed agree, Rochester seemed prejudice-free compared to other areas of the nation. Children felt safe here, and interacted with school mates on a basically equal footing. While prejudice and discrimination existed, Rochester offered apparently golden opportunities for the scholastic success of young African Americans. Yet Rochester combined this liberal, reformist educational pedagogy with a clear and rigid line which relegated African Americans to service employment. You could get a high school education, and you might, if you were one of the lucky few, attend Mechanics Institute or Colgate Rochester Divinity School, but if you wanted to gain the credentials and practice as a doctor, lawyer, or even teacher in Rochester you were basically out of luck.

In the face of these contradictions, Rochester's African Americans turned to their churches to develop the spiritual foundation and material resources to provide their children with educational opportunities. Education, and its accompanying skills of critical analysis, combined with Christian character to create courageous individuals undaunted by the hostile environment they faced. As Elsie Kilpatrick testified, they "knew it was only temporary."

NOTES

1. Walters, *My Life and Work*, 208.

2. The following biographical sketch is based on the author's interview with Ernest DuBois, 12 August 1993.

3. The following biographical sketch is based upon the author's interview with Elsie Scott, 7 October 1993; and Dupree, "Rochester Roots/Routes," (September 1984), 20.

4.See McKelvey, "Lights and Shadows," 6; Laura A. McGregor, "The Early History of the Rochester Public Schools 1813-1850," in Blake McKelvey, ed., "Part I–The History of Education in Rochester," *The Rochester Historical Society Publications* 17 (1939),

58-65; and William S. McFeely, *Frederick Douglass* (New York: Norton and Company, 1991), 161. Frederick Douglass sent his daughter Rosetta to this prestigious private school for girls, only to be dismayed to discover that Rosetta was secluded from the other children in a classroom by herself, because one parent had objected to her presence with white students. Wielding his editorial pen, Douglass took the situation to the Rochester public and the controversy had farreaching effects, namely, the integration of Rochester's public schools.

5. Minutes of the First Meeting, 10 April 1893, Woman's Educational and Industrial Union Papers, Local History Department, Rochester Public Library.

6. Blake McKelvey, "Historical Origins of Rochester's Social Welfare Agencies," *Rochester History* 9 (April 1947), 30.

7. Reese, *School Reform*, 60.

8. Ibid., 61.

9. Ibid., 194.

10. In addition to Reese's extensive discussion of the social center controversy, see Blake McKelvey, *Quest For Quality*, 278-285 and 107-108.

11. For discussions of the meaning of "industrial education" in Rochester, see Georgie C. Hoke and Mark Ellington, "History of the Rochester Athenaeum and Mechanics Institute," *Rochester Historical Society Publication Fund Series*, 14 (1936), 213-216; M. Lucile Bowen, "The Rochester Free Academy," in McKelvey, ed., "Part I–The History of Education in Rochester," 90-92; Stanley V. Levey, "The Last Twenty-five Years in the Public Schools," in McKelvey, ed."Part I–The History of Education in Rochester," 233-237.

12. Arthur J. May, "Oak Hill Becomes the River Campus," *Rochester History*, 30 (January 1968), 7.

13. Ibid., 17.

14.Dupree, "Rochester Roots/Routes" (September 1984), 24.

15. McKelvey "Lights and Shadows," 16; and Dupree, "Rochester Roots/Routes" (September 1984), 24.

16. Undated, untitled newspaper article, ca. 1906, found in Memorial A.M.E. Zion archives in the possession of Charles Frazier.

17.1908 Anniversary Pamphlet found in Memorial A.M.E. Zion archives in the possession of Charles Frazier. "Bishop Addresses Zion Congregation," *Rochester Democrat and Chronicle*, 10 August 1906.

18.James Everett Rose, "The Conception of God in the Book of Job," (Masters of Divinity thesis, Colgate Rochester Divinity School, 1930).

19. Ibid., 15.

20. Undated, untitled newspaper article, ca. 1910, found in Memorial A.M.E. Zion archives.

21. Dupree, "Rochester Roots/Routes (September 1984), 24; and author's interviews with Charles Frazier, 13 May 1993, and Oscar Hawkins, 17 August 1993.

22. "Look Up Lift Up," flyer found in Memorial A.M.E. Zion archives, dated 2 April 1908.

23. Flyer, ca. 1905-1910, found in A.M.E. Zion archives in the possession of Charles Frazier.

24. Warfield with Miller, *William Warfield*, 20.

25. Ibid.

26. Ibid, 32.

27. "Zion Church Has New Parsonage," undated newspaper article, ca. 1910, found in A.M.E. Zion church archives.

28. "Price An Honor to the African Race," undated *Rochester Democrat and Chronicle* article, ca. 1908, found in A.M.E. Zion church archives.

29. Dupree, "Rochester Roots/Routes" (October 1984), 20.

30. Dupree, "Rochester Roots/Routes" (August 1984), 21.

31. See Dupree, "Rochester Roots/Routes" (August 1984), 20; "University's Policy Called Fair, Honest," undated newspaper article in Mt. Olivet archives; and author's interview with Kay Jordan, September 1992.

∽ FOUR ∽
ECONOMIC SELF-DEVELOPMENT

Let us make the best of our opportunities along all lines of industry. Notwith-
standing all the disadvantages under which we have labored, having been robbed
of thousands of dollars by the many unjust systems in operation in the Southland,
we have accumulated over $400,000,000 worth of property, real and personal.
The thing for us to do is to continue to buy land and to build and improve homes,
thus becoming more and more independent.

Bishop Alexander Walters[1]

JESSE STEVENS AND CHARLES PRICE[2]

Charles Price's grandfather, Jesse Stevens, arrived in Rochester in 1883 looking for a place where an enterprising young African American man might
establish a home and raise a family. Two years later he returned to Caroline
County, Virginia and brought back his bride, Maria. The son of a Baptist
minister, who practiced during slavery, Jesse Stevens displayed ingenuity, determination, and vigor in his pursuit of several occupations to support his
family. He worked tirelessly as a baggage coachman, a headwaiter, and a fuel
oil contractor. By the early 1900s, he had opened his own grocery store, lo-
cated throughout the 1920s at the corner of Spring Street and Caledonia Avenue. Maria stayed home to raise a family of ten.

In 1898, Jesse Stevens became one of the founders of the Presbyterian mission that would become Trinity Presbyterian Church in 1902. The church,
Charles Price remembers, was of vital importance to his grandfather, a "Christian individual." Jesse Stevens served as Elder and Trustee of Trinity and expected that his family would attend church every Sunday. Maria became the
"mother" of the church, serving as hostess and premier cook at church events.

Jennie, Charles Price's mother, and Elizabeth, his aunt, played piano during the services and Jennie Price also taught Sunday School. Charles Price remembers that attending church was "a ritual, every Sunday, you got up and you went to church. You were in your spot every Sunday, no ifs ands or buts about it." When Charles Price became the first African American on the Rochester police force and worked seven days out of eight, his mother got his children to church.

Charles Price remembers his grandfather as a stern, quiet man who lived the church from Sunday to Sunday. Worship was a source of inspiration for him, and others in the community. Jesse Stevens taught his grandson how to be satisfied within himself even when "people don't want you, or don't want to acknowledge what you're doing or what you've done." The strength to find such self-worth proceeded from his grandfather's religious background, Charles Price believes, and from the lessons of adversity that his grandfather endured. It took perseverance to migrate from Virginia, establish a base, return to the South to bring a wife to a new and strange city, and work to become financially independent. Charles Price points out that in pre-World War II Rochester, African American men could either work on the railroad or in some kind of service occupation, neither of which offered much financial stability. The only other real choice was to establish your own business. Jesse Stevens was willing to do what he could to support his family. During the Depression, he lost his grocery store, which was called, ironically, the "Progressive Grocery." However stern and quiet a man he may have been, Jesse Stevens had made his store a hub of the informal communications network that notified people within the African American community of one another's needs. His reputation also permeated the white community. During the Depression he gave away food and extended credit to friends and neighbors, black and white, until he went under. Charles Price observed that most of his grandfather's customers were white people, that a black-owned business required a mixed clientele, and that the Depression threw everybody out of work.

Jesse Stevens, however, took pride in having achieved economic independence, and would not accept public assistance. Instead, he did what he had to, in the face of so much unemployment, to continue working throughout those dismal times. He took a job as a bootblack at the Powers Hotel and supported his family with this source of employment until he retired due to illness in the 1940s. He died in 1957 at the age of ninety-four.

Jesse Steven's daughter, Elizabeth Walls, was the second African American to teach in the public school system in Rochester, and was the only African American teaching in the public schools during the 1930s. In 1948, at the age of twenty-six, Jesse Steven's grandson, Charles Price, became the first African

American to serve on the Rochester police force, which, he recalls with feeling, was "tough." Mr. Price did not want to become the first African American anything, and took the civil service exam, which landed him the opportunity to join the force, on a bet. His score, and the possibility it opened up, generated a sense of responsibility and purpose. Mr. Price recalls, "I knew people had to follow me."

Charles Price spoke with reluctance about his own experiences, and with hesitation about what it cost him personally. He gave up a job where he was making twice as much, came up through the ranks, and sacrificed his own aspirations in order to make a difference for his community. When things got "really tough" he drew upon internal resources so that he could go to bed at night and let go of the day's events, telling himself "don't let this kill you."

Charles Price credits his grandfather's lessons in fortitude for providing him the strength to let go of the day-to-day trials he had to endure. His grandfather taught him to be proud of who he was and to believe that "you could make it if you put your nose to the grindstone." Charles Price also acknowledges the guidance of his aunt, who prepared him for what to expect and how to respond. She advised him to "look above the person who's doing this, they are stupid and ignorant, and sooner or later it comes back to them." At times when he wanted to quit, the pastor of his church and other men and women he respected in the community encouraged him to stick it out. He did, and speaks with undisguised pride of his two daughters, their success in college, and their choices to contribute their talents to their community. Charles Price believes that African Americans with strong family and church roots acquire the resources they need to survive these situations. Jesse Stevens, in insisting that his family attend, participate, and contribute to Trinity Presbyterian church, insured such a foundation.

Charles Price is not alone in this assessment. Many of the families most active in the African American church drew upon church teachings and the church community to sustain them in their efforts to break racial barriers and insure a secure economic foundation for themselves and their families. Daniel Garnett, Jr., eloquently recalls the story of his own and his family's efforts.

THE GARNETTS[3]

Daniel Garnett, Jr.'s, parents made their way to Rochester early in the twentieth century. Daniel Garnett, Sr., was born in 1876 and arrived in Rochester in 1912 via South Carolina, where a Rochester family recruited him to work as a live-in servant. Well-to-do families in Rochester commonly recruited from the South, thinking that hiring southern African Americans and enclosing them within solid white neighborhoods would help solve the "servant problem." However, according to Daniel Garnett, Jr., this often didn't work. He describes how his father, feeling lonely and isolated, boarded a trolley one day and started cruising the city, searching for his people. He shouted for joy when he found them at the Majestic Pool Hall near Four Corners. Jubilant with his discovery, he never went back. He met J.W. Thompson, who got him a job at the Powers Hotel, and brought him to Memorial A.M.E. Zion Church.

The next few years were important years for Daniel Garnett, Sr. He established himself economically, leaving the Powers Hotel to work in the Munitions Factory on Culver Road during World War I. There he gained the experience he needed to obtain employment as a skilled worker, becoming the first African American stationary engineer in Rochester. In 1919 he married the woman he had met and fallen in love with on the steps of Memorial Church.

Pearl Garnett migrated to Rochester from North Carolina in 1908. She also had been recruited into private service and worked for a pastor's family. Her employers wanted her to have a church and helped her find Memorial, which she attended regularly. She met her husband on its steps and raised three children in the church. When she married, her husband's wages as a skilled worker allowed her to leave domestic service and stay home. She and her husband rented a house on Ford Street, where Daniel, Jr., was born.

Daniel Garnett, Jr., was born on Mother's Day, 1921. He started working selling magazines when he was nine years old. Memorial A.M.E. Zion recognized and encouraged him in his development of economic responsibility when the Sunday School made him its Secretary-Treasurer, also at the age of nine. When he was eleven years old, Daniel Garnett's father lost his job because he voted for Roosevelt. From 1932 on, Daniel Garnett, Jr., was the major economic support for his family. He peddled newspapers and did odd jobs throughout high school. Upon graduating he got a job with the WPA, went to night school, and earned $13.20 a week. He turned all of his salary over to his parents. By this time he was the Assistant Superintendent of Memorial's Sunday School and he became a Steward of the church at the age of nineteen. That same year, 1940, Daniel Garnett, Jr., became the first African American skilled worker hired by ITECH, one of the most influential and prosperous industrial companies in Rochester. He made twenty-four dollars a week, which enabled his family to buy their own home within eight years.

Daniel Garnett, Jr.'s, life centered around his family and his church. He remembers the importance that both his parents placed on being part of the church community and learning the lessons in faith that active participation encouraged. Daniel's father was President of the Men's Usher Board for as long as Daniel can remember, getting up early on Sunday morning to make sure everything was ready for the services. His mother, Pearl, made the church the focus of everything she and her children did outside the home. Daniel spent all day Sunday in church, going to services, attending Sunday School, and then from about the age of eleven or so, going to Christian Endeavor with the other youth of the church. During the week, Mrs. Garnett took her children to the Gospel Tabernacle so that they would be steeped in Biblical knowledge. Daniel remembers that he and other children from Memorial who got this double dose of religion during the week excelled in their knowledge of the Bible. The Gospel Tabernacle was a white mission in the city, and attending its services opened up important contacts with members of the white community. It was also a source of food and clothing in times of desperate need. The focus for the Garnett family, Daniel emphasizes, was the Biblical base that Pearl Garnett was adamant that her children receive.

Pearl Garnett also participated actively at Memorial. She attended Sunday School and was a member of the Women's Missionary Society. What Daniel remembers most, however, are the things his mother did for people informally, like rounding up the neighborhood children for church events during the week, when their parents had to work and couldn't take them. It was important to Pearl Garnett that no children be left out of what the church could offer and she always made and brought plenty of food for everybody. Why was it so important to her that her own and other African American children be so tied to the church? Mr. Garnett explained: "Church was quite important . . . to keep the kids in the right path, more or less. To keep them spiritually motivated 'cause knowing what you had to tangle with during the week, it would make you much stronger in the week." Pearl Garnett immersed all of her children in the church for that very purpose, and Daniel Garnett, Jr., found this to be of critical importance to him as he entered the working world as an adult.

When Daniel Garnett began his career at ITECH, the white workers spat on him. They threw things at him and created hazardous conditions on the floor. They called him "nigger" and "SOB" and "all this other stuff." Because he had a firm faith, Daniel says, "I could take all those insults, all that spitting on me, spitting at me, calling me all those names, telling the boss that I don't want that nigger working with me, I don't want this and that. . . . It [religious training and constant involvement in the church][4] made me better 'cause I knew when I left there that I went home, I had a happy family, I was taking care of the head of the family—father, mother, sister and brother. I was the breadwinner. I went home with a happy feeling and the services and things fortified me spiritually to know that somewhere in the future there was a better thing for us and so I was able to endure that."

Let there be no mistake. Daniel Garnett is speaking about a real future for himself and his family and other African Americans. "You don't have to wait till you die, you could be getting your rewards on earth, it doesn't mean that you have to die to wait somewhere in eternity to get your reward. You can get it." He understood his role. He knew he was doing something that was larger than just himself, something that had direct impact on those he loved and on the community to which he was committed, wholeheartedly. But even so he didn't know how hard it would be, what he would have to put up with, and what he would lose. And in the face of those realities, as they each visited him, he drew upon his faith to keep him going.

Daniel Garnett remembers that other blacks came and went from ITECH. He watched them break under the pressure, or refuse to put up with the insult to their humanity. He remembers one incident vividly that occurred just after he started working there. Another skilled African American from the South started at about the same time. Daniel recalls, "They were ripping him apart." Told him he wasn't wanted, he wasn't doing good work, nobody wanted him there. And then the foreman handed him a broom and told him to sweep the floors. This man lasted two weeks, took his pay check and left, saying he had lived in the South, he didn't bring the South with him. Now there was only one black man left in the department. The foreman came up to Daniel Garnett and gave him the broom. "Between my God and five other people I said, look, where do you want me to start?" He swept the floors better than those who were paid to do it. What did it matter to him? He thought, "I still got paid the same. I drew my twenty-four dollars. And when I got home I had my family, my God and all. And then, that check fed my family." Daniel Garnett was not only feeding his family. He was feeding his community, and the future. Daniel remembers the strength and pride he gained from seeing the pride his father took in him. With his shoulders back, his father would boast to friends and neighbors, "My son works at ITECH. He makes a difference." And Daniel still feels the pride and satisfaction of being able to see others coming up behind him, passing him, and going on. Daniel Garnett, in the forty years he worked for ITECH, saw other African Americans come into the business and occupy executive positions. He knows that wouldn't have been possible had he not had the faith to endure. He says that he and others like him "scrubbed floors and took the beating," and he takes personal satisfaction in having done so. These are his rewards.

There were times he almost gave up. He remembers, after he had been at ITECH for a couple of years, he complained to the foreman about the treatment he was receiving from the other workers. The foreman interrogated him in front of the shop.

Foreman: When they spit at you, did you stand there?
DG: No, I ducked as much as possible.
Foreman: When they called you all those names, did they lay a hand on you?
DG: No.
Foreman: When they throwed pieces of metal around that would hurt and you saw it coming, you jumped out the way, didn't you?
DG: (I says,) yes.
Foreman: Don't I pay you your same check every week on the same day with the rest of them?
DG: Yes.
Foreman: Darkie, what's your problem?

And the trouble started over again. The boss walked off like this, he don't see nothing, don't hear nothing.

But he never quit. He came close. He talked it over with his mother once, saying he could not take this beating any longer. Some of his coworkers had told him they knew where he could get a job where he wouldn't have to put up with it. His mother asked him, where do these people who are giving you this advice live? Do they own their own home? Why would they want you to leave? Son, what do you mean, quitting? He stayed for forty years.

Daniel Garnett, Jr., is quite explicit in crediting his faith in God, and the expression of that faith through church participation, with making the critical difference for him. "You've got to pay the price in those early years. But you've got to have a foundation . . . to come in here Monday to go to work. Got to. See, 'cause if you don't have nothing to grab onto, you're lost, see. You've got to have something. Even the ones that worship idols and things, there's something other that they've got to grab onto. We might call them atheists or pagans or what. We say our God is the true God. Our God is the living God . . . but they've got to have something to bring them together. And so that's what held me together." Some of his coworkers, the ones who got so they could call him Danny instead of "that nigger," noticed that "every time we see you you've got some church function or church service." He told them point blank that it gave him what he needed to come to work and look them in the eye. They laughed. So, okay, it's a joke to them, he shrugs. "But you do need a savior. You do need a helping hand. You don't realize you take things for granted until these sort of things happen and you have no way else to turn."

Take prayer, for instance. For Daniel Garnett, prayer changed your whole vantage point, shifted your perspective. "When you're in prayer it gives you time in that praying that your mind becomes a little clearer and you can look back at that problem in a different light. . . . And you look from that perspective of looking at things, lights up, all of a sudden you can see that light at the end of the tunnel [where] before [you couldn't] and you come away with that." Daniel Garnett held onto his faith in a God who stood with him in his efforts to create a better future for himself, his family, and his community. He went home and to church from a dehumanizing environment and received nurture, restoration, acknowledgment, and pride in his accomplishments. He attended worship and came away renewed through prayer. He continues to contribute to his church in every way he can. He grieves because so many of this generation, including his sons, look upon the church as an instrument of oppression, and religion as a means to keep control over African Americans. His sons think he was wrong to endure what he did. For them, African American manhood does not have room in its definition for someone who would, with dignity, take a broom to sweep floors for a white bigot. That Daniel Garnett's faith allowed him to do so, is, for them, proof enough of the church's complicity with racism. Yet for Daniel Garnett, and others of his generation, the church held them together and gave them the institutional, spiritual, and material foundation to create and sustain the community, so that their sons and daughters would not have to pick up brooms.

ECONOMIC CONDITIONS IN ROCHESTER

These African American men and women lived within a small city in western New York with a particular economic context that framed their efforts to better their own economic conditions. The African American church functioned as an institution within wider economic realities that placed boundaries on the types of efforts its leaders, organizations and members could make to sustain themselves and prosper. The African American population in Rochester never exceeded one percent of the total population of Rochester prior to 1950. In 1940, there were 3,262 African Americans living in the city.

The Depression of 1891 hit Rochester in 1893, lasted until 1896, and provided the impetus for the recognition of the changing face of Rochester, an examination of its urban and industrial character, and the development of avenues through which the leaders in Rochester would shape the new urban environment. According to Blake McKelvey, immigrants and their children made up seventy percent of the residents of Rochester by 1890, most of whom found employment in the clothing and shoe industries that led Rochester's economy in that day. These immigrants hailed from Western Europe and Britain and contained large Jewish and Catholic contingents. There were five thousand Jews in Rochester at the turn of the century, as opposed to about six hundred African Americans.

One major differentiating factor separating African American migrants and residents from the European immigrants who transformed the character of Rochester from 1900 to 1940 were the sources of employment open to each group. The employment structure of Rochester reflected its industrial development. The lack of ready access to the raw materials to support heavy industrial development shaped the nature of industrial expansion, urbanization, and industrial-labor relations in Rochester during the first decades of the twentieth century. Heavy industry never gained a foothold here and the clothing and shoe industries that flourished did not create the factory and tenement conditions that led to abysmal working conditions and violent labor conflicts elsewhere across the nation. While not exactly tenement- and slum-free, the apparel industries in Rochester tended to confine themselves to small factories and outwork, depending for their profit on the production of high quality merchandise rather than mass production of cheaper goods. Next to these industries, the building trades offered the major source of labor organization and conflict. These industries and their unions consisted of immigrant and native born white labor. While the African American population continued to increase during the first few decades of the twentieth century and provided grounds for concern for the members of that community, foreign immigrants and their relation to the industrial structure became the fulcrum for economic development in Rochester. From 1900 to 1920, Rochester's African American community more than doubled in size while gaining only one-tenth of one percent of Rochester's overall population. These African Americans could not join the unions and neither the factories nor the trades employed them. As Rochester industries struggled to gain economic ascendancy, African Americans remained on the margins of those developments. African Americans drove the coaches, shoveled the coal, stoked the furnaces, cleaned the houses, staffed the kitchens, restaurants, and hotels, and entertained the dignitaries of Rochester. Only once, in a particularly acrimonious labor dispute, did an employer bring in a "gang of Negroes" to break the strike.[5]

During the first four decades of the twentieth century, industrial leaders of Rochester faced the city's limitations in the heavy or mass production of goods. The Chamber of Commerce, under the leadership of men committed to the advancement of research and technology and with a staff of management experts, many brought to Rochester to work for Eastman Kodak, focused on shaping an urban environment conducive to the development of domestic and international markets for quality products that reflected high technological skill. Blake McKelvey notes that while the clothing industry, with its reputation for high-quality products, still led the city's productive forces, "the industries which supplied Rochester with dynamic vitality in these years were

built upon the inventive, managerial, and promotional talents of their managers and on the technical skills of their workers."[6] Immigrants provided those
technical skills. As the industrialists and their managers grew wealthy, they
continued to employ African Americans as live-in servants, chauffeurs, and
cooks. They also gave African Americans jobs maintaining the factories and
transportation networks that insured that their products and customers got
where they needed to go. African Americans swept and polished, hauled and
carried in the factories, and served as porters and redcaps on the railroad. Their
wages remained abysmal (domestic servants were still getting one dollar a day
into the 1940s, while workers at Kodak got between twenty and thirty dollars
a week, not to mention employee benefits). It was a mark of distinction to
have African American servants driving your car and answering your door, and
many recruited their servants from the South. George Eastman brought his
valet up from his "plantation" in North Carolina, and employed the whole
family as servants in his home.[7] However, he was loath to give the sons and
daughters of those servants, or any other African Americans, opportunities to
work in any but manual labor positions in his factories.

African Americans coped with this marginalization through a combination
of industry and ingenuity. Typically, the adults of a family would hold down
two to three jobs, like operating the elevator at the Powers Hotel during the
night shift, and sewing at home for a white seamstress or milliner during the
day.[8] Many African Americans tried to go into business for themselves, serving the needs primarily of the African American community through such
endeavors as rooming houses, restaurants or barber-shops, and then combined
these efforts with wage labor, usually at night.

The color line relegated African Americans to the margins of the economic
structures in Rochester and received support both from the industrialists, like
Eastman, and from the all-white industrial labor force. Any radical impulses
that might have provided immigrant or white allies for the small African
American population in their economic endeavors never had a chance to flourish in Rochester. Throughout the turbulent twenties and the Depression years,
labor and management developed relationships that silenced radical voices.
The brilliant mechanizations of George Eastman established a solidly paternalistic style of treating with labor. The workers who reaped the benefits of
Eastman's model lived through the testing of that model during the Great
Depression when they struggled to maintain their own gains and had little
interest in competing with, or even recognizing the existence of, African
American workers. The hostility to the inclusion of African Americans in the
hegemonic industries of Rochester during the forties stemmed from this un-

derstanding of privilege on the part of white workers whose ranks had been purged of radical or liberal impulses.

The labor disputes that rocked Rochester periodically before World War I in the clothing and building trades proved instructive to George Eastman as he developed the industry in Rochester that defined innovative, quality production. At the first hint of union activity among Kodak employees at the turn of the century, Eastman cut the work day from twelve to ten hours without a reduction in pay, distributed the first of what would become a Kodak hallmark, employee bonuses, and created facilities for his workers that included dining rooms, rest rooms, lockers, reading rooms, and emergency hospital services. Eastman closed out the company division still asking for wage increases, but helped them establish an independent cooperative with a contractual relationship to Kodak. The cooperative served as a "safety-valve" for disgruntled workers.[9]

The labor disputes of 1911 inspired Eastman to create his famous profit-sharing practices and to set up a benefit fund for his employees. Kodak's enormous profits made this magnanimity possible, and created a standard that other Rochester industrialists attempted to meet. Bausch and Lomb reduced hours without a reduction in pay and offered benefit packages to its workers, for example, but no other company matched Eastman Kodak. Eastman's generosity carried a price tag, which became glaringly evident in 1919 when his fear of Bolshevist influence among his workers prompted "a letter to the 'men at the bench' in his numerous plants cautioning them to be wary of agitators with Bolshevist propaganda. A resolution pledging loyalty to the firm and the country was quickly signed by six thousand Kodak workers, many of whom were grateful for Eastman's generous gift of $12 million in common stock to their benefit fund."[10]

Eastman effectively kept unionization out of Eastman Kodak, and the practices he developed and other companies emulated kept organized labor from gaining a foothold in the new technological industries then becoming dominant in Rochester. However, labor still maintained strength in the building trades, and disputes in this arena held up the construction of plants, facilities, and such projects as the construction of the Eastman Theater. His success in labor-management relations at Kodak encouraged Eastman to enter the building trades disputes with a community-wide plan for its solution, a plan that included representatives from labor initially in its development.

Eastman proposed a Community Conference Board which would convene representatives from labor, management, and the community to "study their mutual concerns." The controlling element behind this cooperative effort came to light when, after the failure to restore wage cuts, the Building Trades departed from the Board. The Board then defined its mission as one of "management," focusing on providing building projects throughout the winter months. Eastman Kodak's labor-management techniques sidestepped the unions to meet workers' needs and froze radical contingents out of the process if they continued to be dissatisfied. This strategy pervaded Rochester's developing technological industries.

> [By the late 1920s] few of the 76 labor unions listed in the city directory had any appreciable hold on the city's factory workers. . . . [M]ost of the unions were in the service and building trades, and their only dealings with the leading industrialists came when an expanding company required new factory or office buildings. . . . An increasing number of industrialists and other employers nevertheless recognized the worker's right to security, and three companies followed Eastman in contracting for accident insurance to cover their employees.[11]

The onset of the Depression tested the ability of this strategy to address the issue of unemployment. Blake McKelvey traces the mounting unemployment that Rochester's work force experienced, and the city's response to it. The Chamber of Commerce, Council of Social Agencies, Federation of Churches, Catholic Charities, Industrial Management Council, Central Trades and Labor Council, and the Bureau of Municipal Research established a Civic Committee on Unemployment in March of 1930. This committee encouraged the Community Chest, Council of Social Agencies, and city government to enact programs of both relief and employment. The Committee endorsed the city's work-relief budget and emergency drives to raise Community Chest funds. Rochester's local firms, headed by Eastman Kodak, adopted voluntary programs of unemployment insurance, the first in the nation to do so. These massive efforts drew national attention and the approval of Governor Franklin Roosevelt and his State Industrial Commissioner, Frances Perkins.[12]

George Eastman's suicide left the city bereft of his energy, management, and expansive paternalism. Marion Folsom, the treasurer of Kodak, and president of the Chamber of Commerce, attempted to lead Rochester's industrialists down the road of industrial-government cooperation under the New Deal. Eastman's methods and Kodak's leadership in such innovative programs as unemployment insurance smoothed the way for Rochester to receive government allocations under New Deal initiatives. Rochester's citizens eagerly supported work relief projects, but Marion Folsom put his faith in a national unemployment insurance plan. His strategy seemed more viable as most of the state and federal funds Rochester received went into welfare.

> The number of relief applicants continued to increase until nearly a fifth of the city's population received such assistance. An investigation . . . disclosed the

presence of few "chiselers" but revealed that the major cause was the inadequacy of job opportunities, especially in the white-collar division.[13]

The paternalistic flavor of relief efforts, coupled with the small size of the African American population in Rochester, made possible the equitable distribution of public funds to African Americans. The New Deal federal programs, such as the WPA, provided many African Americans with employment and training opportunities. It was these federal programs that gave many of them leverage to enter occupations formerly closed to African Americans. Daniel Garnett benefited in just this way. African Americans were not included, however, in unemployment insurance plans, or in any rehiring initiatives, since they had not worked at the levels of the corporate structure that provided these measures.

It did not take Rochester industrialists long to react against the New Deal and fall back on patterns they had learned from George Eastman. McKelvey notes that a major source of displeasure for Rochester's businessmen was the New Deal's backing of organized labor. In Rochester, during a labor conflict, Abraham Chatman, the union leader, requested gas masks from the government. "Although the early settlement made the strategy unnecessary, the mere prospect that the War Department might be called to assist rather than chastise a union aroused qualms in Rochester concerning the New Deal."[14] As the economy began to improve, local Rochester industrialists became increasingly critical of the regulatory provisions of the New Deal and organized to turn the city's allegiance to the Republican side, utilizing expansive company programs in the best Eastman Kodak tradition. "Kodak inaugurated a plan . . . to give vacations with pay to all workers who had two or more years of service, and both the McCurdy store and the Gannett Company adopted Eastman's earlier scheme for annual wage dividends."[15]

These patterns of paternalistic philanthropy and expert management through private and public institutions shaped the economic context in which African Americans, struggling to make a living, worked and lived. White Rochester, which included immigrants of every description, controlled the industrial complex, and barred African Americans from participating or acquiring the skills that would equip them to compete adequately with white workers. The technological and white-collar character of the labor force promoted an attitude of privilege, and the material standard of living they enjoyed prompted workers to identify with the management that insured bonuses and profit-sharing. The small size of the African American population made their potential political power to break the color line negligible.

Most families survived through sheer hard work. Buddy Young remembers that his father held down three jobs during the Depression and his mother took in laundry. The kids picked up coal from the railroad tracks after the coal cars had gone by. In the midst of this deprivation, Buddy Young does not remember lacking anything. In fact, his mother took in foster children, all African American, from families who were more destitute. He remembers somewhere around twenty foster children coming into their home over the years. Mrs. Young did it because "she loved children."[16] Jean Kenney remembers that during the Depression, her father lost all the property he had acquired, including the house they lived in. Her sister, Elizabeth Logan, explained that their father then began to work to get the house back. He would go out every day in search of work and come home at night with food for the family. Like the Youngs, the children in the Moore family never felt a lack.[17] For both of these families, and many more, the church played a primary supporting role. In their efforts not only to survive, but to prosper, African Americans relied on their churches to provide the networks, institutional structure, and faith foundation they needed.

THE AFRICAN AMERICAN CHURCH'S ROLE IN ECONOMIC SELF-DEVELOPMENT IN ROCHESTER

All four of the churches that provided data for this study led and exemplified the community's efforts to sustain itself. In each case, a major factor in providing an institutional foundation for the community entailed economic independence. It was of primary importance to the men and women in the pews that they own and operate their own churches. Church leaders expected that financial solvency would relay a message to both the black and white communities. African Americans could take care of themselves, could manage their own affairs, and could establish a viable, responsible presence in the wider community. Owning one's own church was as important as owning one's own home and carried the same symbolic power. Owning the church property, building, and accompanying structures such as a parsonage or manse, proclaimed independence. Independence meant more than providing a foundation for material or social prosperity and equality. For religious African Americans, financial independence insured that the members could freely choose to answer God's call as they perceived it, rather than be materially tied or obligated to white power structures and the perceptions of African Americans conveyed from them. Considering that African Americans could not get bank loans to mortgage their church building projects without a white sponsor, burning the mortgage became one of the most joyful events for the early churches. Establishing a financially independent presence in the community enabled African

American churches to go about their own business and create the institutional and spiritual foundations that the people needed. St. Simon's Episcopal church is an excellent case in point.

St. Simon's began early in the fall of 1921, when "Mother" Dorsey, who had been operating an orphanage for African American children in Rochester, appealed to the Episcopal Diocese to establish a kindergarten for African American children. This effort grew into a mission for African American Episcopalians in Rochester. The Diocese provided services for the burgeoning congregation in the church edifices of other Episcopal parishes, when their churches were not otherwise being used. St. Simon's people met at The Church of the Epiphany, Christ Church, St. Paul's, Church, St. Luke's Church, and Trinity. This practice continued until Father Brown came and began a building fund, raising enough money to begin building a *debt-free* church in 1934, which was completed in 1935.[18] Many of the members of St. Simon's who talked about those early days spoke of the importance of getting their "own" church. It was important not to feel like second-class citizens, not to feel beholden to the white churches for their very spiritual space, not to wonder how long they would be welcome. It is interesting to note that none of the white Episcopal congregations seriously entertained the possibility of welcoming the African American congregants into their midst and into their worshipping community. Once Father Brown had led the congregation in building its own church, the church community really began to flourish.

The efforts on the part of African American churches to acquire financial independence emulated and inculcated economic self-sufficiency. Churches engaged in multiple forms of organized and informal support for individual and communal efforts to better material conditions for African Americans in Rochester. The churches: 1) inculcated values that encouraged economic independence; 2) recognized, encouraged, and supported church members as they sought and achieved material success; 3) found people jobs; 4) supported African American business; and 5) protested economic conditions.

Inculcation of Values

Every single organization within the church, whatever its primary role, had as a secondary purpose the raising of funds. From Sunday School classes to debating clubs, across denominations, every group within the churches raised money to support the pastor, buy their own materials (like books or dishes), increase the poor fund, or support world-wide mission. Men, women, and children all paid dues to any organizations they belonged to. The importance of money to enable people to do good became apparent early in the lives of children and carried through all the years one belonged to a congregation.

While such an emphasis on financial contribution could lead to competition and material pride, the primary focus was not on how much one gave, but on *that* one gave, and that one gave regularly. "People gave what they could," Charles Frazier, the historian of Memorial A.M.E. Zion, recalls.[19] The church taught, by making it imperative that people give financial support to the church at every level, that financial giving was a primary form of service to the community. Every officer of the church had to be a financially contributing member.

Giving to the church reinforced patterns of mutuality in the family. Charles Frazier remembers the way in which children and adolescents who were delivering papers or babysitting or doing odd jobs, would turn their earnings over to their parents, who would then take charge of the distribution of funds.[20] Daniel Garnett followed this model. He turned over his pay check and then went out to do odd jobs to earn his own spending money. When I asked him when he slept, he replied, "Shucks. I was twenty years old. Sun shining both sides of the street." The community, and the family, were more important than the individual's prosperity, but the individual's prosperity was necessary for the health of the community. Consider Jesse Stevens. He worked hard for years to establish his grocery store, but sacrificed his prosperity to help his neighbors out during the Depression. He probably would have gone under anyway, given the economic conditions of the times. His clientele would not have been able to support him. That he *chose*, when faced with the hardship of his friends and neighbors, to extend credit and give away food speaks more to his value system than to the probability that the outcome would have been the same whatever his choice. An African American Christian understanding might even go further in speculating that his continued economic independence proceeded from the quality of the decisions he made. He maintained a strength of character that encouraged him to find work, maintain his independence, and continue to support his family.

The church also taught and promoted the ethic of hard work, relating work more to independence than to wealth. Gladys Scott's Junior Usher Board at Mt. Olivet decided it wanted to purchase a silver tea set for the church. It chose what it wanted to raise money for, organized events to raise the money, and continued to work until the funds were raised. When the tea set was purchased, the Junior Usher Board wanted their names inscribed on it. For this they had to work harder. You have to work hard to get the money you need to do what you want to do. Others in the church wanted the money raised by the Women's Usher Board to go for something else beside the dishwasher they had been working for. The pastor said, uh-uh, what they worked for they should have. They raised the money. They made the decision. Working for something meant that you cared about it. Giving money for the up-keep or improvement of something meant that it was important to you.[21]

The church taught the value of competition tempered by community coop-eration. Competition between individuals over how much people gave could lead to quarreling and dissension within congregations, and while this oc-curred, especially in choosing appropriate officers for the church, this form of competition was frowned upon. Competition flourished, however, around fund-raising events, when congregations divided up into teams. The object was who could raise the most for the community as a whole. Not which person, but which team, working together, could do the most good. Additionally, congregations did not compete against one another, even across denomina-tional lines. Instead, churches supported each other's efforts toward economic independence. Community-wide fund-raising events brought everybody out, including white supporters, if for no other reason than for the food. (People weren't the cooks, chefs, and caterers for the likes of George Eastman for noth-ing.) A.M. Kearney, who acted as pastor of Mt. Olivet off and on between 1918 and 1920, scheduled a rally. A rally was a community-wide fund-raising event. He describes how the other two African American churches existing at that time helped him out.

> At that time there were only two other colored churches in Rochester, the Trin-ity Presbyterian Church with Rev. A. Sellers Mays the Pastor, and the AME Zion with Rev. J.W. Brown, Pastor. They consented to work with Olivet in the rally. I set the time limit of the rally at three months—one month for each Church. Mt. Olivet was to take the third month. At this time final reports were made by the three Churches. . . . The sum total was eleven hundred dollars.[22]

In this case, the churches did more than get their members out to participate. They actually raised money for another church. Eleven hundred dollars was (and for small churches still is) an enormous sum. This spirit of cooperation in an atmosphere of friendly competition pervaded the testimony of those inter-viewed for this study, and is also evident in the state of church records. I found the pamphlet detailing the work of Kearney not in Mt. Olivet's archives, but in Trinity Presbyterian's. I often ran across announcements and reports of events of one church among the papers of another.

The churches, in their fund-raising efforts, communicated values to the white community. Because they initially needed support from the white com-munity to gain access to financial resources, and because the black community as a whole could not survive economically without the jobs and business sup-port that white employers and clientele provided, African American church appeals spoke strongly to their understanding of their own financial character.

In 1909, A.M.E. Zion Church News published an article as part of a fund-raising appeal to reduce their debt on the new church, entitled "The Right Kind of Charity." In it, the author (who was probably J.W. Thompson) reveals the economic values to which the community ascribed.

> The world is beginning to consider "The Right Kind of Charity" to be that which enables an individual or an institution to help themselves. The giving of money, without knowing whether the gift given will help the receiver to expand and enlarge that which he already has is unwise yet, there are still those who give without seeking this information, and those who are constantly begging and receiving—the more they receive the weaker they become.
>
> This certainly cannot be said of the A.M.E. Zion Church of this city. Four years ago a congregation of about 200 people started without a dollar, today they have by their self-sacrificing labors and the assistance of their white friends, erected a modern church building at the cost of $25,000 and have reduced the debt to $6,000, a herculean task worthy of any people. Aside from this they have paid their pastor a living salary, but desire to do more. Kept up the current expenses, fuel, light, organist, janitors' salaries. Interest, insurance and benevolences. We also help the poor of our church and the city.[23]

The help that the author seeks is not charity. He expects that the members of A.M.E. Zion will contribute their own "herculean" efforts to clear the church of debt. This clearing of debt is imperative if the community is to move beyond survival and dependence into prosperity and independence. The church wants to do more than give its pastor a living wage and keep up with current expenses. A pamphlet issued to the wider community laid out some of the church's plans to help "the poor of our church and city." Memorial wanted to provide sewing classes and lectures on domestic science for its young women, a reading room for all its youth, and an employment bureau.[24]

The church inculcated values that defined financial independence as a basis for doing good. Such independence was imperative. One could acquire it through hard work, mutuality, friendly competition, cooperation, and sharing. A firm financial base conveyed a clear message to the wider society of the capabilities of African Americans. This message would, they assumed, open up further opportunities for their people.

Recognizing Accomplishment

A.M.E. Zion offered classes in sewing and domestic science to its young women. This indicates the church's recognition of both the job opportunities available to young African American women in Rochester, and the necessity for them to compete adequately with immigrant labor in a social environment where employers were beginning to regard housework as a "science." Teaching these classes in the church also reveals the church's recognition of the inadequacy of other public institutions to provide this training for African Americans. The church stepped into this breach.

The church took on this secular role, but it also understood the imperative to provide spiritual resources to a people seeking material survival and prosperity. All of the churches under study offered worship services and church events during the week, so that the members who had to work on Sunday could receive this form of sustenance. Usually this happened on a Thursday. The importance of worship to get one through the week surfaced over and over again among the men and women who talked about the church in their lives. The church promoted economic independence by meeting this spiritual need, and through the lessons of the church, allowing those who worked primarily as servants to carry on the work for their children's benefit. Providing spiritual sustenance and practical tutelage reinforced the people's faith in the possibility of an alternative future for their daughters and sons.

When those sons and daughters achieved material success, the church rejoiced and recognized it. Daniel Garnett received position and responsibility in the church as soon as he began to work for a living, and his level of responsibility and acknowledgment increased along with his successes. When people retired or were promoted, the church gave them a party. The Christian Education committee of Memorial recognized Eunice Bullock when she retired from her job. This is significant not only because Mrs. Bullock was active in Christian Education, but because the church community recognized her economic position and success as integral to Christian Education. She embodied important lessons.

Through rejoicing when people found jobs, got promoted, got raises, or retired, the church honored hard work, whatever an individual's occupation. The color line operative in Rochester placed rigid restrictions on what African Americans could do, and the church responded by honoring their members for doing their best at any job. Placing hard-working people in positions of responsibility was one way of doing that. At Mt. Olivet, the church board meetings seated "a paperhanger, seven janitors, an unemployed man, a WPA worker, a factory foreman, a construction laborer, an undertaker, a handyman, two garage workers, a drug store employee, a bank messenger, a butler and a dentist. The majority of the deaconesses are employed housekeepers."[25]

Securing Employment

Finding jobs for members of the congregation was one of the duties of the pastors. Eunice Bullock explained that the pastors would meet on a regular basis to talk over job opportunities in the community and would act as references for their members. White employers would seek out pastors for recommendations. That's how she got her job.[26] Father Brown was quite proficient in this area. He connected many of his members, including Buddy Young and Elizabeth Logan, with job opportunities. Pastors knew the members of their congregations well enough to know what they could and couldn't do and what they did and didn't need.

Pastors were not the only ones who secured employment for other African Americans. J.W. Thompson used his position at the Powers Hotel to secure jobs for people new to Rochester, just getting on their feet, or in desperate need of employment. Daniel Garnett, Sr., Cynthia Lee, and Jesse Stevens all worked at the Powers Hotel at one time or another. Other influential members of African American churches used their connections to secure employment for their family members and friends. The church provided the communications networks that made such connections possible.

Churches also hired their own people to work in their offices and programs. Eunice Bullock served as Memorial's secretary. Harry Bray graduated from the University of Rochester, in 1938, with a B.S. in Sociology. He couldn't get a job as a professional in Rochester, so he did domestic work and worked as a graduate assistant in the Sociology Department of the University of Rochester. After he got his Masters in Sociology at the University of Pittsburgh in 1942, he still couldn't get a job in Rochester until Father Brown hired him to run the Carver House, a program of St. Simon's which began during World War II.[27]

Supporting Business

Members of the African American church expended a lot of energy locating, filling, and even creating jobs for the members of their congregations and community. When employment opportunities were not enough to sustain families, the church also supported independent African American business. It did this in several ways. Buddy Young remembers that Father Brown came to bless his mother's restaurant when she began this business. He recalls that Father Brown was unlike some of the other pastors, who came to get free food. Striking out on one's own by starting a new business took courage, and required spiritual support. Father Brown blessed Mrs. Young and her efforts.

A new business also required patronage. Those "other" pastors might have expected to eat for free, but their presence proclaimed their support of this new business and promoted the restaurant by spreading its reputation. African Americans supported each other's endeavors, filling hair-dresser and barber-shop chairs, soliciting hauling and carting and catering services, and employing dress-makers. The church provided the avenues for the provision of these services through word of mouth and advertising. Directories and bulletins from African American churches are replete with advertisements of goods and services of every description available from African American businesses in Rochester.

The church also provided formal sanction for the organization of African American business in Rochester. J.W. Thompson was the first to organize an African American business league in the early years of the century. He did this at Memorial A.M.E. Zion. African American businesses required reorganization in the 1920s, and once again Memorial took the lead.

> Inspired by the sermon of Reverend Dr. R.R. Bell of the AME Zion Church in 1924, Dr. V.T.Levy, with the encouragement of other black business persons, invited some community proprietors to a meeting at the AME Zion Church in December of 1924. The first meeting of the Negro Business League was conducted in the office of the Roe Window Cleaning Company, 123 West Main Street. The purpose of the League was to "promote better business relations among the colored people of Rochester and vicinity."[28]

The church sanctioned and supported the development of African American businesses, giving the custom of members to those businesses, blessing individual endeavors, and providing both inspiration and meeting space for the promotion of African American business aims. The church recognized independent ownership and operation of business as the foundation for a material existence that would insure the ability of African Americans to exercise freedom: freedom from white domination and freedom to respond to God.

Protest

All of the efforts that African Americans made on their own behalf did not put a dent in the prevailing economic conditions which proscribed African American opportunities in Rochester. African American church leaders were never silent in the face of this discrimination. J.W. Thompson waged an ongoing battle to protest the images of African Americans that reinforced economic strictures. In his appeals for aid, he consistently portrayed his community as hard-working and responsible, intelligent and energetic. He writes, "We want our people in the north to be character builders, home builders and good citizens and it is the mission of the Church to help in these three things. Rochester has a good class of colored citizens and we want to make them better. We have no bar rooms, no dives, no mid-night brawls, no 'black hands' no 'red hands' but are industrious law-abiding citizens. This to our mind is a strong reason why we should be encouraged."[29] J.W. Thompson organized both cooperative business endeavors and political organization to sway Rochester politicians to listen to the concerns of its African American constituency.

By the 1930s and 1940s, African American church leaders were taking a more militant tone in defense of their community's right to equal employment opportunities. Rev. Rose, of Mt. Olivet, proclaimed that "Rochester is one of the worst places for discrimination against the Negro of any city in the North and I'd like to be challenged on that." He cited the laxity of defense industries in Rochester in their employment of African Americans.[30] Rev. Rose, Dr. Lunsford, and Dr. Levy began to seriously pressure Rochester institutions and corporations to open their ranks to professionally trained African Americans. During the 1940s, thanks to this kind of pressure, cracks began to appear.

CONCLUSIONS

The African American church in Rochester, despite a hostile white environment, created the spiritual and institutional foundations for material independence for African Americans during the first few decades of the twentieth century. The people within the churches blended a faith in a God who expected them to live out a vision of equality and justice with practical efforts and programs aimed at sustaining their livelihood. Economic self-sufficiency laid the foundation for the future, and that future included a full and rich life for their children, who would reap the benefits of their hard work. The church provided moral guidance, spiritual sustenance, personal and institutional encouragement and concrete support. It appealed to and protested in the wider community. The African American churches in Rochester and the people within them never rested, and though they sometimes became angry, frustrated, or discouraged, they held on to their vision.

NOTES

1. Walters, *My Life and Work*, 130.

2. The biographical sketches of Jesse Stevens and Charles Price rely upon multiple sources of data, including an author's interview with Charles Price, 1 October 1993, the obituary of Jesse Stevens published in the *Rochester Democrat and Chronicle*, 27 February 1957, announcements and records found in the A.M.E. Zion Church archives in the possession of Charles Frazier, and McKelvey's article "Lights and Shadows."

3. Daniel Garnett is a pseudonym. Mr. Garnett gave permission for his story to be told, but preferred to remain anonymous. I have consequently given fictitious names to the places he (and his father) worked as well. All of the events and situations related here are based on interviews I had with Mr. Garnett, and on substantiating evidence from Memorial A.M.E. church archives and *about . . . time* magazine.

4. The examples and discussion that follow are taken from an interview with Daniel Garnett in which he is replying to the request to describe what he did in the church

during his life and then elaborating from the prompts "How did that affect you?" and "How did that help you?"

5. McKelvey, *Quest For Quality*, 125. This is the book's only mention of the participation of African Americans in Rochester's industries.

6. Ibid., 261.

7. James (Buddy) and Alice Young, interview with author, November 1993.

8. This example is taken from my interview with Cynthia Lee, but many of my informants testified to their parents and grandparents holding down multiple jobs, or trying to run their own business at the same time that they worked for wages.

9. McKelvey, *Quest for Quality*, 253.

10. Ibid., 347.

11. Ibid., 350-353.

12. McKelvey, *Emerging Metropolis*, 56-59.

13. Ibid., 81.

14. Ibid., 73-74.

15. Ibid., 87.

16. James and Alice Young, interview with author.

17. Jean Kenney, interview with author, 20 November 1993, and Elizabeth Logan, interview with author, 17 August 1993.

18. *Passing on Our Tradition, 1817-1992: St. Luke and St. Simon Cyrene Episcopal Church, Rochester, New York, October 1992*, an unpublished bibliography of Historical Materials in church archives, p. 8.

19. Author's interview with Charles Frazier, 20 May 1993.

20. Ibid.

21. Author's interview with Gladys Scott, 12 May 1993.

22. A.M. Kearney, *My Life and Work*, unpublished, undated pamphlet found in Trinity Presbyterian church archives.

23. "The Right Kind of Charity," *The Zion Church News* (September 1909), and A.M.E. Zion pamphlet circulated to relieve the church debt, ca. 1908/1909; both found in Memorial A.M.E. Zion church archives.

24. "The Right Kind of Charity," and A.M.E. Zion pamphlet circulated to relieve the church debt ca. 1908/1909.

25. *Rochester Democrat and Chronicle*, untitled article, 6 March 1938.

26. Author's interview with Eunice Bullock, 21 January 1993.

27. Dupree, "Rochester Roots/Routes" (September 1984), 24.

28. Dupree, "Rochester Roots/Routes" (August 1984), 21.

29. A.M.E. pamphlet circulated to relieve the church debt ca. 1908/1909.

30. *Rochester Democrat and Chronicle*, untitled article, 21 April 1941.

～ FIVE ～
POLITICAL AND CIVIL RIGHTS

Since the Lord has brought us face to face with this great question of equality, and since "premonitory mutterings," indeed, all the indications from the Divine side convince us that He is leading on in this as in the other great events through which He has so miraculously and triumphantly brought us after a long and severe struggle, it is our duty to follow where He leads."

Bishop Alexander Walters[1]

GEORGE BURKS[2]

George Burks created a sensation in Rochester in 1902 when he sued Paul Bosso, an Italian bootblack, for refusing to shine his shoes. That an African American, who stereotypically shined shoes, would sue for this service, caught the attention of the entire community. The case came to trial and was decided in January of 1902. The jury assigned George Burks one hundred dollars in damages (he had sued for five hundred). The *Democrat and Chronicle* article reporting the verdict, and the editorial the next day, reveal both the liberal racial consciousness of Rochester, and its perpetuation of racial stereotypes. The *D&C* stood squarely behind Burks and congratulated the jury for its fair-mindedness. The article also described Burks as the "porter" at the Commercial bank (Union and Trust Company, now Marine Midland), which was not his position, but which revealed the assumptions of the reporter. Burks actually held the position of messenger, which carried more trust and responsibility than that of porter and, by the time he retired, he had achieved the post of assistant teller. Bosso appealed the verdict and the suit eventually reached the State Supreme Court where the original ruling was overturned. New York State did not agree, it seems, with Rochester, and ruled that services could be withheld on the basis of color. Bosso's argument had been that he had the right to refuse his business to anyone he considered "undesirable."

The case rallied the African American community in Rochester. An article in the *Democrat and Chronicle* the week after the original verdict and shortly before Bosso's decision to appeal became public, reported the "stirring" sermon Rev. Adams preached at A.M.E. Zion church in support of Burks and the favorable verdict, while lamenting the possibility of defeat on appeal.

> [T]o my mind when a man's objection is based upon the color of his skin it is a very thin objection. If an individual is allowed to say that the color of a man's skin makes him objectionable they can just as easily say that the color of a man's hair makes him objectionable and our red-haired American will stand a poor chance with the black-haired Italians. . . .
>
> The eyes of all the world look this way because of the honors which have been conferred on Douglas [*sic*], and yet an Italian bootblack is asking the court for the privilege of insulting the race. We know we have not the money with which to buy decisions, and that we are tried by juries on which we are not represented and in courts in which we have no part, but we come to enter most solemn protest against this outrageous insult to our race.[3]

After this rousing sermon, J.W. Thompson introduced a resolution, celebrating the city of Rochester, calling on the memory of the honor and respect Rochester had granted Frederick Douglass, and expressing gratitude for the continued support for African American rights that the municipal court and jury had displayed in their support of George Burks.

At the turn of the century, A.M.E. Zion was the institutional voice for the African American people in Rochester. As such, her pastor, Rev. Adams, and her Board of Trustees President, J.W. Thompson, became the lens through which Rochester's public viewed African American sentiment on this matter. This was true even though George Burks was no longer a member of A.M.E. Zion. He had joined with a cluster of other Methodist Episcopal members in 1898 to form the Presbyterian mission, Trinity Church, which became incorporated in 1902, the same year as Burks's suit.

The reasons for the split from A.M.E. Zion that created the second African American congregation in Rochester seem not to have been recorded and are lost to the memories of the founders' descendants who provided interviews for this study. However, Blake McKelvey records an interesting incident concerning discrimination which could have been the root of dissension. The history of this incident, in and of itself, sheds light on what the African American community in Rochester expected of its church, and its ordained leadership, in defense of African American rights.

Charles Lee, a member of A.M.E. Zion church, "had received an appointment as clerk of the civil service examining board, but his refusal to accept dictation from the party bosses prompted his dismissal" in 1895.[4] In what appears to have been an extraordinarily stupid political blunder, Rev. Ely, then A.M.E. Zion's pastor, endorsed Lee's dismissal, at the request of Republican party boss, George Aldridge. J.W. Thompson and the Douglass League which he headed and which provided political leadership for African Americans in Rochester, condemned the move and Thompson declared what were patently false sentiments for him: that the pastor had no business making political statements to the public. The uproar caused the church to close until the Episcopal District sent James E. Mason, presiding elder, to take Ely's place. Mason proceeded to publicly voice political sentiments at every opportunity, including a statement to the *Post Express* encouraging, among other things, political activity as an avenue for the betterment of the race.

While highly speculative, it seems possible that a portion of A.M.E. Zion's membership were so taken aback by the actions of Ely, and by the machinations of the District, which removed but did not condemn him, that they sought a different denominational polity and a congregation in which the laity had a greater voice. George Burks lived within a community that was often too small to effect political changes in favor of its rights, but was solidly committed to working for them. After the Ely debacle, neither A.M.E. Zion's nor Trinity's pastors disappointed the membership's expectation that the men in the pulpit (and at that point and throughout the time period under consideration, they were always men) would fulfill their role as the voice of political protest, continually calling for justice. The church, with the spiritual support it provided (through, for example, focusing worship on the theme of equal rights and God's expectation of justice, as both Bishop Walters and Rev. Adams's words illustrate), was the institutional vehicle for political protest and civil rights activity.

George and Ernestine Burks were among the number who departed from A.M.E. Zion. As a founder of Trinity Presbyterian church, he served as elder and trustee, and devoted himself to the church day to day, Sunday to Sunday. The memories of his grandson, Alan Adams, who lived with his grandfather when he was a child, record a hard-working, industrious man who provided well for his family and insisted, along with his wife, that they attend church. George Burks typified the dedication and struggle of the hard-working African American men and women in Rochester at the turn of the century. He attempted to make enough money to live on and support his family (his wife, Ernestine, and daughter, Emma) through a combination of service-sector employment and a series of entrepreneurial ventures. His primary source of income came from his job as a messenger for the Union Trust Company. He supplemented this income for a while with a Tonsorial Parlor which was "sanitary and up-to-date" and sold cigars and tobaccos. Later, he became the proprietor of the Douglass Hotel, where his wife, Ernestine, did the cooking. Neither venture remained stable enough to generate sufficient independent income and George Burks concentrated on advancing at the bank.

Alan Adams clearly remembers seeing his grandfather riding his bicycle around town on bank business. The bank replaced Burks's bicycle with an automobile, and Alan inherited the bike. Having a car was an unheard of luxury within the African American community and it is significant of the importance of the church in George Burks's life and his dedicated service to it that he drove the pastor and elders of Trinity to their mission church in Caledonia every Sunday afternoon for worship services there.

Alan Adams remembers the church as being "very serious" for his grandfather, who helped maintain the building. He remembers that his grandparents never missed church, and that he had to go. He went not only to Sunday morning worship, but out to Caledonia on Sunday afternoons, and often to Wednesday evening prayer meetings, which his grandparents always attended. Alan Adams described his grandparents as the heads of a devout Christian family, within a devout Christian community. He recalled that the women of the church made sure that members "didn't have a problem," that they responded readily to those in need and would visit people in the hospital, or in jail. The men made sure the church functioned, made the repairs, kept the boiler going on Sundays, raised the money, and distributed the funds.

George Burks actively participated in Trinity, was a church leader, and gave of himself for the betterment of the community. For the African American community in Rochester, Burks's suit against Paul Bosso was an essential contribution to the community. It is significant that although he eventually lost this suit, he continued to defend African American rights. In 1907, George Burks organized the Afro American Independent Political League of Monroe County, which met on Mill St., but which had the endorsement of both Trinity and A.M.E. Zion churches.[5] The League's program was comprehensive in scope. It proposed an organization "Of Afro Americans, By Afro Americans and For Afro Americans" in order to "organize under its head the entire colored vote of Monroe County for mutual good." The League adhered to no party affiliation, advising the scrutiny of candidates to ascertain which would "guarantee to us such recognition as we seek." The League advocated commercial organization, and by that it meant politically addressing the fact that many commercial enterprises in Rochester profited from African American business, yet did not employ African Americans. Its goal was "to assist our capable men and women in securing employment in these various commercial houses." The League proposed to prosecute all cases of discrimination in Rochester and toward that end expected to raise five hundred dollars for a defense fund. The League espoused unified action, and issued a call for any "loyal reputable Afro American citizen 21 years of age" to become a member.[6]

George Burks's standing in the church and community, and his history of political action, classified him as both loyal and reputable. As President of the League, he exemplified the character needed among African Americans in Rochester who were dedicated to working for justice. Losing the Bosso suit was not as important as voicing the protest, and this attitude indicates a faith in the ultimate triumph of African American rights, through continual protest, even in the face of almost sure defeat. In 1910, George Burks once again brought suit, this time against the Temple Theater, for denying him equal accommodations. He wanted to sit on the main floor and the theater refused to sell him any but balcony seats, though they would seat him in the first row of the balcony if he wanted. This concession was enough for the judge to find in favor of the theater.[7]

Perhaps realizing that the African American community in Rochester was not large or strong enough to successfully fight discrimination without the backing of sympathetic whites, George Burks organized a chapter of the NAACP in Rochester in May of 1919. His address to the annual meeting of the NAACP in Cleveland that year speaks of his, and the branch's, longing to be a part of the "great work" of the NAACP, then just ten years old.

> I laid aside my business and came to Cleveland for the purpose of gaining information that I might carry back to Rochester and enthuse others in this grand work that we are enlisted in, because, in my opinion, more than two-thirds of our people do not realize the immensity of the benefits we achieve by following up this great work, and if we do our duty and do the things necessary to build up this great cause, the result will be so grand and great that every one will be surprised at the achievements thereby resulting from the same.[8]

George Burks cared passionately for the political and civil rights of African Americans. He also cared passionately about Trinity Presbyterian church, as did his wife, Ernestine. When Burks founded the chapter in Rochester in 1919, Ernestine Burks became Vice President. She combined this political work with her position as chair of the Religious Work committee of the YWCA, and her seat on the Board of Trustees of the Dorsey Home. Trinity Church honored her by founding the Ernestine Burks Circle of the Federation of Negro Women's Clubs. The lives of George and Ernestine Burks illustrate the interconnections between church participation, community service, and political involvement which African Americans saw as part of what Bishop Walters had stated to be their duty toward God. Nothing makes this link more clear than that Trinity Church provided the home for the local chapter of the NAACP. Alan Adams remembers his grandparents' household, and he remembers growing up in Trinity. As a child and young adult during the second and third decades of this century (he was born in 1913), Alan Adams absorbed the example of his grandparents and the teachings of his church. He himself is an elder at Trinity now, as is his own son. His testimony of personal faith, moving and eloquent, received its earliest lessons from his home and church environment. When I asked Mr. Adams why the church was so important to him, he replied that religion had always been a part of his life. When the church called, he said, "you just didn't refuse." He explained that he had read the Bible from cover to cover and had taken to heart the understanding that God is there for you when you call. Alan Adams has had many experiences in his life where either his survival or his future were at stake. He is clear in his belief that at those times, miracles happen, because they have happened for him. God intervenes, of this Alan Adams is sure. Whether or not George Burks would express this same faith so eloquently is uncertain. Yet, in the face of continued setbacks in the battle for civil rights for African Americans in Rochester, George Burks persevered. This indicates the presence of faith in the possibility of God's intervention on the side of justice.

REV. JAMES ROSE[9]

In 1920, James Rose ascended the pulpit at Mt. Olivet Baptist church, which had been vacant for a year. He came from a pastorate at the Second Baptist Church in Leroy and during the twenty-two years he served Mt. Olivet he made it the voice of the African American community in Rochester, eclipsing Memorial A.M.E. Zion, which had performed that role since its founding in 1827. His student and successor, Charles Emerson Boddie, remembered him as being "foremost in the rights struggle of his day, in Rochester. . . . The wise race baiter did well to flee before his acrid, unrelenting invective. Perhaps no man ever lashed out against lynching as he did."[10]

Dr. Rose graduated from the Virginia State Normal School and then attended Howard University, where he graduated in 1913. He recalled, "Betwixt working as a janitor in Washington apartment houses, serving as a waiter now and then, and performing as a hotel worker . . . in summers, [I] managed to win a bachelor of arts degree by 1913." While pastor at Mt. Olivet, Rev. Rose attended Rochester Theological Seminary, where he earned his Masters in 1930. Howard granted him an honorary doctorate of divinity in 1932.[11] During the first ten years he preached at Mt. Olivet the membership more than doubled and in the twenty-two years he was there, the congregation gained 808 members with Rose baptising 363 people, in a city in which the African American population never rose above 3,300 during this time. The people who flocked to Mt. Olivet loved and respected him. Many were in awe of him. He laid upon their hearts a simple exhortation: "It is their task, he says, . . . to make the Negro people proud of the name Negro."[12] James Rose understood leadership to mean inspiring such pride. In order to encourage racial pride, James Rose both supported all congregational and community efforts to promote the talents, skills, and industry of African Americans in Rochester and protested vigorously any attitudes or actions within the greater Rochester and national community that conveyed the message that African Americans were inferior.

The dedication ceremony of the new church in 1927 echoed these themes. For the dedication ceremony, Rev. Rose invited Dr. Mordecai Wyatt Johnson to preach. Dr. Johnson was the first African American to become president of Howard University, at the time the largest African American university in the world. He received his education in Rochester, at the Rochester Theological Seminary. Not only was he a close personal friend of Rose's, he exemplified what African Americans could achieve, what African Americans from Rochester could achieve, as he stood before the congregation and advised "the members of his race present . . . to tie up with no economic or intellectual enterprise or concern that has as its aim or object the crushing of other men's wills for personal advancement."[13] Dr. Johnson preached a message that challenged the concept that achievment equaled simple monetary profit, and stated instead that success and advancement required a different measure. People needed to assess their investments based on criteria other than monetary return, criteria that reflected Christian mandates. No institution deserved the support of African Americans if that institution engaged in exploitation.

> Even though your returns bring you 10 per cent, 15 per cent, or even 20 per cent, it does not pay if it comes from an institution that has as its aim merely the maintaining of the present world system. . . . Jesus is concerned with a better world order. You can bear your suffering in this world order if your aim is set on making a better world order.[14]

In inviting Dr. Johnson to preach, in building a new church, in providing every kind of inspiration he could think of, Rev. James Rose was well aware of the forces with which he, and all African Americans had to contend. His political activity was imbued with the understanding set forth by Johnson, that whatever he and other African Americans did for the good of the community had to reflect the Christian concern for justice.

As an indication of the kind of suffering African Americans needed Christian fortitude in order to face, there appeared, opposite the article celebrating the opening of the new church, an advertisement for the Ku Klux Klan. During the 1920s, the Ku Klux Klan maintained a visible presence in Rochester. According to a *Democrat and Chronicle* retrospective,

> the Ku Klux Klan signed up 250 members at an organization meeting here in Malta Hall, in December 1922. There was another such meeting the following year, in the the old Reynolds Arcade and although secrecy was the order of the day, it was learned that more members were signed. The Klan's most spectacular shindig in these parts occurred Sept 25 and 26, 1926, when some 19,000 Knights and their women descended upon a field at Washington and Ivy Streets in East Rochester for a Konvocation.[15]

Against this political backdrop, which included a white community in Rochester that contained a significant liberal minority, Rev. Rose understood as one of his primary political duties to protest, actively, the practice of lynching. He led many anti-lynching rallies during the 1920s, and was joined in the organization of them by other African American leaders in the community.[16] In the 1930s, Rose articulated an analysis of American intervention in Liberia, laying bare American economic expediency and hypocrisy. In response to a U.S. commission's report on conditions in Liberia, Rose challenges:

> We certainly wish that our liberty-loving government would appoint a commission to investigate the peonage system which still holds in the South. We think it is just as outgrown in this civilized age as is the pawning system in Africa. Of course, both of them are wrong; but what right has our secretary to say one word to Liberia, when right here in America Negroes are taken out of prison and turned over to some white man to work off a bail bond . . . against his will, and then cheated in such a way that it takes him years to pay the debt?[17]

His editorial continues along the same vein, challenges the continued practice of lynching, and the denial of equal educational opportunities to African Americans. He ends by accusing the United States of being interested in the clearly oppressive conditions in Liberia only because Firestone had recently acquired rubber interests there. Rev. Rose's political positions always reflected his Christian commitment. This editorial ends with the scathing observation, "Where your treasure is, there will your heart be also."

Rose also excoriated Italy's invasion of Ethiopia. Ocurring in October of 1935, the *Democrat and Chronicle* made the invasion front page news for well over a month before and after Italy's aggression. Every conceivable segment of the Rochester community had something to say about the fascist threat in

Africa, U.S. neutrality, the role of the League of Nations, and/or the role of Great Britain. The *D&C* reported all of it. A large portion of the Italian community in Rochester rallied support for Mussolini. Knowledgable Italian speakers put the case before Rochester. Two of Italy's rationales for the invasion—that Italy was "civilizing" Ethiopia and that Italy needed more land for its surplus population—received the brunt of Rev. Rose's reply.

> Doctor Rose . . . scoffed at Sconfietti's assertion Italy was bound not only on territorial expansion but a civilization mission. "Bombs, poison gas, shot and shell are not the best methods of civilizing", he said, "for civilization, besides meaning enlightenment, is a slow process and cannot be accomplished by shooting down the people for which it is intended."
>
> Italy's argument that her surplus population demands more land is incongruous with Mussolini's campaigns for larger families, Doctor Rose said. He attacked Baron Aloisi's refusal to sit with Ethiopian delegates to the League of Nations as characteristic of Italy's attitude toward the African empire.[18]

This article lacks the fullness of Rose's authorship, unlike the editorial above. Since it is the report of a meeting, rather than an opinion piece, much of what Rose had to say is left out. Still, the tone is clearly one of ridicule and suspicion of not only fascism, but of a European nation's presumption to either "civilize" or take over the territory of an African "empire." Doctor Rose reveals the underlying racism in Italy's behavior not only by pointing out the illogic of expanding a population into Ethiopia, which was of course already populated, but also by calling attention to the refusal of Italians to "sit with" Ethiopians.

Rose asserts that Italy's positions are "illogical," and shows through his analysis the fault in Italy's reasoning. For an African American to claim superior mental acuity to Europeans who were invading an African country took nerve. The reporter of this article was careful to give Rose his full title of *Doctor*, reinforcing Rose's point.

Doctor Rose participated in a number of organizations that gave him access to leadership positions, thus providing public avenues for political analyses. That organizational complexity and professionalization had taken root in Rochester by the mid-twenties is shown in the way Rev. Rose, in his efforts, used several ministerial organizations in which he had attained leadership roles. He held positions as the Moderator of the Baptist Union of Rochester and Monroe County, Vice President of the Rochester Federation of Churches, President of the Rochester Ministerial Association, and President of the NAACP, and he sat on the Rochester City Planning and Housing Council. While other African American pastors had belonged to the religious organizations and some had held office in them, Rose is distinctive both for attaining leadership positions and for the range of organizations in which he did so. The white community may have made Rose Rochester's token African American, but he attempted to fill these positions in ways that further equipped his community for political action. His positions allowed him to focus on local conditions. His analyses linked the treatment of African Americans in Rochester to national and international political realities and emphasized the role of the church. Because he held positions of authority in organizations containing a majority of the white religious leadership in the city, his public pronouncements received attention. For example, the *Democrat and Chronicle* reported that Rose would address the topic of "Race Friendships" in 1932, and "The Inadequacy of the White Ministry" in 1935. These two addresses touch upon two of his deepest concerns, working with people of other races who could help African Americans to full equality, and relying on the leadership of African Americans to accomplish racial goals.

Rev. Rose took advantage of an opportunity to voice these concerns when he encountered the personal brunt of racial prejudice in his capacity as Moderator of the Baptist Union of Rochester and Monroe County. In 1932, that body hosted a national convention of 450 Baptist clergymen. The President of the Southern Convention refused to attend the opening banquet because the presiding officer was a Negro. This incident caught the attention of both the religious and secular press. In an undated and unidentified newspaper article found in Mt. Olivet's archives, Rev. Rose delivered a religious and political indictment of the American Christian church. In "Jesus, Our Way to Brotherhood," Rose declared that "real brotherhood" was more alive in Soviet Russia, or among radical labor, socialist, and communist groups in the United States than in the Christian church. These groups did not remain silent in the face of discrimination or oppression, they registered protests against lynching, and did not exhibit pretensions of racial superiority. He concluded that "the Caucasion race which embraces Christianity in its organized from, cannot practice real brotherhood with the colored races of the earth as long as it feels itself superior to them. You cannot have brotherhood when one brother is admitted to certain places and the other is excluded."[19]

Rose's political positions are instructive. As an African American pastor he took seriously his role as the one who "makes waves" for members of the community who could not do so without serious risk. As Eunice Bullock had observed, taking political and sometimes adversarial stands to protect or advance African American rights, was part of the role of pastor. Rose also went further than any other African American leader in Rochester during this time in his open praise of radical and communist organizations which exemplified his understanding of Christian brotherhood. His stands did not compromise his leadership role; on the contrary, making the practice of racism the ultimate test of the viability of American society fell well within the traditional tenets of African American theology. The ultimate test of Christianity was not doctrine, but behavior. His praise of authentic brotherhood served as a warning that African American loyalty depended upon respecting African American humanity; it was a wake-up call in the finest traditions of African American religious leaders.

Throughout the forty years that span this study, political leaders of the African American community pointed to the participation and patriotism of African Americans as evidence that they deserved respect and the full rights of citizenship. This strategy probably influenced the local African American lack of enthusiasm for socialism. Rev. Rose broke this mold and reversed the understanding of loyalty. It was, in his view, up to American society to show its loyalty to Christian principles by recognizing African American humanity. Rose exemplified the changing social conditions and priorities of African Americans. The first generations of African Americans after emancipation struggled to prove worthiness through personal and communal achievements in education and economic advance. By the twenties and thirties, African Americans had shown such achievement, but still faced hostile racial barriers. Men like James Rose, who encouraged African American racial pride and brought educated and accomplished African American professionals to Rochester, shifted the burden of responsibility for eradicating racial barriers onto the shoulders of white intransigence.

During the incident at the Baptist convention, and in its aftermath, Rose kept his focus on national and international issues and situations. He used the personal slight to stand upon his reputation and position as a respected leader in Rochester and denounce especially the political attitudes of the South, but also the lack of principle within the organized Christian church. Later in the thirties Rose joined with other prominent African Americans in Rochester to deliver an indictment against discrimination in the city.

From December, 1938, through January, 1939, the New York State Temporary Commission Against Discrimination (also referred to as The New York Temporary Commission on the Urban Colored Population) held hearings in Rochester. This Commission was followed by the Federal Fair Employment Practice Committee in 1943 and another State Commission Against Discrimination in 1945. These state and federal bodies were most concerned about the smooth progress of the war effort, and investigated cities across the state to make sure that municipalities and local industries were making all efforts to employ minorities and to keep a lid on any sources of potential domestic unrest. The various hearings created a forum through which African Americans in Rochester could register their perceptions and complaints.

Dr. Charles Lunsford headed a citizens committee that testified for the 1939 Commission. Dr. Lunsford, Dr. Van Tuly Levy, and Rev. James Rose were among the most vocal. The focus of these hearings became the discriminatory practices of the University of Rochester's Medical School, but Rose, in particular, also indicted the entire institutional infrastructure of the city. Rose was also influential in bringing Dr. Lunsford to Rochester. Lunsford had graduated from Howard University's medical school and his friendship with Rose encouraged him to practice here. The citizens committee's accusations, spearheaded by Dr. Lunsford, created a flurry of letters to the editor in the *Times Union*.

The University of Rochester defended its position. President Valentine submitted that the school could not give "adequate instruction to Negroes in some subjects." Editorials in the paper raised the lurid possibility that Negro medical students would be treating white patients, might actually deliver white babies. "Society will not tolerate that. White mothers will not think of having Negro medical students present at, or participating in, the delivery of their babies." Responses poured in from African American and white citizens who lambasted this attitude. William Van Hook declared that "75 years after white and black died so that slavery should be wiped out in our country the entire colored population in the city of Rochester is still denied the right to live as human beings." William J. Pomeroy observed that "Negroes in this city are discriminated against in almost every phase of social activity and practice."[20] Dr. Mordecai Wyatt Johnson concurred when he came to Rochester in January and spoke at the City Club. He attacked the city "for permitting discrimination to gain a foothold in its educational institutions and to win full sway in its great industries and commercial firms."[21]

As a result of these united protests, Edwin A. Robinson was admitted to the University of Rochester's Medical School in 1940. A year later, Rev. Rose took a public stand against the discrimination against blacks in employment practices among the defense industries operating in Rochester. By the time of his death in 1942, James Rose had become the center of a network of vocal African Americans in Rochester and connected to African American leaders in the nation, who spoke out regularly to defend the rights of African Americans in Rochester. His efforts were embedded within a particular political climate and system operative in Rochester and reflected the centrality of the African American church as a voice for protest, often, but not exclusively, led from the pulpit.

POLITICAL CONTEXT IN ROCHESTER

The political history of Rochester reveals an underlying dynamic of strong radical movements countered by a bedrock conservatism that blunted efforts to better the conditions of African Americans in the city. Rochester has a reputation for being a center for abolition, women's rights, the social gospel, school reform, and New Deal innovations in labor relations. Neither Rochester's voters nor politicians backed these movements. Those movements which have garnered the most fame for Rochester, abolition and women's rights, had perhaps the least popular support. A brief discussion of the city's political legacy pertaining to African American and women's rights reveal this long-standing political tendency.

For example, the traditionally Republican city backed Lincoln in 1860 by a mere one percent of the electorate, voted for the Democratic candidate for Congress in 1862, and elected Democratic mayors in 1862, 1863, and 1864, "despite the loud protests of Republican editors against entrusting control of the city . . . to 'Copperheads.'" The city also voted for the 'Copperhead' gubernatorial candidate, Horatio Seymour, for the duration of the war effort, and delivered a plurality of eighty-nine votes favoring McClellan against Lincoln in the 1864 election.[22]

The 1864 election revealed a link between Democratic political leanings and opposition to African American rights. The city voted against the state amendment for Negro suffrage, granting it less than two fifths of the local vote. In 1871, the city defeated Frederick Douglass's bid for the state legislature through a swing vote delivered by local Republicans.[23]

Even more surprising, in light of the honor this city now chooses to bestow upon Susan B. Anthony, is the fact that in both the 1915 and 1917 bids for women's suffrage in New York State, Rochester delivered resounding vetoes. This is true in 1917 even though Rochester elected Socialists to public office for the first time. Socialists had consistently supported women's suffrage in Rochester as elsewhere, but the Socialist victories had more to do with protesting the war than with a change of sentiments concerning women's rights.[24] Until a few years before her death, the majority of Rochestarians considered Susan B. Anthony a figure of ridicule. Not until Anthony's national and international reputation made such responses themselves ridiculous did the city grant the woman, but not her cause, respect.[25] During the early years of the twentieth century, the political movements to reform Rochester society continued to reveal a wall of underlying conservatism, which maintained its hegemony despite fervent, often religiously motivated challenges. Those white reformers who engaged the political system in an effort to better social conditions, displayed racial attitudes that resulted in a failure to ally with African American efforts.

The Social Gospel

Earlier chapters, on human services and education, laid the groundwork for an appreciation of the significance of the social gospel to efforts for social reform in Rochester. The basic religious tenets that infused this movement created a logical connection between social reform and political activity. William Reese, in his exposition of grass-roots movements during the Progressive Era, notes that proponents of the social gospel were in the minority in Rochester, yet wielded an important influence by asking the question of whether or not one could "create a morally just order in a land dominated by the principles of corporate business ownership and management".[26] Walter Rauschenbusch founded a local social gospel organization, The Brotherhood of the Kingdom, which welcomed

> all who believe in a purer, deeper and freer spiritual life; in the unity of Christian men; in the brotherhood of nations under the leadership of Jesus Christ; in the reconstruction of political and social life according to the principles of Christian brotherhood; and in the application of the religious spirit to the regeneration of all human relations . . .[27]

The religious tenets of the social gospel promoted political activity for the reformation of the Kingdom. While the social gospel represented a stream of white Christian thought during the Progressive Era, such religious principles formed the backbone of African American theology. From Bishop Alexander Walters to Mordecai Wyatt Johnson to Rev. James Rose we have heard exactly these beliefs espoused and promoted for the betterment of African American as well as human society.

Ralph Luker described the variety and subtlety of racial attitudes among proponents of the social gospel in *The Social Gospel in Black and White*. Luker argues that far from ignoring racial issues, for which they have been accused, white social gospel leaders grappled mightily to take thoughtful and faithful positions on the proper arrangement of race relations. However, their attitudes revealed the spectrum possible from virulent racism to benign paternalism to complete indifference. Even within such a radical religious movement, African American members found themselves constantly struggling to be heard and consistently holding their white colleagues accountable for their positions. For present purposes, the positions of Walter Rauschenbusch and Algernon Crapsey deserve attention.

Luker notes that Rauschenbusch, the "greatest theologian" of the social gospel, "hesitated to address race relations and did so publicly only in the second decade of the century." Luker justified this hesitancy as stemming from Rauschenbusch's removal from the immediate problem. "Only 600 of Rochester's 162,000 residents, less than 0.5 percent of the city's population, were black." Luker then asserts that while "limited by distance from deep involvement in race relations, Rauschenbusch was yet mindful of American race relations, protested lynching and diverse forms of discrimination, and held to the Christian tenet that "God is the bond of racial unity" because "the recognition of a single God of all mankind lays the basis for an ethical union of all mankind in the future."[28]

Whatever theological views on the subject Rauschenbusch held, he did not involve himself in activities of brotherhood with African Americans in Rochester, and seemed relieved that the small size of the population allowed him this course. As previously noted, Rauschenbusch's report on social conditions in Rochester begins with a demographic breakdown of the city's population, noting that since the African American population was so small, Rochester was manifestly a city of white people. The most pressing social issues then depended upon finding ways for Americans of diverse European backgrounds to live together in harmony. Thus, Rauschenbusch, despite his theological formulations, manifestly ignored the religious motivation, social and political reform activities, and protests registered by a small, but very active local African American community.

Algernon Crapsey was more forthright and direct in his views on a variety of subjects, including race. Luker records two cogent examples, both taking place outside of Rochester, where Crapsey served as priest at St. Andrew's Episcopal church. Invited to conduct an "evangelistic mission" at St. Phillip's, a mission to African Americans sponsored by Trinity Episcopal Church in New York City, Crapsey greeted the senior warden upon his arrival. "Instinctively and without a moment's hesitation" Crapsey stepped forward and laid his hand on the arm of Mr. White, the warden. Crapsey said, "Mr. White, with your permission, I will walk with you; we can talk together as we go along." At the close of his time at St. Phillips, Mr. White said, "Mr. Crapsey, no white man in America ever acted in such a manner toward me as you did on the morning of your arrival." In a less personal, but equally forthright manner, Crapsey preached to a black congregation at Washington's St. Luke's Church at the turn or the century, and addressed a crowd of three thousand at Washington's Metropolitan A.M.E. Church the following Sunday. He exhorted his listeners to defend the integrity of their personalities, and exercise the franchise at every opportunity. For preaching such sentiments, Crapsey endured repuke from the presiding Bishop of the diocese.[29]

Luker describes a contingent of white social gospel leaders who displayed the forthright courage of their convictions, Algernon Crapsey among them. They seemed to be in the minority, however, and the leadership as a whole remained divided on issues of race. As for Rev. Crapsey, his courage and directness not only isolated him from the mainstream in Rochester, but led to a trial for heresy, which he lost, and which also lost him any institutional base from which he may have worked with African Americans in Rochester. The heresy trial resulted from a sermon Rev. Crapsey preached questioning the validity of the virgin birth. Coming from perhaps the most radical of churchmen residing in Rochester, his views, extreme for his time, may not have endeared him to an African American community bent on defending their rights within a system that Crapsey, who became a Socialist, increasingly questioned. He is however, the only social gospel minister who engaged in joint protest activity with African American clergy in Rochester, once to protest lynching, and once to protest racial slurs in the press.

Joseph Alling, a businessman in Rochester who adhered to the social gospel, is one of the few white people recorded as friends of A.M.E. Zion church. He superintended their Sunday School for a while. While the church welcomed his support, the references to Alling place him among those white people to whom the African American members felt beholden, but not close. It seems likely that Alling exhibited the benign paternalism so common among white social gospelers, a paternalism that generally resolved itself into an attitude promoting African American education under white tutelage. For all his seeming paternalism, Joseph Alling felt genuine outrage at the corruption and mismanagement of the municipal government and was the leader in Rochester's first sweeping effort for political reform.

Good Government

The first two decades of the twentieth century in Rochester were heated arenas of political reform. "Boss" George Aldridge controlled the Republican machine here, and wielded control over city government even when he did not hold office. It is not the intent here to describe Aldridge's machinations, but rather to sketch the forces arrayed against him and show how they intersected with African American efforts to gain a voice in the political arena in Rochester.

Rochester's white urban social reformers, infused with the social gospel, cut their teeth on the "Good Government" movement which confronted the political control, manipulation, and corruption of "Boss" Aldridge. The depression of 1893 revealed the inadequacy of public funds and led to a demand for investigations into municipal spending. Corruption and an inadequacy of services abounded, most notably in the public schools, but extending into every avenue of civil service. "Boss" Aldridge and his machine had systematically ignored legal guidelines securing contracts and services. Political intransigence and continued manipulation brought reformers to their feet. Men and women like Joseph Alling and Helen Montgomery turned men's Bible classes and women's clubs into seedbeds for good government clubs in every neighborhood of the city. Usually aligning themselves with the Democrats, the "goo-goos" fought Aldridge tooth and nail. Never in the majority, they nevertheless gained the public's attention and taught Aldridge hard lessons. Aldridge learned to listen and began to clean up his act, at least on the surface. Blake McKelvey, who chronicles the career of George Aldridge, displays a grudging admiration for his ability to learn from his mistakes and outmaneuver his opponents. As the good government forces demanded fiscal responsibility and improved services, Aldridge learned how to "strengthen his hold on the community by the vigor and quality of his services."[30] Thus the challenge to Aldridge's control that began with a fervor of idealism ended in political compromise. The good government movement had forced some concessions and improvements, but left a more wily and efficient Aldridge still in control of the municipality.

African Americans formed their own good government club in 1904, but McKelvey's major discussion of the good government movement in Rochester does not discuss any collaborative activities or direct connections between Alling's movement and the African American community. If the African American club joined with the city's proponents of the social gospel in their political battle, the historical record does not reflect it. It seems likely that, given the African American community's relationship with Aldridge, its good government club would have entered such a partnership readily. That they did not, or that history does not record it if they did, suggests that the wider Rochester community did not consider the African American club a significant factor in the political struggle.[31] The fact that the good government club within the African American commuity found its genesis within Bible classes speaks to the importance of the church to African American political activity. Church archives from this time period are replete with political organizations and activities that better met the needs of African Americans. The next section of this chapter will describe them.

Before discussing socialism, Aldridge's continued control, the shift of power to George Eastman, and how these intersected with the political needs of the African American community, it is necessary to consider the political alliance between the African American community and Susan B. Anthony. As noted previously, women's rights held little favor in Rochester at large, despite its vitality as a radical movement in the city. What distinguishes Anthony from the coterie of social reformers active in Rochester, including other women activists, was her understanding of and unwavering support for African American rights.

Susan B. Anthony and the Political Equality Club

Contemporary African American feminists and historians of the women's suffrage movement have highlighted Susan B. Anthony's willingness to accept racist allies and racist arguments in the name of political expediency during the campaign for women's suffrage.[32] This study does not rehash that history, attempt to analyze Anthony's decisions, or challenge the accuracy of the revisionist argument. However, Susan B. Anthony had a strong, affectionate relationship with the African American community in Rochester and, among the white reformers of her era, was that community's most staunch ally. Rochester's African Americans recognized, and continue to recognize, that allegiance with pride, and chose to honor her memory at Memorial A.M.E. Zion.

The important factor in the relationship between Anthony and the African American community that differentiates her from other white reformers active in Rochester was her willingness to work with African Americans, and by so doing acknowledge their potential for leadership and their right to a voice in policy and decision-making. Susan B. Anthony invited Hester Jerome Jeffreys to join the Political Equality Club, thus acknowledging her social equality with other educated, middle-class women interested in reform. Mrs. Jeffreys accepted the invitation and worked through both the Political Equality Club and the Federation of Colored Women's Clubs for the rights of African American women. The presence of Mrs. Jeffreys among the women in the Political Equality Club indicates a bridge between white and African American reform efforts and could account for the number of African American speakers whom that body, under Susan B. Anthony's guidance, invited to Rochester.

The most celebrated woman among these speakers was Ida Wells Barnett, quite possibly the most radical African American woman of her day, who proffered her friendship to Susan B. Anthony, something she never did lightly. The friendship between Barnett and Anthony offers clues to the high esteem the African American community in Rochester accorded Anthony. Paula Giddings traces the complex interplay between Anthony's personal convictions, and her vacillation concerning, and complicity with, racism on the national suffrage scene, as revealed in Anthony's correspondence with Barnett. When Ida Wells Barnett came to speak in Rochester, she stayed with Anthony in her home. Once, she requested the services of Anthony's secretary, who refused to work for a "colored" woman. Anthony fired her. Once can be reasonably certain that Hester Jeffreys heard about it.

Barnett's intense discussions with Anthony concerning race and women's issues revealed some of the conceptual grounds underlying Anthony's political expediency. Anthony believed that justice would prevail once women got the suffrage, and thus any means to that end would hasten the demise of both racism and sexism. Barnett disagreed. Barnett was also furious with Anthony when she refused to support an African American branch of the National American Women's Suffrage Association. Anthony also asked Frederick Douglass not to attend the NAWSA convention in 1895 as it would be "inexpedient" for him to be there in the presence of the Southern delegation. Once at that convention, Anthony cast her own vote against the racist measures proposed.[33]

At home, Susan B. Anthony freely expressed her personal convictions concerning local race relations. She supported the local African American community and its social and political aims. She made personal contributions, raised money for, and spoke on behalf of the Frederick Douglass monument. She was the only white person recorded as present at the founding of the local chapter of the National Afro-American Council, convened by T. Thomas Fortune. Her last public speech took place in the old A.M.E. Zion church. After Anthony's death, when Memorial A.M.E. Zion built its new church in 1906, it erected a stained glass window commemorating Susan B. Anthony. In the cornerstone of the church, two photographs reside, one of Susan B. Anthony, the other of Rev. Anna Howard Shaw, "with the saying of the suffragist, 'Perfect equality of rights for women, civil and political'." Hester Jerome Jeffreys said of Susan B. Anthony that she "had stood by the negroes when it meant almost death to be a friend of the colored people."[34] In choosing to honor Susan B. Anthony, the African American community in Rochester revealed the characteristics of white support they most appreciated. While having to accept and learn to deal with paternalism and condescension from most white reformers, African Americans in Rochester celebrated the respect and acknowledgment of human potential in every facet of economic and political life which Susan B. Anthony's relationship with them symbolized. As an individual, she exemplified the radical potential of interracial cooperation in a local setting. She took African American struggles for civil and political rights seriously and incorporated that struggle with her own. This could not be said of other reformers in Rochester, no matter how radical.

Susan B. Anthony died early in the time period discussed here, so her possible involvement in the politics of Rochester becomes moot. As an example of an activist who took African American struggles seriously she has no equal in the ensuing decades. Yet Rochester continued to be an arena for reform whose proponents challenged the political machinery in the city. These challenges barely brushed the African American community, but deserve attention with an attempt to describe why progressive reformers, and their reforms, failed to include African Americans.

Socialism, George Aldridge, George Eastman

McKelvey, Reese, and Dutko all concur that socialism never achieved significant electoral power in Rochester, sending its members to office (and none of them to major positions) during only one election, that of 1917. Yet several social gospel advocates displayed socialist leanings, including Rauschenbusch and Crapsey, and many of the women activists were sympathetic. The socialists' major areas of strength were in the labor struggles occurring in Rochester and in the the the area of civic reform, especially within the social center movement. The earlier chapters on education and economic self-development have outlined these pockets of radicalism. Within the political arena, George Aldridge became increasingly annoyed with reformers' challenges and felt some alarm concerning the political clout that socialists wielded, not as a third party threat, but as a coalition movement, whose strength often made a decisive difference, if not in results, then in policy. When one of Rochester's most prominent Socialists, Kendrick Shedd, University of Rochester professor and social center leader, made an ill-considered speech which seemed to denigrate the American flag, Aldridge whipped up a storm of outrage which led to the closing of the social centers, ousted the Labor Lyceum (the organization headquarters of the Socialist Party) from City Hall, and banned political speeches in the schools.[35] Good government forces were also alarmed by Shedd's intemperance and abhorred what they viewed as the socialist influence which contributed to violence within labor disputes. Joseph Allling was instrumental in securing Shedd's resignation from the University, and Algernon Crapsey became disenchanted with socialism during the labor disputes and deserted the party later when it took a stand for peace during World War I. Yet they also deplored "Boss" Aldridge's high-handedness and became convinced that the only way to obtain effective city government was to "remove its functions from political dominance." Consequently they began to explore the possibilities for instituting city management in Rochester.[36]

As outlined in Chapter Four, George Eastman developed a system of labor-management relations that went a long way toward nullifying the influence of both socialism and labor organization in Rochester. Consistent with these methods, Eastman promoted cooperative efforts between business and government in city administration. These efforts received impetus from the war effort, which engaged the industries of Rochester and called for the cooperation of the city government. George Eastman founded the Bureau of Municipal Research in 1915, which engaged the use of experts to investigate more efficent means to deliver municipal services. It proposed "a tighter annual budget, a stricter regulation of city contracts for work and supplies, and a more systematic organization of the comptroller's office. . . . [T]he large tax-payers had a right to demand an honest budget, the bureau maintained, and the reluctance of the political officials to reveal all expected deficiencies in their budgets eventually persuaded the bureau and its backers to seek a more responsible and business-like form of government."[37] Despite popular support, the strength of the Aldridge machine forestalled the implementation of city management until after his death. Then, heated struggles for control of the party both forestalled its implementation and increased popular support for a less partisan form of government. Eastman did not give the city manager movement his wholehearted endorsement until the late twenties, partially as a result of his reaching an agreement with Aldridge on city administration in the postwar years. Yet his stamp was evident in the endorsement of efficiency symbolized in the choice of the first city manager. Stephen Story, previous director of the Bureau for Municipal Research, became the first city manager in Rochester in 1928.

The push for civic reform in Rochester made gains on business, rather than moral or religious, grounds. The leadership shifted from the hands of social gospel proponents and women activists who advocated reform in order to better education, social welfare, health, and municipal services, to those of scientific managers, concerned with the efficient delivery of municipal services that would buttress an industrial base at the least cost to tax-payers. While the earlier movement ignored potential African American allies for good government, the later movement did not spark enthusiasm among African Americans in Rochester. Just as African Americans did not share in the socialist concern for organized labor, being banned from union membership, or become active in a social center movement that did not address their needs, neither did African Americans have a stake in industrial-government cooperation. African Americans neither owned nor worked in Rochester's industries. The municipal projects for improvements only benefited African Americans indirectly as they did not target African American neighborhoods, where African Americans both worked and operated any businesses that they did own. These businesses were small, entrepreneurial, and geared toward the provision of services—for instance, grocery stores and hauling companies. The political concerns of African Americans in the city centered upon such issues as equal accommodations, access to services, discrimination in housing, education, and the professions, and upon the wider political concerns of lynching, the convict-lease system, and disfranchisement. Rochester's white reformers did not begin to address these concerns and as their zeal turned more and more toward industrial growth, African Americans had less and less in common with them. The institution which promoted the development of political activity among African Americans remained the African American church.

The Depression, The New Deal, and the Second World War

The Depression severely taxed the new, more efficient, city manager system. Industrialists and government officials alike maintained that they had the resources and expertise to weather the storm. They established public work-relief efforts and municipal projects, and broke national ground when Kodak instituted a voluntary unemployment program. Such prompt and organized attention to the destitution in the city nipped radical response in the bud. McKelvey notes that a mass protest organized by local "reds" proved disappointing to its leaders. "Most of the unemployed displayed by their absence an eager confidence" in the city's efforts.[38] Rochester's early efforts, especially in the field of unemployment, earned it the attention of Governor Franklin D. Roosevelt and his State Industrial Commissioner, Frances Perkins. By 1932, however, the vast outlays of private and public funds had not stemmed the tide of destitution and city leaders became alarmed while the more conservative called for economy and retrenchment.

When Democrats swept into state and national office in 1933, Rochester still held a Republican majority, and chose to turn its fiscal crisis over to the banks rather than to the government. The city manager, C. Arthur Poole, proposed and received approval from the council to float a $3.6 million bond to fund relief efforts, which, after some hesitation, the banks of Rochester agreed to do. The agreement between the city and the banks left the banks in full control. "The fact that the Rochester banks were strong enough to force the city administration to accept their fiscal leadership contrasted with the situation in many cities where such institutions were insolvent."[39] It was a rare situation indeed, and one which had an influence on Rochester's ability to maintain a certain distance from New Deal programs, while benefiting from state and federal largesse. The pattern of interaction throughout the New Deal was one in which the city developed its own programs, supplemented its needs by applying for federal funds, but bowed out or resisted when government regulations bit too tight. Federal assistance and leadership were most welcome in the welfare field, but in other areas, Rochester balked.

> Many in Rochester were becoming restive under the New Deal. Local compliance with the NRA codes was no longer so encouraging, and many firms were turning back their Blue Eagles. Chamber statisticians, who had noted an occa-

sional upturn in their graphs in 1934, rejoiced when the movement became more pronounced a year later. The need for federal regulation, or even federal assistance, seemed to some less urgent; a few branded such intervention as positively injurious, but the inarticulate majority still accepted both gratefully.[40]

Rochester's Democrats wielded control in the city from 1934 through 1937, but always against a coterie of powerful leaders who resisted, organized reaction to the New Deal, and emerged stronger than ever. By 1938 the Republicans were firmly in control. Reaction to the New Deal notwithstanding, the organizational infrastructure that had arisen among local, state, and federal agencies during the Depression served the city well in mobilizing for the war effort.

Rochester's main contribution to the war effort was once again its technical industries. Contracts exceeding ten million dollars arrived in Rochester in June, 1940, for Bausch and Lomb, Stromberg-Carlson, Taylor Instruments, the physics department of the University of Rochester, and Eastman Kodak. Unemployment virtually disappeared as these and other industries sought skilled workers. Federal and state training programs brought approximately thirty thousand workers into the labor force within two years and "greatly facilitated" war production. As a result of training programs, recruiting women and African Americans into skilled occupations, and devoting its industries to the production of delicate scientific war products, Rochester led the nation in this type of contribution. "The technological competence of its firms brought a flood of orders that totaled $1,215,145,000 by November 1, 1945. And the efficiency with which these orders were filled brought a succession of Army-Navy E awards to 38 local companies . . . [honoring] more than 11 percent of the county's firms, as contrasted with an average of 5 per cent throughtout the country."[41]

World War II cracked the employment ceiling for African Americans in Rochester. Federal regulations combined with a desperate need for more skilled workers fueled this process. Many entered training classes at schools and universities previously hostile to their participation, and found jobs, though not without protest. McKelvey notes that only five Rochester firms "relaxed their resistance to Negro job applicants" (a resistance he had not mentioned before).[42] The African American community's own protest activities in the late thirties and early forties, in cooperation with state and federal investigations, provided the political voice which called for educational and employment opportunities. Rev. James Rose led these political protests.

Throughout the first forty years of this century, Rochester reflected in its political arena the same dynamics existing within the fields of education and employment. African Americans benefited from radical and reform voices and allied with them when they spoke out for African American rights. However, the city displayed a hostility toward efforts by African Americans to advance their rights and better their condition, maintaining racial barriers that kept them in subservient roles. This changed only with the intervention of state and federal mandates coupled with the consistent protests registered by African Americans themselves. Their persistence in demanding their own rights received its support primarily from the institutional and spiritual fortifications of the African American church.

THE AFRICAN AMERICAN CHURCH AS AN ARENA OF POLITICAL ACTIVITY AND PROTEST

The African American church in Rochester promoted the quest for political and civil rights in several ways. It provided space for political debate and activities, it housed, and its leaders led, political organizations, and its ministers took stands from the pulpit and in public both as advocates for rights and as protesters against their infringement.

Space For Political Activity and Debate

Throughout the nineteenth century (since its inception in 1827, founded by a runaway slave, the Rev. Thomas James), A.M.E. Zion served as a station on the underground railroad. When Frederick Douglass published the *North Star*, the basement of A.M.E. Zion housed the printing press. At the turn of the century, the most politically active African Americans in Rochester, J.W. Thompson and Hester Jerome Jeffreys, belonged to A.M.E. Zion. Indeed, the building drive, which Thompson and Jeffreys led, and the new edifice itself, were replete with political activity and meaning. A 1906 newspaper article in the A.M.E. Zion archives describes some of the new features planned for the church. "In the main vestibule on each side of the entrance there will be marble tablets, one to the memory of the anti-slavery agitators, particularly those of Monroe county, and the other to the memory of the men who fought for the cause of the North in the Civil War."[43] In his many appeals for aid in building the new church, J.W. Thompson emphasized the role of Rochester's African Americans in defending the American flag. This strategy, as noted above, rested upon the assumption that African American civil and political equality received legitimation from African American loyalty to and sacrifices for American society and its principles.

The memorial windows that adorned the sanctuary also spoke to the political heritage African Americans wanted to preserve for inspiration. Including that which commemorated Susan B. Anthony, windows also memorialized

Frederick Douglass and Harriet Tubman. The congregation was surrounded every week with figures that the African American community considered sacred, sacred enough to place in stained glass. Three of the eight windows celebrated defenders of African American rights. Thus, the structure of the church itself provided a hospitable space for political expression.

The archives of Memorial also include an announcement for a "debate and trotter supper" held during the pastorate of J.W. Brown (circa1905-1910) with the following subject to be debated: "Resolved that the Republican Party has been more beneficial to the Negro Race since its infancy than the Democratic Party." This was probably not the only political debate sponsored by the Young Men's Guild of the church, which sought to educate and hone political skills. This debate also indicates the criteria upon which African Americans in Rochester judged their political allegiance to any party or cause, namely, its ultimate benefit to African American people.

Political Organizations and Leaders

Throughout the first fifteen years of the century the foremost political leaders in Rochester were J.W. Thompson and Hester Jerome Jeffreys, both of whom were also leaders at A.M.E. Zion. They were joined but not rivaled by George Burks and Rev. Byrd of Trinity Presbyterian Church. The list of their political activities is indeed impressive.

J. W. Thompson led many efforts to organize African American Republicans in Rochester and to align them with African American Republicans across the state and nation. The earliest of these was the Douglass League, formed while the African American statesman was still living, and whose function seemed to be organizing the celebration of emancipation, with appropriate political speeches addressing current issues affecting African American rights. It served as the organizational arm for protest rallies against lynching, and began the effort to erect a memorial statue to Frederick Douglass. It was also the Douglass League that condemned the action of Rev. Ely, when he colluded with "Boss" Aldridge in the dismissal of Charles Lee. Lee originally may have gotten his appointment in part due to the influence of the League, or at the very least of J.W. Thompson, who was so vociferous in his defense. According to A.M.E. Zion historian, Charles Frazier, Thompson had become the political head of the African American community—the one who could get out the vote and influence the outcomes in at least one city ward. Consequently, white Republican party leaders, when they wanted to hear the concerns of African Americans, came to Thompson, and any political appointments probably came from his recommendation as well. This political influence taught Thompson the necessity of organization and unity on the part of the African American community and the need to extend the small influence possible for Rochester population by aligning it with state and national efforts. To that end, Thompson organized what was variously termed the "Colored Republican Club" and the "Colored Voters League." Attempts to get the African American Republicans of Rochester together and align them with African Americans around the state continued into the teens, with J.W. Thompson leading most of these efforts.

The League sought to secure political positions for African American Republicans, but even more importantly, it sought to unify local African American Republicans in order to protect their rights. An undated flyer announced a mass meeting of the "Colored Community Republican Club of Rochester" in order to learn the "great possibilities of the Negro in Rochester as an organized force." Another flyer, announcing the eleventh anniversary of the unveiling of the Douglass Monument in 1910, came from the "Charles E. Hughes Afro-American Republican Club," which would organize for a state-wide effort for the "protection of the Afro-American politically and socially."[44] Both J.W. Thompson and Hester Jerome Jeffreys were instrumental in aligning local African Americans with bi-partisan political organizations whose sole purpose was the promotion of African American rights. Both held office in the Afro-American Council formed by T. Thomas Fortune, and Mrs. Jeffreys was active in the Federation of Colored Womens Clubs. While these various organizations did not always meet in the church, they sometimes did, and the announcements of their activities found in church records indicates that the church acted as both advertiser and sponsor for political organization.

Hester Jeffreys focused most of her attention on organizing the women of her race and creating avenues of cooperation with white women in Rochester, most notably Susan B. Anthony. She was a national organizer for the Federation of Colored Women's Clubs and the New York State President of the Federation of Colored Women's Clubs. She founded the Susan B. Anthony Club at Memorial, which raised money for the church and for the memorial windows in the new building. The club probably focused on the contributions by African American women and the women's-rights movement to the struggle for equality and liberation of African Americans generally. Hester Jeffreys certainly viewed the movements for women's rights and the movement for African American civil and political equality as intimately connected. In this she received the support of her congregation, as attested by the memorial windows to women and the contents of the cornerstone.

George Burks, and other African Americans in Rochester, at least initially differed from J.W. Thompson's approach, in insisting on organizing to support "the man not the party." The Afro American Independent Political League of Monroe County, formed by George Burks after he lost his appeal, made its objectives clear. "In political affairs the League believes that in order to receive the desired recognition, party lines should be obliterated, and the candidate supported that will guarantee to us such recognition as we seek, regardless of his party affiliations."[45] The difference in political approach to the protection of African American rights reflected debates occurring nationally among African American leaders. Bishop Walters was advocating allegiance to the Democratic party as he believed the party of Lincoln had deserted the African American cause. Other leaders advocated political choices based on the individual merits of candidates, much as Burks recommended.

During the twenties and thirties, The NAACP played an active role in Rochester. The branch sent delegates to the national conferences, held mass meetings, celebrated African American accomplishments and delivered protests against discrimination. Rochester sent five delegates to the 1930 convention in Springfield, Massachusetts. These delegates were a roster of the most important political leaders of the African American community: Rev. Augustus E. Bennett, Rev. James E. Rose, Mr. and Mrs. George W. Burks, and Mrs. Martha P. Simpson. Only Martha Simpson's name is unfamiliar.[46] Committed to bettering the condition of African Americans in cooperation with white people, the NAACP consistently drew upon the power and support of sympathetic whites. This was true in Rochester, when in the 1930s, the President of the NAACP was Meyer Jacobstein, and the Executive Vice President Mrs. Helen Probst Abbot.

Political Strategies

The political strategies of Rochester's African American leaders reflect the different approaches and debates then current on the national scene. J.W. Thompson took the stance that in order to succeed, African Americans should align themselves with the most powerful political party. Delivering a small but solid vote, he reasoned, would lead to the political consideration of African American issues. Thus he bent his considerable energies to organizing African Americans for the Republican party. George Burks, on the other hand, advocated the position that African Americans should organize themselves, delineate their own issues, and vote for candidates of any party who would support those issues. A solid African American minority could influence a variety of political and economic issues. Exerting pressure on a white commercial establishment to hire African Americans who, through their custom, supported that establishment, exemplified this strategy. This kind of pressure proved an attractive strategy during the "Don't Buy Where You Can't Work" boycotts of the 1930s in larger metropolitan areas. Also, these campaigns presaged similar demands during the Civil Rights era.

Beginning in the 1920s and throughout the 1930s, Rochester African Americans, again led by George Burks, explored the strategies espoused by the NAACP. Working with white people explicitly committed to the advancement of African American rights, regardless of party affiliation, became a third strategy employed by Burks, Augustus Bennet, the pastor of Trinity church, and James Rose, a frequent officer and/or national conference delegate. The NAACP was a clear organizational presence in Rochester during the twenties and thirties, but remained secondary, even in terms of political protest, to the churches. It seems rather that the NAACP served to keep pastors and lay leaders informed of national issues and strategies (for example, the emphasis on lynching, U.S. involvement in Africa, and the invasion of Ethiopia). It also helped organize interchurch events and activities, and was a bridge between the African American and white communities. The NAACP, and the events it sponsored, like National Negro History Week, and National Negro Health Week, were the avenues through which influential white people could show their support for African American rights in Rochester. Many did so. Meyer Jacobstein, a liberal Democratic leader in Rochester, served as the president of the Rochester branch of the NAACP during the early thirties. Jacobstein had served in Congress in the twenties, taught economics at the University of Rochester, and had moved from being the owner of the Rochester Business Institute to becoming the President of the First National Bank and Trust Company.[47] Interestingly, none of the write-ups of this Rochester reformer mention his involvement with the African American community. NAACP annual conference proceedings and announcements in the *Democrat and Chronicle* provide the information that Jacobstein was involved with advancing the rights of African Americans in the city. Other *D&C* articles attest to the presence of white ministers, reformers, and politicians at events and speakers sponsored by the NAACP. These influential whites expressed deep outrage for the plight of African Americans elsewhere, especially in the South, and looked forward to working with local African Americans.

Working with, or exerting pressure upon the white power structure, were differing strategies with the common political aim of insuring African American rights. While promoting debate within the African American community, allegiance to a particular strategy depended upon its ability to achieve that aim. J.W. Thompson, for example, was no political hack. His ultimate support of the Republican power structure depended upon its willingness to advance African American rights, as his protest of Lee's dismissal illustrates.

He also organized for and took leadership within African American organizations nationally to defend African American rights. He, and other African Americans in the city, were willing to combine strategies and try combinations of political activity to further their aims.

That these strategies would have different effects on the political influence of African Americans in Rochester is less important than the fact that Rochester's African Americans engaged in the political debate, organized according to their positions, and struggled for recognition on the political scene. Despite Burks's early success in the courts, his later reversal and the failure of his second suit indicated the political realities with which African Americans in the city were most concerned. McKelvey downplays this reality. "Although the efforts of several Negroes to secure equal treatment in restaurants and shoe shine parlors failed when the courts managed to dodge the question, the press carried many strong editorials condemning lynchings in the Southern states."[48] More important to local African Americans than the reality that some Rochestarians abhorred lynching, was the fact that despite flagrant discrimination and the political activity and protests that African Americans organized to combat it, none of even the most radical movements in Rochester addressed the issues and conditions of African Americans in the city. For this kind of political support and voice, they looked to the ordained leadership of their churches.

The Power of the Pulpit

The strongest advocates for African American rights in Rochester were the pastors of the churches. The African American church has historically offered avenues for the development of leadership within the African American community, and many politicians started in and remained in the church. The roll call is too lengthy to include. Yet most analyses of this historical process miss the possibility that as interpreters of the word and will of God, African American pastors believed it was their Christian duty to act as advocates for their people.

Many of the editorials that appeared in defense of African Americans in Rochester proceeded from the pens of African American pastors. Rev. W.A. Byrd of Trinity Presbyterian Church delivered a diatribe against disfranchisement and lynching in the South. In this undated editorial appearing in the *Post Express*, Byrd deplores Jim Crow laws, unequal accommodations, mob rule, and disfranchisement. He takes the position that the vote is sacred and if the Negro is not educated well enough to exercise it, then neither are the majority of white people. He ends by professing love for the South and its finest ideals.[49] Byrd linked his protest of southern conditions to the local situation when he joined with Rev. J.W. Brown of Memorial and Rev. Algeron

Crapsey of St. Andrew's to protest disparaging references in the *Herald* to the Negro's qualifications as a voter.[50]

J.W. Thompson, Hester Jeffreys, J.W. Brown, and Rev. Byrd led the political activity within the African American community throughout the teens. During the twenties, that responsibility fell to Rev. James Rose, Rev. Augustus Bennett of Trinity Presbyterian and Father Frank Brown of St. Simon's Episcopal Church. These men had different styles but were revered within their community. People thought Father Brown was a saint. Rev. Rose's efforts on behalf of his people formed part of the introduction to this chapter. His style could be challenging and abrasive, as his editorials clearly attest.[51] Augustus Bennett is the least known of the three, but his continued engagement with the NAACP, offering Trinity as a meeting place, and speaking out on issues of national concern while an officer of that organization, place him among the dynamic African American leaders in Rochester.

In 1933, the second trial of the Scottsboro case was concluded. This case involved nine Negro youth accused by two white women of assault in Alabama. The first youth to be convicted, Heywood Patterson, received a new trial after the Supreme Court set aside the first verdict. In the second trial, one of the women recanted her story, but Patterson was convicted again anyway. This dismal example of justice in Alabama aroused Augustus Bennett, whose thorough knowledge of the case probably came from his connections with the NAACP, since the case received little attention in Rochester.

Alabama dealt a cruel blow to our cherished ideals of justice and fair play in the latest Scottsboro verdict. . . . [A]ll justice-loving people outside of Morgan County, Alabama, had hoped that for once the South would rise above bigotry and prejudice and do a Christian act, that is, try the defendant on the basis of the evidence and not on the question of his color. Hardly any fair-minded person was prepared for the surprise and shock of the verdict announced last Palm Sunday to the worshippers leaving the Decatur churches where Jesus, the Jew, had been preached. What a mockery!

A rank appeal to bigotry, intolerance, prejudice and womanhood—the four horsemen behind which the Southern mob can always be relied upon to ride. It was the same old appeal to the Four Horsemen of the Mob who have been the means by which thousands of Negroes have been rushed out of this world dangling at the end of ropes and trees.

Let us hope that Herr Hitler has been too busy in Germany the past two weeks to have followed the actions of the Nazis in Alabama. . . . While the rest of America protests in righteous indignation against Hitlerism abroad, I wonder if Alabama now has the audactiy to lift its voice against atrocities anywhere. Would it not be a proper course, Mr. Editor, if we ceased fulminating against

Hitler's anti-Semitism thousands of miles away, and give a little more attention to Hitlerized, uncivilized Alabama?

While in 1933 A.D., crosses burn on the clay covered hills of Alabama, thus reminding us of that other Cross on which an Innocent Man was crucified 33 A.D., let us remember that Easter followed Calvary. May this Easter inspire new hope and fresh courage, conviction and committal to all who denounce Hitlerism, whether it be Hitlerism against the Jews in Germany or against Negroes and Jews in Alabama.[52]

In this editorial, Rev. Bennett combines an African American understanding of Christianity, which calls for justice in practice, with a timely political analysis that reveals the primary concerns of African Americans in Rochester and elsewhere in the 1930s. Those concerns were prejudice, racial or religious, and the discrimination and injustice that could be visited on human beings as a result of prejudice. National African American leaders would make much the same point as Bennett makes, decrying the hypocrisy of the American denunciation of Hitler coupled with the practice of racial discrimination here in the United States. These criticisms would last throughout World War II and lead to major efforts of resistance against racial discrimination afterwards.

Bennett also links Jews and Blacks in solidarity in this editorial, and makes the point, not often made during this time period, that Jesus was a Jew. Augustus Bennett served with Meyer Jacobstein as officer of the NAACP, which also defended the Scottsboro boys, whose lawyer was also Jewish. Of any ethnic community in Rochester, at least during the 1930s, the Jewish community seems to have given the most support to the African American community.

Lastly, Bennett calls on the strength of the resurrection and all that it implies. He calls on the promise of Easter to inspire people to resist "Hitlerism" in whatever form it takes. The call of Christ, and thus the responsibility of Christians, is to challenge the hatred and injustice of prejudice. Rev. Bennett, like James Rose, employed the African American pulpit to lead the African American community in Rochester and offer political challenges to the white community.

Father Frank Brown took a different approach, intervening personally as advocate for those in trouble and working to change the negative image of African Americans in Rochester by providing good press. Jean Kenney and Ruth Brown both testified to Father Brown's willingness to visit people in jail, go to court, and come to advocate for any of his parishioners—or for anyone in the community for that matter, black or white—who needed a powerful presence.[53]

The interviews as a whole convey the conviction that it is part of the pastor's job to speak for the people, not only publicly when issues arise, but on an individual basis, when people need help with the political or legal system. Pastors were expected to be there and several people said that the pastor, or someone else in leadership who would then contact the pastor, would be the first person people would call if they were in trouble. Those few who had encountered such incidents within their own families or personal lives, more often than not claimed that the pastor of their church came to their assistance.

Rev. James Rose, in his masters thesis, makes explicit the connections between political advocacy, social critique, and Christian mandates. Rev. Rose understood his political stands in light of his call and duty to God.

> The pages of the book of the prophecies of Amos fairly burn even yet with the indignation of the Lord at the injustice of those who sit in the seats of the mighty. How could the people of Yahweh in the land of Yahweh ever conceive of their God dealing with them as Amos declares in the 4th Chapter of his prophecies? Famine, drought, blastings, mildew, pestilence, reverses in battle, overthrow of their cities, repudiation of their sacrifices are all considered by this prophet as visitations from Yahweh because the rulers are not dealing justly with the people. . . . He is to be made known through righteousness and justice to the oppressed.[54]

This biblical interpretation indicates that Rev. Rose understood his prophetic role to include calling both African Americans and white Americans to social responsibility. It echoes Bishop Walter's query "can we remain silent?" in the face of God's mandate for Christian transformation in human relations. For Rev. Rose, it is the responsibility of African American pastors to model Christian brotherhood through their unwavering advocacy for African American rights, both individually and communally, and to call white Americans to responsibility. That responsibility consisted of delivering justice to the oppressed. Otherwise, as the Old Testament prophets had forseen, society as a whole would suffer the wrath of God. Through the pulpit and the press, African American pastors like Rev. Rose, Rev. Bennett, and Father Brown strove to do their Christian duty.

CONCLUSION

The African American people in Rochester lived within a community which supported individual struggles for freedom and against discrimination, and which provided an integrated school system and an atmosphere of acceptance for African Americans at the same time that it created rigid racial barriers that perpetuated systemic discrimination. One of the most intriguing dynamics revealed in the interviews is the tension between—on the one hand—the safety and acceptance that African Americans experienced in Rochester, especially when young, and—on the other—the virulent racism they also encountered, often after they started working or attempted to break into educational or professional fields. Charles Price, Elsie Scott Kilpatrick, and William Warfield, to name just three, all described how they grew up in an atmosphere free of discrimination, unlike the experience of African Americans elsewhere in the country. Yet they and others also recount painful memories of racial slurs, closed doors, and impossible barriers. At the same time that Charles Frazier described his friendships with white classmates, he also made the point that if he and I, as adults, had met and stopped to chat downtown during the 1930s, a policeman would have come along and told us to go on about our business. The assumption would have been that I was soliciting, since no white woman would otherwise stop to greet a black man on the street. Charles Price recalled the camaraderie he experienced belonging to a white YMCA and playing on their basketball team, juxtaposed to the response of white players on other teams who "called me everything but a child of God on the court."[55]

African Americans were relatively safe in Rochester. They weren't getting lynched, they could make a decent living, their children could attend school, and the small size of the population, while hampering much of their organized efforts to better their condition, also protected them from organized overt racial hostility. A significant minority of the white community considered itself liberal on race, and those who were most concerned with reforms either had personal relationships with African Americans, worked cooperatively with them, or allowed the small size of the population to give them an excuse not to listen to African American concerns. The solid majority in Rochester expressed the subtle, and sometimes overt, racism that maintained the position of African Americans throughout the 1930s.

Faced with a mostly intransigent white community and hampered by small size and internal diversity, African Americans, through their churches, persisted in challenging the community to grant them their rights. That they had the stamina to do so over the course of these generations speaks to the power of their faith.

NOTES

1. Walters, *My Life and Work*, 125.

2. The following account is derived from several sources: 1) author's interview with Alan Adams, 24 July 1993; 2) documents in the possession of Alan Adams (advertise-

ment for Excelsior Tonsorial Parlor, photograph, mementos); 3) Trinity Presbyterian Church archives; 4) *Rochester Democrat and Chronicle* articles, 8, 9, 13 January 1902; and 5) McKelvey, "Lights and Shadows," 16-17.

3. *Rochester Democrat and Chronicle*, untitled article, 13 January 1902.

4. McKelvey, "Lights and Shadows," 14-15.

5. I found flyers and information concerning the league in A.M.E. Zion archives and among the papers of Trinity members.

6. "Afro American Independent Political League of Monroe Co.," pamphlet found in A.M.E. Zion church archives.

7. McKelvey, "Lights and Shadows," 18.

8. National Association for the Advancement of Colored People. *Annual Report of the National Association for the Advancement of Colored People*, New York (1919), microfilm, reel 10.

9. The sketch of James Rose is drawn from Mt. Olivet church records, newspaper articles, and interviews with Mt. Olivet members. Specific sources will be footnoted.

10. *Mt. Olivet Baptist Church 75th Anniversary Booklet* (1985), 4; found in Mt. Olivet Church archives.

11. *Rochester Democrat and Chronicle*, Sunday Magazine section, 6 March 1938.

12. Ibid.

13. "Large Crowds at Opening of Mount Olivet," *Rochester Democrat and Chronicle*, 24 January 1927.

14. Ibid.

15. Bill Beeney, "Conversation Pieces," *Rochester Democrat and Chronicle*, 26 March 1964.

16. *The Third Ward and Its Corn Hill Historic Preservation District: 150th Rochester Celebration*, Pamphlet, undated, found in Mt. Olivet archives, Community Miscellaneous File.

17. "Directs Attention to Oppressed Negroes Here," *Rochester Democrat and Chronicle*, 16 January 1931.

18. "Pastor Raps Italy's Logic on Conquest," *Rochester Democrat and Chronicle*, 25 November 1935.

19. This editorial has the appearance of the secular press, both in typeface, columns, and headline. Additionally, it incorrectly identifies Rose as the pastor of Parsells Avenue Baptist Church, which tends to confirm its secular source.

20. The accounts of the various commissions are found in McKelvey's "Lights and Shadows" 21-25; Dupree's "Rochester Roots/Routes" (September and October 1984); various newspaper articles found in Mt. Olivet archives. The letters quoted are from "Readers Forum, letters to the *Times Union*" undated, ca. 1939, from Mt. Olivet archives.

21. McKelvey, "Lights and Shadows," 23.

22. McKelvey, "Rochester's Political Trends: An Historical Review," *Rochester History* 14 (April 1952), 6-7.

23. Ibid., 7.

24. John Dutko, "Socialism in Rochester 1900-1917" (Master's Thesis, University of Rochester, 1951), 220-221, 225-232.

25. McKelvey, *Quest for Quality*, 194-195, 304.

26. Reese, *School Reform*, 80.

27. Blake McKelvey, "Walter Rauschenbusch's Rochester," *Rochester History* 14 (October 1952), 14.

28. Luker, *The Social Gospel in Black and White*, 315, 317, 321.

29. Ibid., 171-172, 228.

30. McKelvey, *Quest for Quality*, 73-88.

31. McKelvey, *Quest For Quality*. See Chapter 3, and McKelvey, "Lights and Shadows," 18.

32. See Ellen Carol DuBois, *Feminism and Suffrage: The Emergence of an Independent Women's Movement in America 1848-1869* (Ithaca: Cornell University Press, 1978); Aileen Kraditor, *The Ideas of the Woman Suffrage Movement: 1890-1920* (New York: Columbia University Press, 1965); and Giddings, *When and Where I Enter*.

33. Giddings, *When and Where I Enter*, 125-126.

34. "Bishop Addresses Zion Congregation," *Rochester Democrat and Chronicle*, 10 August 1906, and "Are Memorials to Three Woman," *Rochester Democrat and Chronicle*, 21 August 1906.

35. Reese, *School Reform*, 197.

36. McKelvey, *Quest for Quality*, 113.

37. Ibid., 316-317.

38. McKelvey, *Emerging Metropolis*, 57.

39. Ibid., 70.

40.Ibid., 78-79.

41. Ibid., 149.

42. Ibid., 140.

43. "New Church for Afro-Americans," unidentified newspaper article, 26 May 1906, found in A.M.E. Zion archives.

44. "Colored Republican Clubs Form League," unidentified newspaper article and flyers announcing league activities found in A.M.E. Zion archives.

45. "Afro American Independent Political League of Monroe Co."

46. National Association for the Advancement of Colored People. *Annual Report of the National Association for the Advancement of Colored People*, New York (1930), microfilm, reel 12.

47. McKelvey, *Rochester on the Genesee: The Growth of a City* (Syracuse: Syracuse University Press, 1973), 170.

48. McKelvey, *Quest For Quality*, 157-58.

49."Letter to the Editor," *Post Express*, undated, found in A.M.E. Zion archives.

50. McKelvey, "Lights and Shadows," 18.

51. "Directs Attention to Oppressed Negroes Here."

52. Augustus Bennett, "Hitlerism in Alabama Term Used for Scottsbor Verdict," Letters from Readers, *Rochester Democrat and Chronicle*, 14 April 1933.

53. Jean Kenney, interview with author, 12 November 1993, and Ruth Brown, interview with author, 19 August 1993.

54. Rose, "The Conception of God in the Book of Job."

55. Charles Price, interview with author, 10 January 1993.

～ SIX ～
CONCLUSION

The history of the African American church in Rochester during the first four decades of the twentieth century highlights the importance of faith in the day-to-day struggles for human fulfillment in a society permeated by racism, restriction, and oppression. The African American church articulated the tenets of that faith and provided the institutional infrastructure for its practice. The women and men who occupied the pews and pulpits of Memorial A.M.E. Zion, Trinity Presbyterian, Mt. Olivet Baptist, and St. Simon's Episcopal churches interpreted their communal roles and tasks in light of that faith.

This inquiry into the historical development of the African American church in Rochester has employed diverse sources of evidence to articulate the connections among personal faith development, institutional expression, and social engagement and challenge. Bishops, ministers, and lay people expounded the theological tenets that shaped the personal convictions expressed in the interviews. The reliance on prayer, worship, and consistent church attendance inspired the daily lives and activities of the people who struggled for human fulfillment within their communities and strove for wider social recognition of their humanity on the basis of equality and liberation from oppression. The achievements of these people speak to the strength of their faith against overwhelming odds. An explication of those odds, and how they presented themselves within a particular local setting, framed the argument.

The African American church, and its faith foundations as a consistent source of social challenge, deserves serious historical investigation. An illumination of the personal faith and day to day lives of African American lay people is especially important in order to address the charge that African American mainline churches serve an accommodating and supportive role in sustaining the social structures of oppression. Peter Paris, C. Eric Lincoln, Lawrence H. Mamiya, and Gayraud Wilmore have all made this charge to varying degrees.

These scholars, to be sure, place the church's accommodating stance within a historical dialectic in which, as Wilmore explains, "even when the Black church was quiescent the seed of radical resistance to oppression was being harbored in its depths."[1] In their explication of dialectic polarities within African American religion, Lincoln and Mamiya maintain that

> every black person and every black institution has participated in making compromises between these two poles. The pole of accommodation means to be influenced by the larger society and to take part in aspects of it, however marginal that participation may be. In their accommodative role, black churches have been one of the major cultural brokers of the norms, values, and expectations of white society. Black churches are seen as "mediating institutions." For example, after the Civil War the church was the main mediating and socializing vehicle for millions of former slaves, teaching them economic rationality, urging them to get an education, helping them to keep their families together, and providing leadership for early black communities. . . . But the pole of resistance meant that it was possible to resist the accommodative forces and pressures of the American mainstream. Resistance meant affirming one's own cultural heritage, in this case an African American or black heritage. As one of the few totally black controlled and independent institutions, black churches played a major role in resistance.[2]

And Peter Paris, who emphasizes the liberation theme within African American religious tradition, describes the dialectic which allows for accommodation in the following way:

> Scholarly opinion regarding the relationship of the black church to American society can be classified as compensatory and political. The former contends that black religion is basically an otherworldly preoccupation seeking relief from the cruel realities of historical existence, while the latter views it as a dynamic agency for social change. . . . [I]t is the essence of every religion to be related to history in two ways: (1) to espouse a positive view of some distant future which serves as a lure for its adherents; and (2) to exhibit the basic sociocultural forms and values relative to its specific location. The former designates an eschatological vision of the final end of humankind while the latter expresses the nature and meaning of historical experience.[3]

Peter Paris and Gayraud Wilmore, who deal most extensively with early twentieth century church development, argue that the church did, indeed, prove more accommodating than resistant during this time period. Paris contends that the desire for a fully integrated society where race did not matter influenced the black church's adherence to prevailing white behavioral norms, which took precedence over "the original purpose of the black church independence movement which aimed at religious, moral, and political freedom from racial oppression." African Americans, through becoming "law-abiding, respectable citizens," contributed to the maintenance of peace and harmony between the races, which "constituted no threat to the oppressive structures of the larger society but in a sense contributed unwittingly to the maintenance of the status quo." Identifying ignorance as the source of racism and oppression, African Americans "for several generations" produced empirical evidence of their worthiness and believed that whites would "forthrightly alter their racial attitudes and practices."[4] For Paris, such strategies were at best misguided in that they both failed to perceive the racism endemic to white Christian theology and placed an emphasis on integration rather than racial development.

Gayraud Wilmore is a harsher judge of African American church leadership and its accommodative stance from the turn of the century to World War II, terming its behavior during this time an "obsequious adjustment to white oppression."[5] Wilmore's social analysis of this period faults African American church leaders who, even when they opposed Booker T. Washington's accommodation to white racism in the South, came to regard "civil rights agitation as a means of entering the mainstream of American society rather than a tactic for confronting the basic assumptions of the American system." He cogently outlines the hostile social forces that confronted African Americans during the "nadir" and then blames the lack of militant church leadership for failing to overcome these forces.

> The resistance of Black leadership to the direction which the nation was moving was consistent but moderate. Washington's gradualism, while opposed by a few . . . was adopted by most Black preachers not only because they lacked the courage to fight back, but because it was entirely consonant with the ethics of the white Christianity which increasingly influenced them. The picture of the nonviolent, self-effacing, patiently suffering white Christ which was held up by the conservative evangelicals and ethical revivalists became for Black preachers the dominant image of what it was like to be Christian.[6]

Wilmore presents a complex analysis of the movements and organizations within the black community which contributed to the co-opting of mainline African American Christianity. Among these he cites the rise of secular organizations, alternative religious sects, and a growing body of disaffected and militant urban migrants who found their voice within Marcus Garvey's United Negro Improvement Association (U.N.I.A.). The combination of a lack of church leadership with viable alternatives resulted in "the independent Black churches of the United States . . . becoming respectable institutions. . . . The dominant influence of clergymen in the social betterment and civil rights groups helped to keep these organizations on an accommodationist path."[7] Wilmore concludes his chapter on the "Deradicalization of the Black Church" with the following observations:

> Attacked by both the "nigger" on the block, who abandoned the too-removed, too-unjust God of white Christianity, and by the educated class of New Negroes, who imagined themselves superior to preachers and too sophisticated for religion, many Black ministers retreated to what they knew best—preaching and raising money. With a few outstanding exceptions, their churches turned inward to the spiritual needs of a deprived and oppressed people. . . . [T]he deradicalization of the Black church . . . was almost complete by the middle of this century. Although many perceptive observers recognized the unique role it continued to play and its freedom from some of the sins of the white church, it could nevertheless be said, with a note of disappointment and nostaligia that "in relations with the white community [the Negro church] has been for the most part a defensive and accommodating institution."[8]

Charges of "obsequious" accommodation, political expediency, and cowardice do not ring true for the African American church in Rochester. The theological position of the African American church during the period under discussion included a different stance, which influenced the relationship of the church to white society. African American theology, which viewed racism as sin, understood the challenge to racism as a call for redemption. The future of white society, and the Christian commitment of African Americans, depended upon challenging the sin of racism, leaving open the question of redemption of white society through conversion. Certainly not all African Americans or their church leaders adhered to this theology. Yet, the tendency of the historical record to portray the African American church in the early twentieth century as inwardly-focused, relying upon a theology that counseled otherworldly rewards and patient suffering, and embraced white priorities for African American social inclusion goes much further than a critique of political strategies. It distorts the historical record and misinterprets the character and motivation of African American Christians.

At this juncture it is important to consider the meaning and implications attached to "accommodation," and to reconsider the role of the African American church as a bulwark against racism. The evidence from the African American church in Rochester provides insights for this consideration. Lincoln and Mamiya's understanding of accommodation—"to be influenced by the larger society and to take part in aspects of it, however marginal that participation may be, [and to act as] one of the major cultural brokers of the norms, values, and expectations of white society"—resonates with the experience of the African American church in Rochester. African Americans here, in their search for equality and liberation, "rejected neither the basic religion nor the basic political orientation of the nation," as Paris asserted.[9] Yet accommodating to behaviors and values that they believed would gain them access to avenues for the fulfillment of human potential did not mean accommodating to racism, nor did it mean an uncritical embrace of white middle-class values.

The African American community in Rochester did not experience the extreme social forces mitigating the power of the church in other localities, as Wilmore describes. The Great Migration did not create such an influx of migrants that the church could not meet their needs; the secular institutions that the community developed worked in tandem with and expressed the combined forces of the churches; alternative sects did not drain membership from mainline churches; and Marcus Garvey did not promote a following here. By its very atypicality, the African American church in Rochester provides an example of an institution which continued to provide leadership through a sustained process of engagement in and challenge to wider social forces. African American lay people in Rochester were definitely concerned with social uplift, with claiming the benefits of American society for themselves; and their leaders, with the possible exception of James Rose, emphasized loyalty to American principles and causes as one basis for inclusion.

Yet important distinctions between accommodation and cowardice remain cogent, especially in light of what Higginbotham noted was the subversive quality of claiming equality on the basis of excellence. Her discussion of the "politics of respectability" is noteworthy:

> With regard to the black Baptist women's movement, such a politics did not reduce to an accommodationist stance toward racism, or a compensatory ideology in the face of powerlessness. Neither did it reduce to a mindless mimicry of white behavior or a "front" without substance or content. Instead, the politics of respectability assumed a fluid and shifting position along a continuum of African American resistance. Through the discourse of respectability, the Baptist women emphasized manners and morals while simultaneously asserting traditional forms of protest. . . . The women's movement in the black Baptist church reflected and reinforced the hegemonic values of white America, as it simultaneously subverted and transformed the logic of race and gender subordination.[10]

Higginbotham could well be describing the African American church in Rochester when she describes the subversive implications of otherwise accommodationist strategies. These strategies signified "the search for common ground on which to live as Americans with Americans of other racial and ethnic backgrounds.

This search for common ground . . . occurred as the nation worked assiduously to deny this possibility by isolating the 'Negro's place' within physical and symbolic spaces of inferiority."[11] The preceding chapters have illustrated the racial barriers operating in Rochester which served to isolate African Americans within subordinate economic, social, and political enclaves. African Americans here never accepted these barriers. Instead, they consciously built networks and infrastructures centered in the church that nurtured the skills and abilities so that they could challenge these restrictions at every turn.

Certainly the articulation of those skills and abilities resided within an effort to develop Christian character, a character which reflected white middle-class norms. However, African Americans in Rochester drew upon another stream of values that flowed from their common struggle and heritage, values that fed their understanding of themselves as a people and fueled their resistance to white dominance. Christian character and social betterment depended as much upon mutuality, reciprocity, cooperation, and self-sacrifice as it did upon individual restraint and competition. The behavioral norms emphasized by African American leaders blended these streams to create a community of people who valued each other as persons regardless of levels of social and material success, even while they strove for that success. Exemplifying white behavioral norms gave African Americans in Rochester leverage to hold white society accountable, while African American communal norms provided an essential buttress for human worth when these efforts proved fruitless. Underlying all their efforts to build "character," strong enough to both succeed and endure, rested the Christian mandate: to work for justice, to challenge racism, to promote equality, to further the creation of a society where all people could respond to God's call through the exercise of their own human potential.

The African American Christian community in Rochester did not hold to an image of a meek and mild, obedient to the Master, long-suffering but patient Christ. They believed in a Christ in whom all things are possible, including, possibly, the redemption of white society. Redemption for whites remained, however, secondary, something that could follow from, and indeed depended upon the realization of, liberation and equality for African Americans. Remember the words of Bishop Caldwell: "'He shall not fail or be discouraged until judgment is set in the earth, and the isles shall wait for His law.' He shall not fail as the emancipator." and Bishop Walters: "Since the Lord has brought us face to face with this great question of equality, and since 'premonitory mutterings,' indeed, all the indications from the Divine side convince us that He is leading on in this as in the other great events through which He has so miraculously and triumphantly brought us after a long and severe struggle, it is our duty to follow where He leads." Such an understanding of Christ's mandates for liberation and equality led directly to political and social action. Bishop Walters' impassioned plea, "Can we remain silent?" in the face of the multiple injustices of the age, calls for all African American Christians to question and combat manifestations of racism when they appear. And Rev. Rose's theology made the challenge to oppression the foundation of African American, as well as white, redemption.

The African American community in Rochester both inspired and responded to such leadership. They did so within proscribed social realities which included small size and rigid racial barriers operating against them. Their practical assessment of the odds against them and their faithful response in light of those odds certainly accommodated to their surroundings. The result, however, was neither cowardly, inwardly focused, self-serving, short-sighted, nor expedient. In fact, the African American community's response to the only instance on the record of "obsequious adjustment to white oppression" is instructive. Rev. Ely's attempt to gain favor with the white political machine at the expense of another African American brought swift condemnation, his removal from the pulpit, and the political and religious reorganization of the African American community in Rochester, including the proliferation of its second church, Trinity Presbyterian.

African Americans in Rochester dealt with the economic and political necessity of white patronage and evinced gratitude in their acceptance of white financial and social support. Yet their assessment of white colleagiality, those with whom they felt and honored a relationship of mutuality, depended upon different standards. The community had to put up with white condescension and paternalism, but they gave respect only to those who respected them as equals. During this time period, the only white person in Rochester who received the wholehearted respect of the African American community was Susan B. Anthony. The comunity was clear about the characteristics that garnered that respect. Susan B. Anthony worked for justice, equality, and liberation for African Americans. She treated them as full human beings.

The African American community in Rochester was most concerned with the issue of assimilation, but there was nothing obsequious about that concern. To begin with, assimilation for them meant assimilating newcomers into the existing African American community. Historians have portrayed this concern as having as much to do with established African Americans' fear of losing their standing with the white community as a it did with a concern for the conditions facing migrants to the city. If white people made sweeping generalizations on the basis of the newcomers' "lazy, ignorant, or raucous" behaviors, the entire community would suffer. If white people chose to interpret claims for equality to mean a quest for "social equality" (sexual relations with white women) it could prove detrimental to the always precarious economic and political standing of established African American elites. Perhaps a less flagrantly self-serving or class-biased concern for conformity also revealed interest in maintaining social control; that is, if African American leaders could not maintain the stability of their own community, they knew that white people were capable of taking measures that would affect the entire community.

African American religious leaders in Rochester took issue with white characterizations of African American motives, values, and behaviors. Their pronouncements established solidarity with, rather than a critique of, less educated or assimilated members of their own community. Rev. J.W. Brown, in an article seeking white financial support for the construction of Memorial A.M.E. Zion, boldly confronted the fear of "social equality."

Why should we want to marry white women? While it is true they possess many virtues, there is only one color from which to select. In our own ranks we have a variety, from the fair skinned, blue-eyed and flaxen-haired, with all the variation of the rainbow between to the fast black, guaranteed to hold her own under all climatic conditions. Let the agitation cease. Give the negro an industrial education, give him higher education with equal privileges in the pursuits of life; but before all and with all give him a moral and religious education. That we may have such in Rochester we beg of our white friends to help us complete our new church where we may worship God in the front seats if we so desire and where lessons of righteousness and morality may be learned.[12]

This pronouncment has amazing implications. Rev. Brown scoffs at white fears of racial assimilation at the same time that he "begs" for financial support. He is calling for justice and claims for his community access to all the avenues necessary for obtaining that justice. His vision encompasses African Americans of diverse talents and potentials, capable of governing themselves and achieving equality through the creation of a church where they can nurture righteousness and morality. Critical to this effort is a place where African Americans can view themselves as full human beings, separate from white control and connected to a God whom they can worship "in the front seats." J.W. Brown is concerned with creating an inclusive African American community, which, through the inculcation of racial pride and Christian responsibility, can gain equality in all the "pursuits of life."

During the 1920s, Rochester attracted a stream of southern migrants, and while the newcomers did not create the tensions and problems of assimilation on the same scale here as elsewhere, African American leaders expressed concern. Once again, this concern promoted solidarity with, rather than a fear of, unassimilated newcomers. Rev. Jones, pastor of Memorial A.M.E. Zion, expressed the only instance in the historical record indicating a fear of the "race problem." "We don't want too many of them here," he said. "We have no race problem in Rochester and we don't want to bring that problem here."[13] While this pronouncement may indicate a concern for stable race relations, the tenor of Rev. Jones commentary displays a much stronger concern for the well-being of the migrants, and the need for them to find a footing within the Rochester African American community. Problems of employment, housing, health, and integration with community norms headed the list of his concerns. In his depiction of conditions, Jones cites the inability of white employers to overcome prejudice or understand the needs of the migrants. The article emphasizes the unfamiliarity with northern conditions, the severity of the winters, for one, and the type of education needed to enter the job market here. Jones coordinated an effort, centered in the churches and incorporating the resources of institutions such as the "colored" YWCA, to bring the migrants into the community as participating members. His basic concern is for newcomers to find welcome and aid among their own kind. While his tone carries a certain condescension, in that he views the responsibility of Rochester's African Americans to teach and guide the migrants, his efforts are also embued with a compassion for and understanding of the frustration and difficulties they face. He does not belittle or denigrate their behaviors at the same time that he encourages community-wide efforts to aid migrants in establishing themselves in "useful and profitable" occupations. He locates the problems involved in accomplishing this task in the resistance of the white community to accept the humanity of southern negroes who differ in work habits and expectations from their northern counterparts, not in the character of the migrants, who he finds willing and eager to fulfill the promises held out by northern industry.

FAITHFUL STRATEGIES FOR JUSTICE

African American communal efforts to work for justice in Rochester evinced a strategy of gradual advancement along educational, economic, social, and political lines. African Americans understood the route toward advancement to include suffering and sacrifice, and they drew upon spiritual resolve to keep them going. A recognition of the reality of suffering does not mean giving in to that suffering or accepting the legitimacy of the oppressive structures that create it. Drawing upon the resources of faith within a community of human beings who offer alternative understandings and appreciation of human worth also mitigates against a wholesale acceptance of white middle-class values. To put it in theological terms, African Americans in Rochester understood the reality of the cross, while remaining focused on the resurrection.

The evidence of the daily lives and the faith pronouncements of African American lay people in Rochester provides a foundation for assessing the nature of their commitment to social and human transformation. These stories are eloquent illustrations of courage and self-respect, not cowardice and self-effacement. Daniel Garnett endured psychic and physical assaults upon his humanity as he strove to better his economic condition in Rochester. Subjected to racial slurs, white spittal, and denigration, Daniel Garnett submitted to these conditions and held onto both his job and his dignity. The courage he manifested in picking up a broom to sweep floors was born in his faith and succored in his community. Prayer and worship gave him the inner resolve to persevere. Daniel Garnett's assessment of his trials and their influence upon his life, his family, and his community reveal African American values, African American definitions of self-worth, and African American social and political priorities that rest upon a faith in a God who calls people to fulfillment and rewards them for struggles against injustice. What did he care how he was treated at work? When he got home he had his family and his God. He was feeding his family and providing a home for them. His father and mother were proud of him. With their support, he never gave up. His church honored him and gave him positions of authority and respect. These were his daily rewards—that he was changing the existential conditions in which his family had to live. As his faith pronouncements explained, you don't have to wait for heaven to get your reward. Prayer, worship, and church involvement shored up his inner resolve, true enough, but only so he could face what he had to in order to serve his community. Over the course of his life, he understood his personal sacrifices to benefit not only his own family and community, but the future of his people as well. His trials made it possible for other African Americans to break even tougher racial barriers.

Daniel Garnett accommodated himself to the exigencies of his times and accepted personal suffering as a necessary condition to overcoming oppression. His faith in a God who eventually overcomes racism is echoed in the life of Elsie Scott Kilpatrick. For forty years she labored against racial barriers in Rochester to first become a nurse and then practice her profession. From an early foundation in Mt. Olivet, she drew upon her faith so that she wouldn't waver in the face of the evils that surrounded her. She likened her situation to Job, and maintained a commitment to a God who worked in God's own time. She knew her trials were "only temporary."

Other individuals whose stories appear in preceding chapters evinced the same kind of Christian faith embedded in African American community values. Jesse Stevens, who lost his store, the basis of his economic independence, while retaining his dignity and supporting his family by shining shoes, instilled in his grandson, Charles Price, the understanding that no matter what occurred, he could claim an inner sense of dignity and self-respect even when "people don't want you, or don't want to acknowledge what you're doing or what you've done." And Charles Price drew upon these lessons to see him through the tough times on the Rochester Police Force, because he knew that "others had to follow him." Again and again, people testified that it was faith, through prayer and worship, that "got them through." But this faith was never so inwardly focused that people turned their eyes only toward heaven, or looked to the peace of an insular community. Religion "wasn't an excuse for anything," Ernest DuBois admonished. Prayer both clarified and fortified you for a course of action, as Elizabeth Logan explained. The lesson that through God you learned to love everybody became manifest through practice, in the service of others in your community.

The African American church in Rochester housed, articulated, nurtured, and sustained the faith of people who strove, in their daily lives, to live out the mandates of a liberating and redemptive God. The church provided both the center of an African American community where African Americans could express themselves as full human beings and provided them with spiritual and practical tools to challenge restrictions to that expression in the external, white-dominated world. The church provided the institutional base for a generational strategy of persistent social challenge. The Stevens family offers an example of generational strategy within the supportive infrastructure of the church. Jesse Stevens strove for an economic foundation, and received nurture and authority within the church. His daughter, Elizabeth Stevens Walls, achieved educational success and became the first African American teacher to retain a teaching position in the Rochester public schools. She honed her skills at Trinity, and honored the educational acccomplishments of others through the vehicle of the church. Charles Price, Jesse Steven's grandson, became one of the first African Americans to enter the professions when he joined the Rochester police force. He also found support and acknowledgement within the church. The African American community as a whole, centering its resources within the church and drawing upon them, exhibited a generational pattern that follows the Stevens model: first, economic self-sufficiency whenever possible, then educational attainment to whatever degree, and finally professional certification. By the 1940s, the Rochester African American community had a cadre of educated professionals, belonging to the church, leaders within the church, who led organized protests against racial exclusion in employment and education.

The church, through its multiple informal networks and formal programs of support for economic and educational achievement, provided a human reserve of individuals able to take advantage of any opportunities when they arose. Pauline Moore had her teaching degree when her community needed it. Elsie Scott Kilpatrick was hired as a nurse as soon as that racial barrier came down. Edwin Robinson entered the University of Rochester Medical School, with the proper undergraduate credentials, as soon as those doors were open. What is critical to understand here is not that these people stood ready, as if they were doing nothing else, and waited for white doors to open. In the face of continued exclusion, they drew upon African American notions of self-worth and community involvement to contribute their talents and skills in ways that benefited their community. Additionally, the leaders of that community, most particularly its pastors, continually agitated for the opening of doors. Father Frank Brown and Revs. Rose and Bennett speak to this pattern in their visible community involvement and their challenge to both racism and exclusion.

The relative cohesiveness of the African American community in Rochester provides an unusual opportunity for examining the role of supposedly white middle-class values in shaping African American norms of behavior. There were very few unemployed African Americans and no stratum of individuals visibly more well-off than others in Rochester. The solid, working-class, and entrepreneurial community valued hard-work, temperance, diligence, honesty, thrift, etc., but these values did not primarily channel elitist efforts for social control either within the African American community itself or from a white power structure. First of all, there weren't that many elite. Secondly, there seems to have been unanimity regarding these values; a sub-stratum of unemployed or disaffected African Americans did not exist. Clearly, African Americans understood these norms as the foundation for social advancement. More importantly, they viewed them as evidence of Christian character. Again, the Christian character that African Americans attempted to develop served the dual purpose of inculcating behaviors that would lead to individual achievement and would support the channeling of individual talents and resources into the community. The African American work ethic, as it operated in Rochester, served both to cement the community and to support individual striving. The involvement of Gladys Scott with the junior usher board of Mt. Olivet illustrates this point. Her deliberate consecration and induction of the youth describe her Christian commitment. Her understanding of the sacredness of hard work delineates the connections between serving God, practicing habits which dignified labor as personally gratifying and mutually sustaining, building upon these personal habits to achieve educational and professional success, and continuing to serve the community.

The small size and cohesiveness of the African American community in

Rochester also created a high degree of Christian solidarity and cooperation. While it is possible that the people interviewed for this study simply did not reveal community in-fighting, the documentary and personal evidence supports the image of a solid and mutually supportive community. Churches supported one another's efforts to raise funds, advertised one another's events, and lauded the accomplishments of African American members of other congregations. Family members within and across generations belonged to different congregations, seemingly without raising any fuss. What appears to be more important was that one belonged to the church in which one felt most comfortable. J.W. Thompson was the rock of Memorial; his daughter, Pauline Moore, was one of the first members and leaders of St. Simon's. Ruth Brown and Buddy Young both began to attend St. Simon's as young people, with the blessing of their families, who attended other churches. While such religious integration may be idiosyncratic of a small, tightly knit community, religious rivalry is not unknown within small communities. The solidarity in Rochester suggests a high degree of overarching Christian commitment to the nurturance of the people, who because they had basic agreement upon their Christian mandates could work together for common goals.

The history of the African American church deserves the attention of historians in order to bring into the historical record evidence of African American efforts to achieve justice for themselves through an institution neglected through secular bias. The importance of faith as a source of persistent, generational resistance to oppression requires serious attention. The lay people in the African American churches in Rochester were active, vocal, and committed in their struggles against racial restrictions. The scope and degree of their involvement in the church and the world indicates their commitment to the concept of Christian justice.

NOTES

1. Wilmore, *Black Religion and Black Radicalism*, 101.
2. Lincoln and Mamiya, *The Black Church in the African American Experience*, 14-15.
3. Paris, *Social Teaching*, 1.
4. Ibid., 44-45.
5. Wilmore, *Black Religion and Black Radicalism*, 168.
6. Ibid., 188, 194.
7. Ibid., 197.
8. Ibid., 226.
9. Paris, *Social Teaching*, 71.

10. Higginbotham, *Righteous Discontent*, 187-188.

11. Ibid., 188.

12. "To Meet Need of Zion Church," unidentified, undated newspaper, ca. 1906.

13. "Negro Exodus to this City is Finished," *Post Express*, ca. 1920.

BIBLIOGRAPHY

PRIMARY SOURCES

Interviews

Cultural Informants

I interviewed Frederick Jefferson, Jesse Moore, Juanita Pitz, Mildred Reynolds, Betty Anderson, Alean Rush, and Eugene DuBois during the Spring of 1992. These interviews were informal and not recorded.

Church Members, Primary Informants

All interviews took place in Rochester, New York; all were taped except where noted.

Adams, Alan. Interview with author. 24 July 1993.
Anderson, Kitty. Interview with author. 2 December 1993.
Brown, Ruth. Interview with author. 19 August 1993.
Bullock, Eunice. Interview with author. 11 May 1992, 21 January 1993.
Coles, Howard. Interview with author. 21 April 1992.
DuBois, Ernest. Interview with author. 12 August 1993.
Frazier, Charles. Interview with author. 12 April 1992, 11 May 1992, 18 May 1992, 13 May 1993, 20 May 1993.
Garnett, Daniel. Interview with author. 13 May 1993, 20 May 1993.
Hawkins, Oscar. Interview with author. 17 August 1993.
Jacque, Mildred. Interview with author. Date not recorded; not taped.
Jordan, Katherine. Interview with author. 1 August 1992.
Kenney, Jean. Interview with author. 11 December 1993.
Lee, Cynthia. Interview with author. 4 February 1993.
Logan, Elizabeth. Interview with author. 17 August 1993.

McDaniel, Francis. Interview with author. Date not recorded; not taped.

Pitz, Juanita. Interview with author. 18 May 1992.

Price, Charles. Interview with author. 1 October 1993.

Sanders, Mrs. Joe. Interview with author. 8 May 1992.

Scott, Elsie. Interview with author. 7 October 1993.

Scott, Gladys. Interview with author. 12 May 1993.

Scott, Harriet. Interview with author. 30 September 1993.

Thompson, Mary. Interview with author. Date not recorded; not taped.

Young, James (Buddy) and Alice. Interview with author. Date not recorded.

Books

Johnson, Robert Ross. "The Mountain of Olivet: A Historical Sketch of Negro Baptists in Rochester, New York." Master's thesis, Colgate Rochester Divinity School, 1946.

Rose, James Everett. "The Conception of God in the Book of Job," Master's thesis, Colgate Rochester Divinity School, 1930.

Walters, Alexander, A.M., D.D. *My Life and Work*. New York: Revell Company, 1917.

Newspapers

Democrat and Chronicle. Rochester, New York.

Post Express. Rochester, New York.

Rochester Herald. Rochester, New York.

Union and Advertiser. Rochester, New York.

Pamphlet

Thompson, J.W. *An Authentic History of the Douglass Monument: Biographical Facts and Incidents in the Life of Frederick Douglass, His Death at Anacosta, D.C. and Funeral at Washington D.C. and Rochester, N.Y. together with Portraits and Illustrations of Important Incidents of the Four Years' Struggle to Complete the Work*. Rochester, N.Y.: Rochester Herald Press, 1903.

Articles, Historical Publications

Hoke, Georgie C., and Mark Ellington. "History of the Rochester Athenaeum and Mechanics Institute," *Rochester Historical Society Publication Fund Series* 14 (1936).

McKelvey, Blake, ed. "Part I—The History of Education in Rochester," *The Rochester Historical Society Publications* 17. Rochester, N.Y.: Historical Society, 1939.

Church Records, Manuscript Collections

Memorial A.M.E. Zion church records, Rochester, in the possession of Charles Frazier.

Mt. Olivet church records, Rochester, at Mt. Olivet.

National Association for the Advancement of Colored People. Annual Reports, 1919-1940. Microfilm.

St. Simon's church records, Rochester, housed at St. Luke-St. Simon's Episcopal Church.

Trinity Presbyterian church records, Rochester, in the possession of Mildred Jacque.

Woman's Educational and Industrial Union Papers. Rochester Public Library, Local History Department.

SECONDARY SOURCES

Books

Axinn, June, and Herman Levin. *Social Welfare: A History of the American Response to Need.* 2nd Ed. New York: Harper and Row, 1982.

Baer, Hans A., and Merrill Singer. *African-American Religion in the Twentieth Century: Varieties of Protest and Accommodation.* Knoxville: University of Tennessee Press, 1992.

Blair, Karen J. *The Clubwoman as Feminist: True Womanhood Redefined, 1868-1914.* New York: Holmes & Meier, 1980.

Borchert, James. *Alley Life in Washington: Family, Community, Religion, and Folklife in the City, 1850-1970.* Urbana: University of Illinois Press, 1980.

Burkett, Randall K., and Richard Newman, Eds. *Black Apostles: Afro-American Clergy Confront the Twentieth Century.* Boston: G.K. Hall & Co., 1978.

Carlisle, Rodney. *The Roots of Black Nationalism.* N.p.: Kennikat Press, 1975.

Childs, John Brown. *The Political Black Minister: A Study in Afro-American Politics and Religion.* Boston: G.K. Hall & Co., 1980.

Cone, James. *For My People: Black Theology and the Black Church.* New York: Orbis Books, 1984.

Davis, Allen. *Spearheads for Reform: The Social Settlements and the Progressive Movement 1890-1914.* New York: Oxford University Press, 1967.

DuBois, Ellen Carol. *Feminism and Suffrage: The Emergence of an Independent Women's Movement in America 1848-1869.* Ithaca: Cornell University Press, 1978.

Du Bois, Eugene E. *The City of Frederick Douglass: Rochester's African-American People and Places.* Rochester: The Landmark Society of Western New York, 1994.

Du Bois, William E.B. *The Souls of Black Folk.* In *Three Negro Classics.* New York: Avon Books, 1965.

_____, Ed. *The Negro Church.* Atlanta: Atlanta University Press, 1903.

Duster, Alfreda M., Ed. *Crusade for Justice: The Autobiography of Ida B. Wells.* Chicago: University of Chicago Press, 1972.

Dutko, John. "Socialism in Rochester 1900-1917." Master's thesis, University of Rochester, 1951.

Etter-Lewis, Gwendolyn. *My Soul is My Own: Oral Narratives of African American Women in the Professions.* New York: Routledge, 1993.

Farley, Ena. *The Underside of Reconstruction New York: The Struggle Over the Issue of Black Equality.* New York: Garland, 1993.

Fausett, Arthur Huff. *Black Gods of the Metropolis: Negro Religious Cults of the Urban North.* Philadelphia: University of Pennsylvania Press, 1944.

Fordham, Monroe. *Major Themes in Northern Black Religious Thought, 1800-1860.* Hicksville, N.Y.: Exposition Press, 1975.

_____, Ed. *The African American Presence in New York State History: Four Regional History Surveys.* Albany, N.Y.: African American Institute of the State University of New York, 1989.

Franklin, John Hope, and Alfred A. Moss, Jr. *From Slavery to Freedom: A History of Negro Americans.* 6th Ed. New York: Alfred A. Knopf 1988.

Frazier, Franklin. *The Negro Church in America.* C. Eric Lincoln, *The Black Church Since Frazier.* New York: Schocken Books, 1974.

Gatewood, Willard B. *Aristocrats of Color: The Black Elite 1880-1920.* Indianapolis: Indiana University Press, 1990.

Gatewood, Willard B. Jr. *Black Americans and the White Man's Burden 1898-1903.* Chicago: University of Illinois Press, 1975.

Gaudet, Frances Joseph. *"He Leadeth Me."* New York: G.K. Hall & Co., 1996.

Genovese, Eugene D. *Roll, Jordan, Roll: The World The Slaves Made.* New York: Vintage Books, 1974.

Giddings, Paula. *When and Where I Enter: The Impact of Black Women on Race and Sex in America.* New York: Bantam Books, 1984.

Gottlieb, Peter. *Making Their Own Way: Southern Blacks' Migration to Pittsburgh, 1916-30.* Urbana and Chicago: University of Illinois Press, 1987.

Gregg, Robert. *Sparks From the Anvil of Oppression: Philadelphia's African Methodists and Southern Migrants, 1890-1940.* Philadelphia: Temple University Press, 1993.

Grossman, James R. *Land of Hope: Chicago, Black Southerners, and the Great Migration.* Chicago: University of Chicago Press, 1989.

Grover, Kathryn. *Make a Way Somehow: African American Life in A Northern Community 1790-1965.* Syracuse, N.Y.: Syracuse University Press, 1994.

Higginbotham, Evelyn Brooks. *Righteous Discontent: The Women's Movement in the Black Baptist Church 1880-1920*. Cambridge: Harvard University Press, 1993.

Jones, Jacqueline. *Labor of Love, Labor of Sorrow: Black Women, Work and the Family from Slavery to the Present*. New York: Vintage Books, 1985.

Kemp, Leatrice M., and Victoria Sandwick Schmitt. *Images "Afro-Rochester" 1910-1935: From the Albert Stone Negative Collection*. Rochester, N.Y.: Rochester Museum and Science Center, 1996.

Kraditor, Aileen. *The Ideas of the Woman Suffrage Movement: 1890-1920*. New York: Columbia University Press, 1965.

Kusmer, Kenneth L. *A Ghetto Takes Shape: Black Cleveland, 1870-1930*. Urbana: University of Illinois Press, 1976.

Lasch, Elisabeth Dan. *Black Neighbors: Race and the Limits of Reform in the American Settlement House Movement, 1890-1945*. Ph.D. diss., University of Massachusetts, 1990.

Lincoln, C. Eric, and Lawrence H. Mamiya. *The Black Church in the African American Experience*. Durham, N.C.: Duke University Press, 1990.

Luker, Ralph. *The Social Gospel in Black and White: American Racial Reform, 1885-1912*. Chapel Hill: The University of North Carolina Press, 1991.

Malson, Micheline R., Elisabeth Mudimbe-Boyi, Jean F. O'Barr, and Mary Wyer, Eds. *Black Women in America: Social Science Perspectives*. Chicago: University of Chicago Press, 1990.

Mays, Benjamin Elijah, and Joseph William Nicholson. *The Negro's Church*. New York: Arno Press, 1969.

McFeely, William S. *Frederick Douglass*. New York: Norton and Company, 1991.

McKelvey, Blake. *Rochester: The Quest for Quality 1890-1925*. Cambridge: Harvard University Press, 1956.

_____. *Rochester: An Emerging Metropolis 1925-1961* Rochester, N.Y.: Christopher Press, Inc., 1961.

_____. *Rochester on the Genesee: The Growth of a City*. Syracuse, N.Y.: Syracuse University Press, 1973

Meier, August. *Negro Thought in America 1880-1915; Racial Ideologies in the Age of Booker T. Washington*. Ann Arbor: University of Michigan Press, 1963.

Nelsen, Hart M., Raytha L. Yokley, and Anne K. Nelsen, Eds. *The Black Church in America*. New York: Basic Books, Inc., 1971.

Nielson, David Gordon. *Black Ethos: Northern Urban Negro Life and Thought, 1890-1930*. Westport, Ct.: Greenwood Press, 1977.

Osofsky, Gilbert. *Harlem: The Making of a Ghetto: Negro New York, 1890-1930*. New York: Harper and Row, 1963.

Ovington, Mary White. *Half A Man: The Status of the Negro in New York*. New York: Longmans, Green, and Co., 1911.

Paris, Peter. *The Social Teaching Of The Black Churches*. Philadelphia: Fortress Press, 1985.

Peterson, Paul E. *The Politics of School Reform 1870-1940*. Chicago: The University of Chicago Press, 1985.

Raboteau, Albert J. *A Fire in the Bones: Reflections on African-American Religious History*. Boston: Beacon Press, 1995.

_____. *Slave Religion: The Invisible Institution in the Antebellum South*. New York: Oxford University Press, 1978.

Reese, William J. *Power and the Promise of School Reform: Grass-roots Movements during the Progressive Era*. Boston: Routledge & Kegan Paul, 1986.

Sanders, Joe L. *Rochester Black History 1795-1990*. Rochester, N.Y.: Sanders Publishing, 1990.

Sernett, Milton C., Ed. *Afro-American Religious History: A Documentary Witness*. Durham, N.C.: Duke University Press, 1985.

Sobel, Mechal. *Trabelin' On: The Slave Journey to an Afro-Baptist Faith*. Westport, Ct.: Greenwood Press, 1979.

Swift, David E. *Black Prophets of Justice: Activist Clergy Before the Civil War*. Baton Rouge: Louisiana State University Press, 1989.

Taylor, Clarence. *The Black Churches of Brooklyn*. New York: Columbia University Press, 1994.

Three Negro Classics, Avon Books, 1965.

Trotter, Joe William. *Black Milwaukee: The Making of an Industrial Proletariat, 1915-45*. Urbana: University of Illinois Press, 1985.

Vincent, Theodore G. *Black Power and the Garvey Movement*. N.p.: The Ramparts Press, n.d.

Warfield, William with Alton Miller. *William Warfield: My Music and My Life*. Champaign, Ill.: Sagamore Publishing Inc., 1991.

Washington, Booker T. *Up from Slavery*. In *Three Negro Classics*. New York: Avon Books, 1965.

Washington, Joseph R., Jr. *Black Religion: The Negro and Christianity in the United States*. Boston: Beacon Press, 1964.

Weisenfeld, Judith, and Richard Newman, Eds. *This Far By Faith: Readings in African American Women's Religious Biography*. New York: Routledge, 1996.

Weiss, Judy. *The National Urban League, 1910-1940*. New York: Oxford University Press, 1974.

Weldon, James. *The Autobiography of a Black Man*. In *Three Negro Classics*. New York: Avon Books, 1965.

Wilmore, Gayraud. *Black Religion and Black Radicalism*. New York: Doubleday and Co., Inc., 1972.

Woodson, Carter. *The History of the Negro Church*. 3rd Ed., 1921. Reprint,

Washington, D.C.: The Associated Publishers, Association for Study of Negro Life and History, 1972.

Woodward, C. Vann. *The Strange Career of Jim Crow*. New York: Oxford University Press, 1966.

Journal Articles, Chapters in Anthologies

Cash, Floris Barnett. "Radicals or Realists: African American Women and the Settlement House Spirit in New York City." *Afro-Americans in New York Life and History* 15 (January 1991).

Diner, Steve. "Chicago Social Workers and Blacks in the Progressive Era." *Social Service Review* 44 (December 1970).

Gordon, Linda. "Black and White Visions of Welfare: Women's Welfare Activism, 1890-1945." *Journal of American History* (September 1991).

Greenbaum, Susan. "A Comparison of African American and Euro-American Mutual Aid Societies in 19th Century America." *Journal of Ethnic Studies* (Fall 1991).

Harley, Sharon. "For the Good of Family and Race: Gender, Work, and Domestic Roles in the Black Community, 1880-1930." In Micheline R. Malson, Elisabeth Mudimbe-Boyi, Jean F. O'Barr, and Mary Wyer, Eds. *Black Women in America: Social Science Perspectives*. Chicago: University of Chicago Press, 1990.

Kogut, Alvin B. "The Negro and the Charity Organization Society in the Progressive Era." *Social Service Review* 44 (March 1970).

May, Arthur J. "Oak Hill Becomes the River Campus." *Rochester History* 30 (January 1968).

McKelvey, Blake. "Historical Origins of Rochester's Social Welfare Agencies." *Rochester History* 9 (April 1947).

_____. "Lights and Shadows in Local Negro History." *Rochester History* 21 (October 1959).

_____. "Rochester's Political Trends: An Historical Review." *Rochester History* 14 (April 1952).

_____. "Walter Rauschenbusch's Rochester." *Rochester History* 14 (October 1952).

Moore, Jesse. "Resolving Urban Racial Problems: The New York Urban League, 1919-1959." *Afro-Americans in New York Life and History* 4 (January 1980).

Morial, Ernest. "Black Religion and Civil Rights." In Joseph R. Washington, Jr., Ed., *Black Religion and Public Policy: Ethical and Historical Perspectives*, N.p., 1978.

Proctor, Samuel D. "Black Protestants and Public Policy." In Joseph Washington, Ed., *Black Religion and Public Policy: Ethical and Historical Perspectives*, N.p., 1978.

Rochester Metropolitan Area Studies. (Spring 1957).

Rouse, Jacqueline. "The Legacy of Community Organizing: Lugenia Burns Hope and the Neighborhood Union." *The Journal of Negro History* 69, nos. 3-4 (1984).

Williams, Lillian. "And Still I Rise: Black Women and Reform, Buffalo, New York, 1900-1940." *Afro-Americans in New York Life and History* 14 (July 1990).

Pamphlets

Dupree, Adolph. "Rochester Roots/Routes." *about . . . time magazine* (August-October 1984).

Lewis, LiAni. "African American Sites of Significance in Rochester, New York 1900-1940." Rochester, N.Y.: The Landmark Society of Western New York, 1992.

THE AFRICAN AMERICAN CHURCH
COMMUNITY IN ROCHESTER,
1900–1940

INDEX